UNIVERSITY OF NORTH CAROLINA
STUDIES IN THE ROMANCE LANGUAGES AND LITERATURES
Number 75

THE POETICS AND THE POETRY
OF RENÉ CHAR

THE POETICS AND THE POETRY OF RENÉ CHAR

BY

VIRGINIA A. LA CHARITÉ

CHAPEL HILL
THE UNIVERSITY OF NORTH CAROLINA PRESS

DEPÓSITO LEGAL: V. 3.438 - 1968

ARTES GRÁFICAS SOLER, S. A. - JÁVEA, 30 - VALENCIA (8) - 1968

TO MY MOTHER
Virginia Nelson Anding

ACKNOWLEDGMENTS

I wish to express my appreciation to Carlos Lynes, Jr. of the University of Pennsylvania under whose guidance and generous assistance this study was prepared. I am also greatly indebted to my husband, Raymond, for his careful reading and affectionate criticism of the manuscript; his confidence and patience made this study possible.

TABLE OF CONTENTS

	Pages
ACKNOWLEDGMENTS	9
INTRODUCTION	13

CHAPTER

- I. 1907-1930: A POETICS OF THE ACT OF POETRY ... 15
  - 1907-1930: The Early Years ... 16
  - 1922-1927: *Les Cloches sur le coeur* ... 19
  - 1927-1930: *Arsenal* ... 29
- II. 1930-1936: A POETICS OF CREATIVE ACTIVITY ... 40
  - 1930-1934: *Le Marteau sans maître* ... 42
  - 1935-1936: *Moulin premier* ... 67
- III. 1936-1947: A POETICS OF MORAL RESPONSIBILITY ... 77
  - 1936-1939: Awareness of the Menace ... 78
  - 1939-1944: Fraternal Action ... 88
  - 1944-1947: Glorification of the Menace ... 99
- IV. 1947-1952: A POETICS OF INTERDEPENDENCY ... 109
  - Nature and the Contemporary World ... 112
  - Reconciliation of Man with Nature ... 131
  - *Pauvreté et Privilège* and *Art bref* ... 142
- V. 1952-1961: A POETICS OF FUSION ... 152
  - The Synthesis of *Lettera amorosa* ... 153
  - 1953-1961: The Necessity of Poetry ... 165
- VI. CONCLUSION: 1962-1966: A POETICS OF RENEWAL ... 195
  - *Commune présence* ... 196
  - Char's Present Position ... 201

LIST OF APPENDICES

- I. POEMS: KNOWN DATES OF COMPOSITION ... 207
- II. EDITIONS OF CHAR'S POEMS ... 212
- III. VARIANTS ... 220

BIBLIOGRAPHY

- A. Works by René Char ... 247
- B. Critical Works ... 251

INDEX ... 255

INTRODUCTION

The poetics and the poetry of René Char are characterized by a thematic and stylistic unity which obscures any idea of a linear development from youth to maturity in Char's conception of poetry and in his poetry itself. Char insists upon the organic unity of his work by arranging his poems in successive anthologies and collective editions. This procedure disregards the chronology of the composition in order to emphasize the unified structure of his poetic universe: "il n'y a pour lui de poème qu'anthologique." [1]

Nevertheless, Char the man and Char the poet exists in history; his individual poems and their incorporation into larger editions have also existed and do exist in history. While study of the totality of Char's work is very valuable in literary criticism, it seems that a close examination in a historical perspective can throw new light on Char's poetic development, on how Char became Char, and contribute to a better understanding of Char's thematic and stylistic unity.

Very little historical data on René Char is available. This lack of information is due to Char's refusal to discuss himself other than in his role of poet and his personal wish that the unity of his poetry not be limited by details of his historical existence:

> je suis un homme comme les autres, aussi partial et utopiste que les autres, je vous assure, pas meilleur... Ah! non. [2]

---

[1] Georges Blin, "Préface," *Commune présence* (Paris, 1964), p. vii.
[2] Pierre Berger, "Conversation avec René Char," *La Gazette des lettres* (15 juin 1952), p. 8.

Char's concern for the preservation of the organic quality of his style and themes has thus far tended to limit criticism and scholarship to the following four categories: 1) studies on Char's poetic unity and his affirmation of poetic totality; 2) stylistic studies of vocabulary, imagery, phraseology, and structural form; 3) examination of a particular collection of poems; and, 4) attempts to determine and discuss one given theme or stage of thematic concern in his poetic development. These critical essays are helpful in tracing the general points of emphasis of Char's work, but, with the exception of the two presentations of Char in the *Poètes d'aujourd'hui* volumes by Pierre Berger in 1951 and Pierre Guerre in 1961, there have been few efforts to examine Char's development in a chronological perspective.

It is the purpose of this study to examine the poetics and the poetry of René Char from his poetic debut in 1923 to his most recent works, *L'Age cassant* (1966) and *Retour amont* (1966). Despite a lack of material on Char's artistic development, this writer finds that one can trace his poetic growth through an examination of his thematic and stylistic evolution which reflects shifts of emphasis, through the study of those poems and works whose dates have been established, and through detailed analysis of the textual variants and revisions which reveal the direction of his growth. In fact, this method is suggested by Char:

> Mon passé est trop entamé, éffrité, hors de vue, pour que je sois tout à fait sûr de l'exactitude et de l'intérêt de ce que je pourrais rapporter. Chacun, au cours de ses saisons, donne ce qu'il peut. A vos questions, chemin faisant, depuis trente ans, mes ouvrages se sont efforcés de répondre.[3]

The writer of this study hopes to present a more complete view of Char the poet through the chronological examination and elucidation of the successive stages of his poetic development.

---

[3] Interview with René Char as reported by Pierre de Boisdeffre in "Poésie vivante - René Char," *Les Nouvelles littéraires* (12 février 1959), p. 7.

CHAPTER I

1907-1930: A POETICS OF THE ACT OF POETRY

René Char began writing poetry at an early age. His earliest known poem, "Jouvence," was written when he was 16 years old, while his first published poem, "Témoignage de grandeur," appeared when he was 20. At the age of 21, he published his first collection of poems, *Les Cloches sur le coeur* (1928), which was followed one year later by the first edition of *Arsenal* (1929). *Arsenal* brought him to the attention of the Surrealist group and led to his temporary adherence to that movement.

Char's early writings reveal an interest in poetry as a means to discover the truth of reality. This goal is announced in 1924 in an untitled prose poem:

> Toute poésie doit naître libre et un peu folle, tendre et rebelle aux mains qui la mettent au monde; elle doit ignorer la course du bien et la ronde du mal; c'est pour cela et sans ce souci qu'elle est humaine. Arbre nocturne, elle pousse au centre du jour. Elle sert à nos métamorphoses parce qu'elle dit vrai ou le croit. Et tous les opprimés sentent et savent qu'elle est leur soeur et le frais talus de leur chemin.[1]

This text demonstrates Char's early concern for poetry, its role, its value, and its possibilities. It indicates that Char's work will explore and assess poetry and its relationship to human existence: "elle sert à nos métamorphoses parce qu'elle dit vrai." This poem

---

[1] This poem was published by Georges Mounin in his article "Situation présente de René Char," *Les Temps modernes* (juillet-août 1957), pp. 277-278.

even suggests that poetry can serve man in the determination of his moral conduct, "la course du bien et la ronde du mal," and possibly justify his existence, "soeur et le frais talus de leur chemin." "Toute poésie" [2] is a significant poem because it indicates that Char's thematic goal is a fusion of poetry and life; this poem contains the first evidence that organic unity is essential to his poetics and poetry. Furthermore, study of Char's first two collections, *Les Cloches sur le coeur* and *Arsenal*, reveals how his style, that is, the poet's role of communication, is to contribute to the presentation and eventual achievement of that goal.

René Char's first stage of development dates from 1907 to 1930. During this time, he views poetry as an instrument with which to detect and depict human reality as having an objective existence. Char concentrates on the act of poetry, not as the act of an individual man, but as the act of the poet's discovery which may help individual man. Throughout his first period, Char manifests interest in poetry as a possible tool for the establishment of truth. It is a period of "trial and error," a youthful period of experimental procedure in the field of poetry. This stage may be divided into three parts: 1) 1907-1929, Char's formative years as a historical individual; 2) 1922-1927,[3] his first appearance in print as a poet, represented by *Les Cloches sur le coeur*; and, 3) 1927-1930, his initial assessment of the possibilities of poetry in the first two editions of *Arsenal*.

1907-1930: THE EARLY YEARS

René Emile Char was born at Isle-sur-Sorgue in Vaucluse on June 14, 1907. His surname, Char, is an abbreviated form of Charlemagne, which was first shortened to Char-Magne and later to Char.[4] René Char is the only son[5] of Emile Char, a manufac-

---

[2] I have chosen the title "Toute poésie." Char occasionally designates a poem according to its first words.

[3] There is an overlap of dates between the first two stages because I find it more feasible to treat Char's first two works as poet apart from the discussion of his youth.

[4] P. A. Benoît, *Bibliographie des oeuvres de René Char de 1928 à 1963* (Paris, 1964), p. 11.

[5] Char has an older sister, Julia, about whom there is no information.

turer who also served as mayor of Isle-sur-Sorgue, and of Marie-Thérèse-Armande Rouget de Cavaillon, daughter of a mason. In 1918, when Char was 11 years old, his father died, leaving him to the guidance and care of his mother: "et j'appelle en vain mon père." [6] Although the extent of the effect of his father's death on Char's childhood is not known, he does indicate that this event caused him some difficulties during his adolescence: "Que d'années à grandir, / Sans père pour mon bras." [7] Moreover, in the discussion of "Jacquemard et Julia" in *Arrière-histoire du Poème pulvérisé* (1953), a work which was not published until after his mother's death, Char describes his mother as having been always "bonne pour moi, bien que maladroite parfois." This comment suggests that he was never able to be close to his mother. The death of Char's father and the subsequent uneasy relationship with his mother may have been the determining factors in Char's early exploration of the world of nature and his friendships with the men who live close to nature; he honors these men in *Soleil des eaux* (1951). In the "Pourquoi" of this work, he pays hommage to the men of La Sorgue for "un apprentissage privilégié."

Char's childhood was spent in Isle-sur-Sorgue, where he gained an understanding of nature and its manifestations, an accurate knowledge of agriculture, and a deep respect for the inhabitants of the rural region of Vaucluse. His affection for this area and for nature permeates the vocabulary of all his works; this is particularly true of *Les Matinaux* (1950) and *La Paroi et la prairie* (1952). Even today, Char divides his time between Paris and Isle-sur-Sorgue.

Char's closest childhood friend seems to have been Louis Curel, who incarnates human freedom and action in "Louis Curel de la Sorgue" (*Seuls demeurent*, 1945), and to whose father, François Curel, Char wrote throughout World War II of the lessons contained in nature for man. [8] In addition, it was Louis Curel who

---

No doubt, she was named for Char's mother's sister and Emile Char's first wife who died after one year of marriage ("Jacquemard et Julia," *Arrière-histoire du Poème pulvérisé*, 1953).

[6] "Présence chère qui n'est plus," *Les Cloches sur le coeur* (Paris, 1928).

[7] "Le Deuil des Névons," *La Bibliothèque est en feu et autres poèmes* in *La Parole en archipel* (Paris, 1962).

[8] "Billets à F. C.," *Recherche de la base et du sommet* (Paris, 1955).

aided Char in his characterizations of L'Armurier and Apollon for *Le Soleil des eaux*.[9]

There is little information available on Char's formative years. He attended first the Ecole communale of Isle-sur-Sorgue and later the Lycée d'Avignon where he studied for the Baccalauréat. The exact dates of Char's attendance at this Lycée are not known, but he seems to have spent two to three years there from 1922 or 1923 to 1925, the years during which he read Reverdy [10] and composed most of *Les Cloches sur le coeur*. Mounin suggests that Char first began to write poetry during his studies at Avignon; this evidence is found in the text "Ce Soir..."[11] This poem was later published in *Le Feu* in April, 1929:

> Le chèvrefeuille en fleurs frissonne, languissant,
> Au vieux mur décrépi, tout boursouflé de pierre;
> Les volets se sont clos ce soir à ma prière,
> Le chèvrefeuille en fleurs se dresse éperdûment
> L'âme de tes parfums erre en ce doux moment,
> Je devine ta voix en ce soir de misère,
> Mon coeur est cet enfant tout délirant de fièvre,
> Et qui clame sa peur de mourir, grimaçant.
> Quelque chose a glissé sur ma joue, lentement,
> Un cyprès quelque part apaise un cimetière;
> Ton souvenir est là qui rôde et qui espère,
> Je suis lâche ce soir, hélas! je t'aimais tant!
> Et sur mon désespoir la nuit grave s'étend.

Mounin describes "Ce Soir..." as "un poème de collégien" characterized by "une vieille prosodie."[12] It is probably one of Char's earliest texts, but Mounin errs in dismissing it as "un sonnet mallarméen."[13] In "Ce Soir...," as in "Toute poésie," one finds an indication of Char's ultimate poetic vision. While "Toute poésie" emphasizes the role of poetry, "Ce Soir" suggests how the poet

---

[9] Louis Curel, "Evocation de l'Armurier et d'Apollon," *Témoignages et documents* in *Le Soleil des eaux* (Paris, 1951), pp. 154-156. Char also mentions that Jacques Dupin, the musical composer of *Le Soleil des eaux*, found it valuable to speak with Louis Curel ("Pourquoi du 'Soleil des eaux'," p. 150).
[10] Mounin, p. 282.
[11] *Ibid.*, pp. 276-282.
[12] *Ibid.*, p. 277.
[13] *Ibid.*

may make this role meaningful for man. Char addresses "tu," his muse of inspiration, as a woman who alleviates man's loneliness and isolation even in her absence: "Je devine ta voix en ce soir de misère." This text foreshadows Char's later poetry: the importance of absence ("ton souvenir"), the role of desire ("délirant de fièvre"), the use of "tu" as the poet's companion, and interest in the present time demonstrated by the prevailing force of the present tense. In fact, these thematic and stylistic concerns characterize all of Char's work, and it is interesting to note their early appearance in his poetics and poetry.

In 1925, Char enrolled at the Ecole de Commerce in Marseille, and he may have attended the Université d'Aix;[14] between 1925 and 1926, he completed *Les Cloches sur le coeur*. From 1927 to 1928, he did his military service as an artilleryman at Nîmes, where he began the first edition of *Arsenal*. After his discharge from the army, Char returned to Isle-sur-Sorgue where he served until 1930 as editor of a literary review, *Méridiens*: "Revue mensuelle de tendance et d'expression modernes. Vers et proses. Direct.: René Emile Char."[15] Other than a trip to Tunisia in 1924, Char seems to have spent the first period of his life in the southern part of France, in Vaucluse, Avignon, Marseille, and Nîmes.

1922-1927: *Les Cloches sur le coeur*

Les Cloches sur le coeur (1928) is Char's first published volume of poems. Most of the 153 copies of this work were destroyed by Char as an act of repudiation of the traditional prosody which characterizes the edition. Char later recognized that his early poems suggest the eventual direction of his poetic development, and accordingly, he republished some of them in *Premières alluvions* in 1946: "Ce n'est que plus tard que l'objet de mon embarras m'apparut sous les traits ruisselants et tout aussi ambigus de poème."[16] *Premières alluvions* is a description of the poet's first

---

[14] *Who's Who in France 1955-1956* (Paris, 1955), p. 723.
[15] *Nomenclature des journaux et revues en langue française paraissant dans le monde entier* (Paris, 1930-1931), p. 707.
[16] "Je me voulais événement...," *Premières alluvions* (Paris, 1946).

attempts to build under the influence of poetic inspiration; what remains are the alluvia or increases of land formed by the flowing waters of poetic activity. This 1946 work is usually the only one available for the study of Char's poetic debut, but it is not an accurate presentation of this early stage in Char's evolution. On the contrary, *Premières alluvions* represents Char's retrospective appraisal of his early stage of development, for only 11 of the original 38 texts are included, and, of these 11, all but one were revised between 1928 and 1946.[17]

Furthermore, Char includes in *Premières alluvions* one poem, "Jouvence I,"[18] which does not appear in *Les Cloches sur le coeur*. The date of "Jouvence I" is 1923-1925, the earliest specific date given for a poem by Char. "Jouvence I" praises those poets who endeavor to infuse a new spirit in poetry, one which will give man a new understanding of his existence: "...l'oeil unique/Et leur taciturne horizon." Significantly, this early text represents Char's first known expression of artistic responsibility, a theme which is assumed but neither affirmed nor even discussed in *Les Cloches sur le coeur*.

"Jouvence I" and "Toute poésie" are Char's earliest available texts. Both poems treat poetry as an instrument for the discovery of reality. Neither text was published during Char's first period of development although they underlie his early commitment to poetry, represented by *Les Cloches sur le coeur*, as well as by the first two editions of *Arsenal*.

The revisions which mark the early texts included in *Premières alluvions* consist primarily of deletions rather than textual revisions.[19] Char eliminates the awkward phraseology, banal images, and superfluous elements which characterize to a large extent *Les Cloches sur le coeur*. These changes reflect a shift in Char's attitude

---

[17] "Prêt au dépouillement" is the only text which remains unchanged. The other poems included in *Premières alluvions* are: "Harmonium" as "14 Juin 1924," "Morte-saison," "Profession de foi" as "Poème pour la voir," "Sillage" as "Sillage noir," "Intérieur" as "Le Veilleur naïf," "Parallèle du coeur" as "Le Sol de la nuit," "Témoignages de grandeur," "Présage" and "Pour une vierge" as "Fanemousse"; "Sans pardon" appears only in the 1950 edition of *Premières alluvions*.

[18] "Jouvence II" appears once in the 1950 edition of *Premières alluvions*; only "Jouvence I" is definitely dated and can be positively included in a discussion of Char's earliest stage of development.

[19] See Appendix III.

toward life, demonstrated by the 1928 text, "Harmonium," and its 1946 form as "14 Juin 1924." The last four lines of "Harmonium" were:

> Qu'importe si laide sera notre joie
> Avenir enfante passé
> Epelle l'amour sur les doigts
> Mais tous les doigts sont mutilés.

The 1946 text emphasizes the constructive value of the poet's efforts:

> Epelle l'amour sur les doigts
> Lorsque les doigts sont mutilés
> Aussi fervente sera ta joie
> Aussi fertile ta journée.

The 1928 text suggests that Char believes in the poet's creative force as a possible means of making the present acceptable in the present, while the 1946 version affirms that poetic activity is the only means to attain a better present and future; this concept does not fully emerge in Char's work until his third period of development, 1937-1947, during which he prepared *Premières alluvions*.

Premières alluvions contains the poet's view of his early efforts, his first work, his foundation. In this respect, it is an interesting work, for it reveals what Char had announced in "Toute poésie" and "Jouvence I" and had hoped to achieve in *Les Cloches sur le coeur*. By 1928, he was aware of the inherent possibilities of poetry in general and sensed his own artistic direction in particular; this is illustrated by the 1946 revisions. Nevertheless, *Premières alluvions* is no more than a work of salvage and reconstruction. In a sense, it is a distortion, but a distortion of conscious effort and love by the poet in order to show on the one hand that his poetic debut is in keeping with his later work and on the other that his poetics and poetry were influenced by the nineteenth and early twentieth century's concept of "modernité," and not by the Surrealist movement.[20]

---

[20] P. A. Benoît, Pierre Berger, and Georges Mounin are the only critics who recognize the value of Char's pre-Surreal poetic formation.

According to Benoît,[21] *Les Cloches sur le coeur* was composed between 1922 and 1926, a period which Mounin describes as "l'avant-garde non-surréaliste,"[22] that is, Char wrote his first work "dans l'ignorance du surréalisme."[23] Char's "ignorance" of Surrealism is important to an understanding of *Les Cloches sur le coeur*, for this work shows clearly that Char's literary antecedents are found outside the Surrealist movement and are independent of the Surrealists' appraisal of nineteenth and early twentieth century writers. In *Pauvreté et privilège* (1955), Char confides his admiration for Baudelaire, Rimbaud, and Apollinaire and their efforts to free poetry from conventional rules and subjects. The influence of these three poets is unmistakable in Char's first work.

The main theme of *Les Cloches sur le coeur* is the hostile passage of time. "Les cloches" refers to bells which mark the passing of man's life, represented by "le coeur." As each bell strikes, it reminds man that he is mortal, fragile, and condemned to death. Man's only certainty is that he will die. Char's title and the dominant theme of his work specifically recall these lines from "L'Horloge" by Baudelaire:

Horloge! dieu sinistre, effrayant, impossible.
Dont le doigt nous menace et nous dit: *Souviens-toi*!

Tantôt sonnera l'heure...
Où tout te dira: "Meurs, vieux lâche! Il est trop tard!"[24]

The theme of time and inevitable death in Char's work is reinforced by a vocabulary of oppressive funereal terms: "mort," "bière," "cadavre," "meurtri," "morbide," "moribond," "cortège," "tombe," "trépas," "râle," "mortel," "glas." These terms, which also mark much of Baudelaire's poetry, are juxtaposed with a satirical use of a religious vocabulary: "supplice," "ange," "rosaire," "mi-carême," "foi," "crèche," "hérésie," "hymne," "messe," "stigmatiser." The satire of religion is reminiscent of Rimbaud's demand that the poet replace God, a view shared by the young

---

[21] Benoît, p. 11.
[22] Mounin, p. 282.
[23] *Ibid.*, p. 276.
[24] Charles Baudelaire, "L'Horloge," *Les Fleurs du mal*, ed. Antoine Adam (Paris, 1959), p. 87.

Char who is in rebellion against modern man's fear of life. Terms which denote sailing ("mât," "nacelle," "marin," "môle," "cale," "voilier," "navire") evoke both Baudelaire and Rimbaud and their use of the voyage to escape and show the decadence of man's existence. Char continues their insistence that the poet discover how to free man from his fear of life. Throughout *Les Cloches sur le coeur*, Char evokes Baudelaire's "spleen" in the spirit of Rimbaud's revolt. Char joins in Baudelaire's attack on "ennui" and Rimbaud's depiction of "désarroi." For Char, as for Baudelaire and Rimbaud, there must be more to life than agony and death; behind the externals of the world, "l'ennui de sable," [25] there must be a unity which makes it possible to reverse the limits of man's condemnation to decay: "Au même passé au même avenir." [26]

Char concentrates on the despair of man's mortality: "Les hommes porteurs de trépas." [27] He observes that "qui se concrétise ... se meurt." [28] Like Baudelaire, Char finds that no experience is free from the threat of destruction: "Sur un clavier la mort joue des airs drôles." [29] Even physical love is accompanied by the knowledge that flesh decays, that there is no escape from death: "Au creux du lit annexe du tombeau." [30] In fact, the event of life is often more depressing than the state of death: "J'ouvre à la vie et c'est le pire." [31]

Like Baudelaire and Rimbaud, Char is disgusted by life as he sees it. He is "le scribe honteux de la terre" [32] who "parcourt les rues," [33] seeking some hope which will enable him and others to raise the "ancre de désespoir." [34] His examination of man's behavior reveals debauchery, prostitution, murder legalized by war, spiritual disease; corruption even threatens the innocence of childhood. Despite the fact that men "tonnent un hymne nostalgique" [35] for purity and happiness, the poet finds only moral de-

---

[25] "Harmonium," *Les Cloches sur le coeur* (Paris, 1928).
[26] "Morte-saison."
[27] "Rappel."
[28] "Tenailles."
[29] "Sonatine."
[30] "Progressivement vers la passe."
[31] "Présence chère qui n'est plus."
[32] "Aumône d'hier."
[33] *Ibid.*
[34] "Dupe de la couleur."
[35] "Rappel."

generacy and "plaisir morbide." [36] This observation disgusts Char as it did Mallarmé: "Mon esprit tournoie dans le vide/Mon espoir tournoie d'être vide." [37]

The central problem of *Les Cloches sur le coeur* is the replacement of "le vide" by the discovery of "latentes réalités" [38] which will permit man to overcome his fear of life and live more meaningfully in the present. Religion fails to construct a better present because it promises a better future: "la promesse d'être aveugle." [39] Individual man can only experience life; the state of death is not "sa véritable image." [40] It is impossible to "descendre dans la certitude du demain," [41] for only the *hic et nunc* confronts man. Like Apollinaire, Char wants to establish a modern myth for the acceptance of reality and human existence:

> La véridique histoire d'un siècle
> De décrépitude pour regénérer
> Une légende nourricière. [42]

Moreover, the starting point of this "légende nourricière" is found in the everyday world of man: "La feuille refuse à un rêve/Qui n'est jamais redescendu." [43] Within man's immediate grasp, the poet must find a means "que le vide soit meilleur." [44]

Char's first proposed solution for the improvement of daily life, "le coeur," and the abatement of oppression, "les cloches," is love. Physical love is an individual means with which to reach the "latentes réalités" of man's own being. There is a beneficial and strengthening quality to be gained from the experience of passion: "Sirène au ventre du désir/Boit l'horizon..." [45] It is an act which leads to fulfillment and an act which demands that each participant go beyond self-interest and be oriented towards another being:

---

[36] "Tenailles."
[37] "Sans pardon."
[38] "Arrière vertige des tremplins."
[39] "Constitution de l'autre terre."
[40] "Intérieur."
[41] "Constitution de l'autre terre."
[42] "Flexibilité de l'oubli."
[43] "Naissance du jour."
[44] "Parallèle du coeur."
[45] "Présage."

> Pour que mon amour revienne
> Me labourer le coeur
> A cette cheminée qui fume
> A cette maison qui saigne.[46]

Furthermore, sexual love is also a possible condition for fulfillment beyond the physical: "Ce rêve l'amour l'amitié."[47] The de-emphasis of the sexual aspect of love later becomes a general characteristic of Char's work and provides him with the basis for fraternal exchange.

Another concern which will receive further development in Char's poetics and poetry is the effort to reveal the instant of becoming. In the poem "Intérieur," Char attempts to capture and immortalize one link in a chain of events which is that event at the moment of occurrence: "A l'instant ne fut que la chose."

In addition, Char's interest in the particular as representative of the general character of existence appears throughout *Les Cloches sur le coeur*. This is indicated by the title of the poem, "Un Oiseau suffit à la vie." Moreover, *Les Cloches sur le coeur* begins with a quotation attributed to William Blake, who endeavored to reveal the universal harmony of existence through the examination of one of its component parts: "Ne comprends-tu pas que le moindre oiseau qui fend l'air est un immense monde de délices formé par tes cinq sens." Char's citation of Blake also serves three other purposes. First, it emphasizes the poet's awareness of the literary activities of his time, for Blake was not introduced into French literature until the 1920's. Secondly, a reference to an eighteenth-century English writer universalizes the scope of the problem treated in *Les Cloches sur le coeur*. Thirdly, and most importantly, this quotation announces the revelation of a unified reality behind contradictory appearances, a reality which can be discovered through man's conscious experience.

The problem of contradictory appearances and possible fusion of these opposites is frequently posed in *Les Cloches sur le coeur*. This interest in the problem of opposites is expressed in several ways: reality versus appearance, absence versus presence, life versus death, destruction versus construction, particular versus gener-

---

[46] "Parallèle du coeur."
[47] "Sans pardon."

al. In brief, it is the impossible versus the possible. Each contradiction is a continuing one of concern in Char's poetry and is further developed in his later works. In *Les Cloches sur le coeur*, the problem is posed, but it is not solved. This problem is to be the major goal and connective force of Char's poetry: "Par ce temps de soleil veule, de douceur sans contrariété, il est inacceptable que la distance soit telle."[48]

In general, the vocabulary of *Les Cloches sur le coeur* is oppressive. Expressions of death, anguish, suffering, hopelessness and despair dominate. It is this emphasis on the dismal aspects of man's existence which distinguishes *Les Cloches sur le coeur* from the rest of Char's work. While Char will consistently view man and his world without illusions, his basic attitude becomes one of optimism rather than pessimism. This attitude is present in his first work in the tone of disbelief which underlies his use of terms of death and futility. Significantly, this tone of indignation is most frequently used in conjunction with expressions drawn from the physical world of matter. Within nature, the young Char senses a feeling of permanence and hope through recurring phenomena: "champs," "germe," "soleil," "graine," "tige," "feuille," "arc-en-ciel." The use of a vocabulary based on nature and cosmic elements becomes one of the chief characteristics of Char's work in general.

Char's admiration for Baudelaire, Rimbaud, Apollinaire and, to a lesser degree, Mallarmé is seen in his vocabulary and imagery, as well as in his themes. Some of his lines can be traced directly to them. The best example is this line from "Profession de foi" which recalls Mallarmé's "Brise marine": "Souvent ai-je tracé sur le/Papier vierge..." One also finds overtones of Mallarmé in Char's use of a pane of glass as a transparent object and as an obstacle, the mirror, in "Intérieur" and "Caesia."

The direct influence of Baudelaire's "Au lecteur" appears in several poems, particularly in these lines of "Sans pardon":

> Où s'attise le repentir
>
> Le lâche qui suivra sa bière
> N'aura plus droit à la lumière.

---

[48] "Prêt au dépouillement."

Additional similarity is found in the treatment of sensuality in Baudelaire's "La Chevelure" and Char's "Caesia" and "Pèlerinage." On the other hand, Apollinaire is reflected in Char's efforts to treat a trivial event of daily life in "Un Oiseau suffit à la vie" and "Ravages de la lune" and in his use of terms of modernity: "oiseau saturé d'électricité," "sun-lights."

Three of the 38 texts of *Les Cloches sur le coeur* are prose poems: "Prêt au dépouillement," "Variation en caractères," and "Un Oiseau suffit à la vie." In general, the poems in verse are characterized by uneven metric lines; however, almost one-third of them are marked by octosyllabic meter. Only two texts, "Présage" and "Ravages de la lune," are in ballad form. Despite similarities in theme and style, it is interesting to note that Baudelaire's use of the alexandrine line and the sonnet form has little influence on Char's first volume of poems.

There is much end rhyme in *Les Cloches sur le coeur*, and the most frequent schema used are: abba, ababcc, aabb, aabccb. However, Char often seems to make a conscious effort to disrupt rhyme patterns with the following irregular schema: abcdd, aaba, abac, abcca. Many of the texts appear in free verse form, and it is this form which will characterize the first edition of *Arsenal* and the whole body of Char's poems in verse. After *Les Cloches sur le coeur*, very little end rhyme and formal metric rhythm mark Char's poetry.[49]

Although formal conventions of style distinguish *Les Cloches sur le coeur* from Char's later works, the use of the free verse form, the prose poem, and irregular metric and rhyme patterns shows that Char is moving away from a traditional prosody toward an undefined, unlimited, and, above all, independent style of poetic composition. In fact, *Les Cloches sur le coeur* contains evidence of the style that will later identify Char's work.

The main tense of *Les Cloches sur le coeur* is the past tense because it is the past which has brought about the oppressive present which confronts the poet. The past has generated man's current fear of life and his feelings of inadequacy and futility in the face of constant death. Yet, man lives in the present. Therefore, the poet must reject not only the past, but also the future

---

[49] After 1928, the major reoccurrence of end rhyme and formal metric patterns is found in *La Sieste blanche* in *Les Matinaux* (1950).

and all promises of a better tomorrow; he must concentrate on the present if he is to enable man to live meaningfully. Although past tenses statistically dominate *Les Cloches sur le coeur*, it is the problem of action in the present which actually prevails: "Ce n'est plus possible .../D'ouvrir à la vie un coffret." [50] Recognition of the need to live and act in the present indicates that Char's later texts will be characterized by the present tense.

The most significant stylistic trait of *Les Cloches sur le coeur* is the use of "tu," which appears not only throughout this work, but also marks all of Char's poetics and poetry. This "tu" of poetic address is a nameless companion who accompanies Char in the communication of his discoveries. It is of, to, and about "tu" that most of Char's poetry is composed; "tu" represents the best that the poet possesses, his creative force, his poetry:

> Ta voix est décharnée intraduisible et c'est tout juste en l'écoutant si cette verge dont je me cingle le mollet ne devient pas le plus vil instrument de supplice. [51]

Les Cloches sur le coeur is the work of a zealous young poet who resents the futility of daily life. In its ardent response to those poets who first recognized man's hopelessness and tried to reintegrate man with his world, *Les Cloches sur le coeur* is a work of hommage to Baudelaire, Rimbaud, and Apollinaire. However, this work is above all a declaration of determination to continue the work of those who preceded. The tone which underlies every text is one of anguish without resignation; it is not a tone of hostile anger, but one of resolute protest, which refuses to accept a degenerate and condemned existence of instability, chaos, and moral decrepitude: "un suicide moral ne pouvait me suffire." [52] It is an announcement that Char the man and Char the poet is to dedicate his work to the constructive discovery of a homogeneous reality through the destruction of contradictory appearances. In *Les Cloches sur le coeur*, Char indicates that he will answer the challenge to confront the present in the present and make it acceptable to individual man through poetry.

---

[50] "Profession de foi," *Les Cloches sur le coeur*.
[51] "Prêt au dépouillement."
[52] Epigraph.

1927-1930: *Arsenal*

Char completed *Les Cloches sur le coeur* in 1926 or 1927 and began *Arsenal* in 1927. Like *Les Cloches sur le coeur*, the first two editions of *Arsenal* (1929, 1930) [53] retain an interest in love as a possible condition for poetry and in the role of the poet to discover reality. In addition, *Arsenal* represents Char's break with traditional poetry, for no rules of versification or structure are observed.

However, unlike *Les Cloches sur le coeur*, neither edition of *Arsenal* was composed "dans l'ignorance du surréalisme." [54] On the contrary, *Arsenal* shows that the Surrealist movement appealed to Char during the late 1920's. This is evident not only in the form and content of the first two editions, but also in Char's decision to send a copy of the 1929 volume to an active member of the Surrealist group, Paul Eluard. It is significant to note that Char selected the poet Eluard rather than André Breton, the author of the *Manifeste du surréalisme* (1924) and the acknowledged leader of the Surrealist group. Char's choice of Eluard indicates that his primary concern was the composition of poetry rather than the establishment of theory. In other words, Char already felt that he knew what he wanted to express in poetry; his problem was one of communication. Char desired criticism of his work by an established poet, and for this role he chose Eluard. Moreover, in 1929, Eluard was more actively engaged than Breton in the liberation of poetry through the act of poetry, the actual writing of poems. [55]

---

[53] The third edition appears in *Le Marteau sans maître* (1934), which represents Char's Surrealist texts. The first two editions are pre-Surreal and belong to Char's first stage of poetic development.

[54] Mounin, p. 276.

[55] This is not intended to minimize Breton's literary activity before 1929. However, Breton was more active in the organization of his group, in the promotion of his movement, and in the publication of documents than in the composition of poetry. In fact, Breton had published very little poetry before 1929. His major works in the early years of the Surrealist movement, 1924-1929, consisted of one novel, *Nadja* (1928), and several documents: *Manifeste du surréalisme* (1924), *Légitime défense* (1926), *Introduction au discours sur le peu de réalité* (1927), and *Le Surréalisme et la peinture* (1928). On the contrary, Eluard had published several works of poetry, notably *Mourir de ne pas mourir* (1924), *Capitale de la douleur* (1926), *Les Dessous d'une vie ou la pyramide humaine* (1926), and *L'Amour la poésie* (1929).

Char's admiration for Eluard's work is not surprising, for there are definite affinities within their poetic visions. The young Char envisaged poetry as a means to discover the truth of reality and enable man to enter into meaningful relationships with others; this is suggested in his treatment of love in *Les Cloches sur le coeur* and in the 1929 edition of *Arsenal*. These general aims also characterize Eluard's concern with the immediacy of life, stress on the real world, effort to use a language common to all men, and desire to expand poetry in order to integrate man and poetry.

Eluard reacted favorably to Char's 1929 edition of *Arsenal* and went to Isle-sur-Sorgue to see Char and invited him to visit Paris.[56] In 1929, Char took his first trip to Paris where he met Breton and other leading Surrealists. In 1930, he returned to Paris to join the Surrealist group.

Between his two trips to Paris, Char revised the first edition of *Arsenal* and published it in 1930. While both the 1929 and 1930 editions reflect Char's interest in the new spirit in poetry proclaimed by the Surrealists, the changes between the two editions reveal his movement in the Surrealist direction. However, it is important to note that Char was not a member of the Surrealist group when he prepared the texts of the first two editions of *Arsenal*.[57]

One poem, "Flexibilité de l'oubli," marks the specific character of the turning point in Char's poetic development toward the unlimited possibilities of poetry as envisaged by the Surrealists. In retrospect, this poem seems to represent Char's earliest Surrealist text, but it was originally published in *Les Cloches sur le coeur* (1928), that is written during his period "non-surréaliste."[58] In "Flexibilité de l'oubli," Char shows interest in the search for the marvelous in the everyday existence of man, an interest shared by the Surrealists. However, examination of the text reveals that Char was probably influenced by Baudelaire, Rimbaud, and Apollinaire and not by the Surrealists, although certain analogies with Surrealism are possible, particularly the exploration of the subconscious as a possible means to attain man's ultimate and true reality.

---

[56] Benoît, p. 11.
[57] Maurice Nadeau, *Histoire du surréalisme* (Paris, 1964), p. 503.
[58] Mounin, p. 276.

"Flexibilité de l'oubli" is concerned with the role of the poet in the dream world of hallucinations. The poet wanders in the world of sleep where new perspectives of reality may come into view:

> Sans l'écumeur de mémoire
> Avide de ce qu'il ne comprend pas
> Vorace de ce qu'il redoute.

The poet is a "pèlerin" in an urban environment: "cité," "gratte-ciel," "grabat," "portes-cochères." In his inner voyage for "mers intérieures," he finds that he remains preoccupied with the real world of everyday existence: "Boule élastique ce coeur / Percé de flasques mamelles." The "putains" recall the real, as dawn approaches and the dream ends: "A chaque coup de sonnette/ Une morte." The poet's experience in the unfamiliar dream world has been a temporary wandering away from the memory of the known, but this "oubli" is adaptable to modification; it is flexible and pliant; it yields readily to the real. The poet "avance en chantant" this experience in the concrete form of a poem.

The style and, above all, the images of "Flexibilité de l'oubli" reflect the possible influence of Reverdy,[59] whose definition of the image was also adopted by the Surrealists: "Plus les rapports rapprochés seront lointains et justes, plus l'image sera forte."[60] Char's early images, in this text as well as in both editions of *Arsenal*, seem to reflect an effort to master Reverdy's theory of the image. His juxtaposition of images to express the penetration of the extraordinary and yet unite the real and the dream worlds is demonstrated in these lines:

> Gratte-ciel saute d'étoile en étoile
> Comme nacelle à bout de lest
>
> Horizontale à même le grabat
> Les pieds de salpêtre qui neige la toiture
>
> Les putains...
> Se lancent leurs linges fumants.

---

[59] Char was well acquainted with Reverdy's work by 1925 (Mounin, p. 282).
[60] Pierre Reverdy, quoted by André Breton in the 1924 *Manifeste du surréalisme* (Paris, 1963), p. 31.

In general, the vocabulary of "Flexibilité de l'oubli" is not as simple and elementary as that which dominates *Les Cloches sur le coeur*. The vocabulary of this text and of both editions of *Arsenal* is more abstract as if to grasp the intangible aspects of life: "écumeur," "vapeurs," "déséquilibre," "plaintes." However, concrete terms prevail to express the importance of this experience in the immediacy of man's reality: "bras," "gratte-ciel," "nacelle," "cheminée," "pieds," "boule," "linges," "candélabres," "mains," "lèvres," "épaules," "instrument." The immediacy of the experience is reinforced by the present tense which is the only tense used in the poem. Past participles appear as adjectives to erase past time and to place emphasis on the present correction of past experience.

"Flexibilité de l'oubli" is the only poem which was included in *Les Cloches sur le coeur* and the first two editions of *Arsenal*. In 1928, the text consisted of 11 stanzas; in 1929, four (V, VI, VIII, IX) were completely omitted and 13 lines of three other stanzas were also omitted,[61] but very few textual changes occurred.[62] The significance of these deletions is best demonstrated by these lines from the 1928 text: "Fardeau de génie bossu/Borgne qui fume l'alcool des déroutes." In 1929, Char suppresses all references to hallucinations experienced in the states of drunkenness and preserves only those lines which suggest disorder attained through sleep and dreams. This emphasis on the unconscious as it functions in the world of sleep reveals Char's growing interest in the activities of the Surrealists. In other words, the 1929 revisions of "Flexibilité de l'oubli" point directly to Char's movement toward Surrealism.

Moreover, "Flexibilité de l'oubli" was slightly revised between the 1929 and 1930 editions of *Arsenal*. In both editions, this poem consists of seven stanzas. In the seventh stanza, the position of the last line, "Candélabres en mains les étreignant," was changed to become the first line of that stanza. The relocation of this line to an initial position emphasizes Char's interest in discovering the real world; the subconscious or dream world has meaning only in its clarification of the real. In the last stanza, Char deleted

---

[61] See Appendix III.
[62] Plurals become singulars and the line length changes in some instances, but these revisions are minor. See Appendix III.

the third and fourth lines: "Clown musical/Aux braises des sunlights." In the 1928 and 1929 text, these lines satirize the poet's role, while their omission in 1930 indicates that Char has become confident in his chosen role. This confidence may well have been one of the results of Eluard's 1929 visit to Isle-sur-Sorgue and Char's subsequent introduction to the Surrealist group.

Additional revisions between the 1929 and 1930 editions of *Arsenal* are found in "La Tête sous l'oreiller" and "Le Grand travail." In "La Tête sous l'oreiller," Char deleted the middle stanza:

> Nos mains qui fouillent l'édredon
> Provoquent les anges en délire
> Or combien d'anges ont pour rire
> Fendu leurs lèvres d'un juron?

This stanza serves merely as a transition between the two parts of the poem, "le rire" and "le coeur." It explains how the two aspects of the text are actually one action experienced concurrently by the same individual. The omission of these four lines is further accompanied by a rearrangement of the poem on the printed page and represents one of Char's earliest successful uses of space through form. In 1930, he divides the poem into two parts; he places "le rire" at the left margin as a subtitle and indents the description of lines 2-4 under it; this procedure is followed in the second stanza with "l'amour." The transitional stanza ceases to be necessary; through spatial typography, Char juxtaposes two opposites, reveals them as representative of one experience, and supplants the need for transition. The elimination of transition is a trend by the end of Char's first period of development.

In "Le Grand travail," Char rewrote the last stanza. The 1929 text, "On voit la tête/calculer," was significantly changed in 1930 to "Tête à tête/N'est pas calculer." The 1929 form implies that the poet attempts to calculate reality, that is make reality acceptable through a process based on the poet's estimate of the facts. In 1930, Char corrects this through the negatives "ne... pas"; the poet's "grand travail" is not to calculate but to decipher; he must discover and interpret reality as it is, not forecast it. This revision announces Char's concern with doing as opposed to being, with discovery as opposed to creation or invention.

The 1929 edition of *Arsenal* consisted of 16 poems; 14 were included in the 1930 edition, and of these 14 texts, 11 remained unchanged.[63] These 11 poems indicate that Char's poetry is moving away from a treatment of an act itself and toward the expression of activity. This evolution from act to activity begins in the first two editions of *Arsenal* and distinguishes them from *Les Cloches sur le coeur*, while Char's actual rejection of act and adoption of activity marks these two editions of *Arsenal* from those written during his Surrealist period.

For Char, the difference between act and activity is mainly temporal. An act refers to a function performed, an effect produced, an achievement attained. Its duration is measurable, for an act is the result of something done in the past. On the other hand, activity cannot be measured, for it refers to the state of actual doing in the present. Activity denotes movement, and it often suggests the occurrence of change through the exertion of energy. An act is "being," while an activity is "doing."

An act of poetry is the written poem, the result of the poet's activity. The activity produces the act. Therefore, the activity is more important than the act. Char's shift from act to activity is first noted in his predilection for the present tense and verbs of motion: "passe," "tire," "délivre," "tourne," "pousse," "libère," "avance," "marche." In the first two editions of *Arsenal*, the present tense is clearly associated with verbs of motion or "doing" as opposed to the past tense and verbs of description, "being," which characterize *Les Cloches sur le coeur*.

In both editions of *Arsenal*, three themes, previously noted in *Les Cloches sur le coeur*, are connected to Char's growing interest in activity: the poet as the discoverer of reality, love as a condition for poetry, and the liberation of poetry from a traditional prosody. Moreover, these three themes begin to converge with each other for the first time.

In order to discover reality, the poet must be free in his activity: "L'oiseau maquis de paradis/Tire la corde de tumulte."[64] He must reject rules and conventions of composition and of form. The expression of thematic freedom is found in the treatment of physical love as a source of human fulfillment, proclaimed by

---

[63] The 11 poems are: "L'Emploi," "La Vérité," "Possible," "Probable," "Puissance négative," "La Guerre sous roche," "L'Exhibitionniste," "L'Embaumé." "Singulier," "Leçon sévère," and "La Plus heureuse."
[64] "La Vérité," *Arsenal* (Nîmes, 1929 and 1930).

1907–1930: A POETICS OF THE ART OF POETRY 35

Apollinaire and others, as well as by the Surrealists. Char uses this theme, but it is significant that his only exploration of physical love in and of itself appears in *Les Cloches sur le coeur*, where he also first senses the possible expansion of sexual love as a condition for an act of poetry. In *Arsenal* (1929 and 1930), physical love is treated only in its poetic application: "L'amour enseigne." [65]

Poetic freedom and physical love are two of the materials in the poet's "arsenal" for his discoveries. Another important source at the poet's disposal is free and uncontrolled inspiration: "Elle mange à sa faim." [66] Like the Surrealists, Char is also interested in seeking a new order or a new perspective of order through the world of sleep; this is noted in "L'Emploi," "Le Grand travail," and "Flexibilité de l'oubli." He even examines automatic writing:

> On libère le bras qui tombe sous les sens
> On retourne le doigt
> Le coup part au poignet. [67]

However, despite the appearance of these Surrealist traits in both editions of *Arsenal*, the 1930 edition is closer to Surrealism than the first edition; this is represented by the omission of two poems from the 1929 edition and the addition of six texts in 1930. [68] The two texts deleted in 1930 are "Récit funèbre prend forme de poème" and "La Délivrance naturelle." Both texts seem to have been replaced in 1930 by "Bonne aventure," which modifies the form of the first and the content of the second. Like "Récit funèbre prend forme de poème," this text expresses emotion by typography rather than by content; in both poems, details return over and over as the details of life are said to flash before a drowning man. The major difference between the two texts is reflected by their respective titles; the 1929 title, "Récit funèbre prend forme de poème," is more pessimistic than the 1930 title, "Bonne aventure." Moreover, the problem posed in 1929 is answer-

---

[65] "Leçon sévère."
[66] "Singulier."
[67] "La Guerre sous roche."
[68] The six texts added are: "Le Sujet," "Bonne aventure," "Masque de fer," "L'," "Amour," and "L'Egalité." These texts were placed at the beginning of the volume, preserving the order of the 14 texts included from the 1929 edition.

ed in this 1930 text in a line taken from "La Délivrance naturelle": "gagner le soleil." The poet's RECHERCHE d'un emploi du TEMPS" in the dream world fails in 1929 as a "récit funèbre"; his release from the limits of the real world, his search for "la délivrance naturelle" in sleep, results in distortion but not in new knowledge. In "Bonne aventure," he succeeds in finding value in a distorted view of reality; the dream becomes a "bonne aventure."

Between the 1929 and 1930 editions of *Arsenal*, Char becomes convinced of the possibility of attaining knowledge through the subconscious. Unlike "Récit funèbre prend forme de poème" and "La Délivrance naturelle," "Bonne aventure" is a "récit de rêve," as it is envisaged by the Surrealists, and it represents Char's first attempt in this area.

Char's interest in the new perspective which is possible through the disorder of the dream and his exploration of the subconscious in "Bonne aventure" is reinforced by "Masque de fer" and "L'Egalité," also added in 1930. In "Masque de fer," Char stresses the value of free inspiration, "viande secrète," a description first found in "La Délivrance naturelle" in 1929. In "L'Egalité," he criticizes efforts to restrain inspiration and control the poet's activity, "la bouche en chant."

The desire to fuse opposites in *Les Cloches sur le coeur* continues in the first two editions of *Arsenal* in "Puissance négative." But, in the 1930 edition, Char links for the first time this vision of fusion with the theme of love; this is demonstrated by "L'" and "Amour." "L'" acknowledges the necessity of a sexual union between man and woman, but within this union a notion of dependency of one participant upon the other overrides and weakens the idea of a joint but equal union: "N'attends rien de toi-même/qui ne soit passé par moi-même." In "Amour," the seeking of a union is associated with a concept of absence: "C'est ne rien entendre à toi-même." Although neither concept of union, man and woman, absence and presence, is developed in this work, it is significant to note their appearance in Char's poetry by 1930.

The most significant text added to the 1930 edition of *Arsenal* is "Le Sujet," for it represents Char's earliest known use of the aphoristic form. Written in a short abbreviated prose form, "Le Sujet" consists of ten aphorisms on the nature of poetry and the role of the poet. The primary emphasis of "Le Sujet" is literary freedom; the poet has the right to compose freely and repudiate all existing rules. Moreover, this artistic right is necessary to explore all ways and means of poetic activity in order to discover the possibilities of poetry. In "Le Sujet," Char rejects his early poetry and proclaims his own poetic liberation: "Je touche enfin à cette Liberté entrevue ... sur le déclin d'une adolescence ...fort peu méritoire." The adverb "enfin" is probably a reference to Char's 1929 visit to Paris and to his decision to return there to join the Surrealist group:

> Je m'applique à marcher sur les mains quitte à tout prendre au-delà d'un silence ou la Liberté pourtant démunie étouffe l'irréductible *vacarme*.

By definition, an aphorism embodies a general truth, and in the case of "Le Sujet" this truth is the necessity of artistic freedom. However, the "je" of "Le Sujet" is personal; it expresses neither the "je" of the impersonal poet, nor of the poet as man in general. It is the "je" of René Char as a young poet who yields to his "plus secrètes espérances," defends the new attitude in literature, and derides its critics as "Idiots." The personal tone and style of "Le Sujet" show no evidence of the objectivity which characterizes Char's later aphorisms; in fact, "Le Sujet" seems to have been written in haste as a personal declaration of artistic freedom. Not until the publication of *Moulin premier* in 1936 does Char's use of the aphoristic form attain the general and impersonal character that will identify Char. Nevertheless, it is significant to note Char's early use of the aphorism to assess and evaluate poetry and the poet's role.

In the first edition of *Arsenal*, Char initiates his examination of the new spirit of poetry in the hope of discovering a poetic avenue to man's reality. In 1929, the poet's "arsenal" of materials includes: free use of inspiration, dream experience, physical love, and fusion of opposites. The 1930 edition retains these same sources, but they are no longer treated separately. On the contrary, Char begins to juxtapose them through one major theme, activity. His failure in "La Délivrance naturelle" and "Récit funèbre prend forme de poème" to construct a new perspective in the dream world is overcome in "Bonne aventure" because the poet is moving from a description of the experience or act to an evocation of the activity involved. This trend is also found in the other poems added to the 1930 edition, and particularly in "Le Sujet" and its demand for "le Mouvement Perpétuel."

The increasing distinction between act and activity in the 1930 edition of *Arsenal* marks Char's movement toward Surrealism. The revisions which appear in this edition were undertaken in full knowledge of Surrealism and probably coincide with Char's decision to join that group. In any case, the 1930 *Arsenal*, and specifically "Bonne aventure," contains many traits analogous to Surrealist writing: unlimited freedom, rejection of all restraints, dream world, subconscious, automatic writing, uncontrolled inspiration, fulfillment through physical love. Furthermore, the variants which occurred between 1929 and 1930 reveal an endeavor to capture what Breton terms "L'assemblage aussi gratuit que possible." [69] The effect of spontaneity, the appeal to the imagination, and the effort to find new affinities between words are Surrealist characteristics which distinguish the 1930 edition from the preceding 1929 work.

However, the 1930 edition also contains evidence that Char will never fully adhere to the Surrealist movement. In his treatment of the problem of the real versus the worlds of dream and sleep, he evidences a preference for the real. He even suggests that the unreal worlds of sleep and dream cannot establish a new and more acceptable order of reality. On the contrary, he intimates that the poet must never disassociate himself from the real; this notion is demonstrated by his omissions of "La Délivrance naturelle" and "Récit funèbre prend forme de poème." Moreover, the variants of the 1930 edition signify that Char will not accept the Surrealist disdain of literary revision, that Char will effect spontaneity rather than compose spontaneously.

At the end of his first period of development, Char is already becoming Char the poet rather than Char a Surrealist poet. Stylistically, he has announced his three forms of composition (prose poem, free verse poem, aphorism) and his interest in an economy of language to eliminate the superfluous, in organic consistency of theme and style, and in the suppression of particular details to emphasize the general aspects of experience. Similarly, his major themes of this period remain through the whole body of his

---

[69] Breton, p. 56.

work: discovery of the real, need for freedom, love as a condition for poetry, fusion of opposites into one entity or totality.

Char's ultimate poetic vision appears before his participation in the Surrealist movement. His first three works indicate that his Surrealist period can be no more than an apprenticeship of exploration and experimentation, an immediate opportunity to pursue his personal quest for objective reality through poetry.

CHAPTER II

1930-1936: A POETICS OF CREATIVE ACTIVITY

René Char's second chronological stage of development, which dates from 1930 to 1936, is characterized by the theme of creative activity. Between 1923 and 1930, Char's poetry was evolving in a twofold direction. In the first place, he was moving away from a traditional prosody toward an unrestricted one, and in the second place, he was becoming more concerned with poetry as activity than with poetry as act. These two poetic concerns were compatible with the general aims of the Surrealist movement and led Char to sign the "Prière d'insérer" on the handbill of the second *Manifeste du surréalisme* (1929) and adhere to that group from 1930 to 1934.

According to the Surrealists, authentic poetic activity is the only means by which the truth of existence can be established, for this activity overcomes contradictions and reveals reality as an individual totality: "la vérité... est à la base de toute activité valable."[1] Only spontaneous activity by the poet can reintegrate man with his environment and justify human existence in the modern world:

> la poésie est un moyen de connaissance ...un moyen d'action. Les poètes d'autrefois ont été inspirés de temps à autre...; mais le poète d'aujourd'hui non seulement l'est toujours, mais objet devient sujet ...C'est lui qui change la vie, le monde, qui transforme l'homme... Il fait de l'homme à son image une unité indestructible.[2]

---

[1] André Breton, *Manifeste du surréalisme* (Paris, 1963), p. 142.
[2] Maurice Nadeau, *Histoire du surréalisme* (Paris, 1964), p. 21.

1930-1936: A POETICS OF CREATIVE ACTIVITY

To the young Char, the Surrealist movement appeared as a dynamic and needed literary force which represented best the new spirit in literature that had already attracted him. In 1930, this movement offered him an immediate opportunity to pursue his quest for the nature of poetry and the role of the poet in the contemporary world.

Char was a formal member of the Surrealist group from 1930 to 1934. He owes much of his poetic growth to his affiliation with that movement. The Surrealists were the first critics to recognize Char's creative genius, for one of Char's earliest Surrealist activities was *Ralentir travaux* (1930), written in collaboration with Breton and Eluard. However, Char's adherence to Surrealism was never one of total commitment. On the contrary, Char spent these four years in independent exploration and evaluation of the theme of poetic activity as proclaimed by Surrealism but not limited to it. While this theme evolved in large part during his formal contact with Surrealism, it is the very theme which led him beyond Surrealism as early as 1931 at the height of his participation in the movement. Moreover, this theme of creative activity is not fully developed in *Le Marteau sans maître*, a collective volume of Char's texts written between 1930 and 1934; its ultimate form and position in Char's poetics and poetry does not appear until *Moulin premier*, written immediately after Char ceased to be an active Surrealist:

> ce n'est pas le surréalisme qui servira de pierre de touche à la poésie, mais au contraire la poésie qui va servir de pierre de touche au surréalisme.[3]

Study of *Le Marteau sans maître* and *Moulin premier*, the two major works composed during Char's second period of development, reveals the evolution of his theme of creative activity as well as the independent character of his Surrealist experience and its position in relation to his total poetic production.

---

[3] Georges Mounin, *Avez-vous lu Char?* (Paris, 1946), p. 72.

1930-1934: *Le Marteau sans maître*

Le Marteau sans maître is a collective edition of poems which marks what is generally considered as Char's formal Surrealist period. This collection was originally published in 1934, and revised editions appeared in 1945 and 1963. The title *Le Marteau sans maître* is in itself a Surrealist image; the "marteau" represents the hammer or instrument with which a poem is forged, while the modifier, "sans maître," implies the notion of free creative activity. When the hammer of poetic inspiration strikes the poet, the poem explodes into being without restraints and without control.

Not only does the concern with the Surrealist notion of poetry as spontaneous activity dominate *Le Marteau sans maître*, but there is of equal importance a restlessness on the part of the poet to establish a basic working principle of poetry. This restlessness is seen in the revisions that occurred from 1930 to 1934 and in those made for the 1945 edition.[4] Furthermore, this restlessness has a twofold thematic direction. It recognizes and affirms a Surrealist victory in the liberation of the poet and of the activity of poetry. It also suggests the inadequacy of Surrealism to define poetry and to integrate man and reality into an absolute totality.

All editions of *Le Marteau sans maître* consist of five parts: 1) *Arsenal*; 2) *Artine*; 3) *L'Action de la justice est éteinte*; 4) *Poèmes militants*, and 5) *Abondance viendra*. Each section contributes to the unifying theme of poetic activity, and each attests to Char's progressive movement through and beyond Surrealism.

The 1930 edition of *Arsenal* appears to have been prepared before *Le Tombeau des secrets* (1930) and *Artine* (1930). This observation is based on the fact that "Flexibilité de l'oubli" was omitted in 1934; this poem deals with the same problem of attachment to the real versus the value of dream experience as treated in *Artine*, but it lacks the cohesive unity which characterizes *Ar-*

---

[4] The few revisions which appear in the 1963 edition tend to restore minor deletions which were made for the 1945 edition. These changes are listed in Appendix III. However, it is through the 1934 and 1945 revisions that one can accurately establish Char's poetic evolution, and it is these two editions that I have used in this chapter.

tine. In addition, six of the poems of *Le Tombeau des secrets* were incorporated into the 1934 edition.

Every poem in the 1930 volume of *Arsenal* was changed in some form before its republication in 1934; these changes include the omission of ten texts,[5] major variants such as line or stanza deletions and additions in six poems,[6] and three title changes.[7] Form and punctuation changes occur in "Possible," while only one poem, "L'Exhibitionniste," remains unchanged between 1930 and 1934. One text, "Détachement," appears for the first time in the 1934 edition.

The numerous revisions made between 1930 and 1934 indicate a definite change of direction from Char's earlier poetic concepts. The title becomes more important because it begins to contain in summary form the meaning of the poem. This characteristic is first noted in the 1934 revisions of *Arsenal*. "La Vérité continue" is the best example of this trend, for its title change also reflects an increasing concern on Char's part to communicate a constant truth which can be discovered through poetry. The original title was "La Vérité"; as the 1930 title implies, this truth is universal in scope, but the 1934 addition of "continue" extends it to represent an eternal, unchanging truth. It is this quality of continuity, which suggests a unity in the world through poetry, that gives the poetic truth its human value and significance. The verb "remonte" of the first line reinforces the cyclical nature of this truth. The concreteness of the vocabulary of the poem further attests that it is within the realm of human possibilities to attain a degree of this truth through participation in the union that is formed in the physical act of love.

Another major trend in Char's poetics between 1930 and 1934 is a new concentration on the agent of the action and the activity of creativity rather than interest in the act itself. The variants of the first line of "La Vérité continue" mark this shift. In 1930, the

---

[5] The ten texts omitted are: "Le Sujet," "Bonne aventure," "Probable," "Amour," "La Tête sous l'oreiller," "Puissance négative," "Flexibilité de l'oubli," "L'Embaumé," "Le Grand travail," and "L'."

[6] The six poems are: "L'Emploi," "La Vérité," "Masque de fer," "Egalité," "Singulier," and "Leçon sévère."

[7] The three title changes are: "La Vérité" to "La Vérité continue," "La Guerre sous roche" to "Transfuges," and "La Plus heureuse" to "A l'horizon remarquable."

line indicated a clearing away only of formerly accepted poetic perspectives, not the initiation of a completely new act: "L'oiseau maquis de paradis"; the revised line in 1934, "Le novateur de la lézarde," emphasizes the agent, the active innovator who positively asserts a new perspective by pulling upon "la corde de tumulte" which Surrealism offers. The 1934 version is stronger and more vigorous through its emphasis on the agent of the action. Similarly, the title of "Les Poumons" reflects this new stress on the agent; the original title in *Le Tombeau des secrets* was "La Respiration," which referred to the act being performed; the 1934 change to "Les Poumons" suggests the agent, in this case organs, which perform the act of breathing.

In the 1930 *Arsenal*, the attempt to fuse opposites is particularly noticeable in the poems "Puissance négative," "L'," and "Amour." However, all three poems were omitted in the 1934 edition in favor of poems where the union of two different entities is more developed. "Amour" and "L'" were replaced in 1934 by the poem "L'Amour" from *Le Tombeau des secrets*: "Etre / Le premier venu." "L'Amour" successfully combines the concept of union by the term "premier," which suggests the presence of more than one, and the concept of absence by the past participle "venu"; "L'Amour" offers more possibilities for individual action than "Amour" and "L'."

Although the 1930 edition of *Arsenal* espouses certain aspects of Surrealism, it also maintains an interest in the role of the real as opposed to the unreal. This concern for the concrete world foreshadows *Artine*. In the 1930 *Arsenal*, the poems "Flexibilité de l'oubli," "La Tête sous l'oreiller," and "Le Grand travail" treat the problem of the real versus the unreal and indicate a preference for the real; these three poems reveal a sustained interest on Char's part in discovering the real because these poems were also published in the 1929 edition prior to Char's formal adherence to Surrealism; these same three poems were omitted from the 1934 edition of *Le Marteau sans maître* probably because *Artine*, which is included, elaborates and treats this problem more fully.

In the 1930 and 1934 editions of *Arsenal*, Surrealism is welcomed as a liberating literary force, but much of the youthful exuberance and enthusiasm of the 1930 edition is suppressed in the 1934 edition. Study of *Le Tombeau des secrets*, published in 1930, already reveals this shift in tone as well as an important new emphasis on man.

Le Tombeau des secrets had a single publication in 1930; as a separate volume of poems, this work is neglected by the critics,[8] perhaps because six of the ten poems of this edition were revised for the 1934 edition of *Le Marteau sans maître* in which they were included as a part of *Arsenal*. These poems are: "Bel édifice ou les pressentiments," "L'Amour," "Sosie," "L'Ambition," and "La Respiration"; the sixth poem, "L'Illusion imitée," does not reappear as an individual poem; it was condensed and incorporated into the revised form of "Bel édifice ou les pressentiments." The poem "A l'horizon" is a revised form of "Jouvence I"; it was written between 1923 and 1925, but not published before 1930.

Three poems, "Mauvaise nature," "La Peine de mort," and "Le Solitaire," were omitted in 1934. Significantly, these three poems treat the same aspect of Surrealism, an effort to free the subconscious. However, the poet fails to attain the surreal in these poems; instead, he finds that complete liberation from the physical world is impossible. The poet's attachment to the real and his inability to reach a new reality through his subconscious are summed up by "Mauvaise nature":

> Inutile d'étendre les mains
> Pour éclairer ce visage
> A perte de mémoire
> Le jour suffit à sa tâche.

Char's recognition of the importance of the real and concrete to poetic inspiration is present but not stressed in these three poems of *Le Tombeau des secrets*. These poems were probably omitted from the 1934 edition because Char had already composed *Artine* which anticipates his rejection of Surrealism on this point. The poems retained from *Le Tombeau des secrets* are in general an extension of *Arsenal* and its examination of the materials that Surrealism offers to the poet.

Le Tombeau des secrets resembles the 1930 *Arsenal* in content, as its title suggests: a monument to the unknown but valuable repository of the mind. However, "tombeau" is a more restrictive

---

[8] *Le Tombeau des secrets* is not discussed by a single critic.

term than "arsenal," for "tombeau" refers to a withdrawal from the conscious and objective world to the subconscious world. In *Le Tombeau des secrets*, Char seeks access to an expanded reality, specifically the surreality, through the use of the unreal and the imagination, and he stresses the role of the poet to decipher and communicate this new perspective of reality.

"A l'horizon" is dedicated to André Breton and acknowledges that the future of poetry is indebted to the efforts of the Surrealists, notably Breton, to liberate the poet: "A l'avenir.../Ouverte à l'oeil unique." Inherent in the poem is a belief in the possibilities of man to attain new vistas of experience. In 1923 when this poem was first composed, the "oeil unique" praised the new poets; in the 1930 publication, it is Breton's prophetic vision of the future of poetry which is singled out and honored; in the 1946 edition of *Premières alluvions*, the "oeil unique" is rejected in favor of an "oeil multiple." This progression is also reflected in the title changes: "Jouvence" in 1923 represented the youth of poetry, the promise of the future; "A l'horizon" in 1930 is a salute limited to Breton and his Surrealist group; the return in 1946 to "Jouvence" implies a rejection of Surrealism and a recognition of the youth of the poet, which the second stanza further clarifies in its expression of Char's aesthetics as of 1946, "oeil multiple." "A l'horizon" is an important poem in *Le Tombeau des secrets* because it affirms that Char's early poetic attempts were directed towards the future of poetry and because it firmly acknowledged that this direction took the form of his adherence to Surrealism, the attainment of one goal.

Prior to *Le Tombeau des secrets*, Char concentrated on the act of poetry; he was involved in a quest for poetic activity which was connected solely to creativity on the part of the individual poet. *Le Tombeau des secrets*, particularly the poem "Sosie," marks a shift of focus to man and an indication that Char's poetic interests are to become increasingly commited to the cause of man. Char's awareness of human duality is first seen in "Sosie," whose theme is that of man as a miserable animal who will be made known through the efforts of the poet.

This new interest in man is further linked to the search for truth which was announced by "La Vérité" in the 1930 *Arsenal* and which is continued in *Le Tombeau des secrets*, particularly in "Bel édifice ou les pressentiments" and "L'Illusion imitée." In 1930, "Bel édifice ou les pressentiments" consisted of two stanzas; a middle stanza, which is a condensed version of "L'Illusion imitée," was added in 1934. In "Bel édifice ou les pressentiments," man's illusions hinder his search for truth; the poet seeks to be a "bel édifice" which will contain this truth, but his "pressentiments" prevent him from succeeding in this search: "La mer morte vagues par-dessus tête." This text presents an either-or situation; either the poet is the only possibility for the residence of this truth or he only offers the foreboding that this truth is illusory due to the nature of man. The 1930 form of "L'Illusion imitée" further accentuates the ominous nature of this search; the poet is certain that truth exists within him, but he fears that it is illusion which he imitates, not truth; he wishes to combat the illusions:

> Revenir là où je n'ai jamais été
> En rapporter ce que j'ai déjà vu
> Aux prises avec l'ignorance.

"L'Illusion imitée" recognizes the problem of discovering and communicating the truth offered by poetry. In the 1934 text, Char acknowledges the nature of his quest by consolidating "Bel édifice ou les pressentiments" and "L'Illusion imitée" into "Bel édifice et les pressentiments." The change from the conjuction "ou" to "et" reveals Char's earliest acceptance of man's duality and shows his growing interest in justifying man and directing his conduct through poetic activity. The poet remains aware that he is the only possibility within which this truth may dwell openly and that illusions are obstacles to the attainment of this truth. However, the added stanza explains his duality: "Enfant la jetée-promenade sauvage/Homme l'illusion imitée"; truth is within because its possibility is first contained within the child and is then retained in the adult who was the child, although man has since turned to illusion. The "pressentiments" arise because of man's penchant for the illusion, but these forebodings, while encumbering the poet, are not unconquerable, for each adult retains the "yeux purs" of the child with which to perceive truth and reality. It is the role of the poet to recognize that the contradiction of "bel édifice" versus "pressentiments" is merely superficial and that he must express the totality that is man and help him discover his inner truth. This truth is not easy to obtain, and only the poet can express it: "Des yeux purs dans les bois/Cherchent en pleurant la tête habitable." The phrase "en pleurant" was added in 1934 in order to emphasize the urgency of the need to expose and overcome this problem.

The importance of *Le Tombeau des secrets* in Char's poetic formation lies in the fact that, while Surrealism is further praised and explored, there is an indication that the unreal has no value unless it is firmly rooted in the concrete world of man. The quest for poetic truth is continued, but now for the first time Char recognizes that poetry must be joined to the cause of man.

The 1934 edition of *Arsenal*, through its revisions of the 1930 edition and its incorporation of two-thirds of *Le Tombeau des secrets*, becomes an evaluation of Surrealism and its contribution to poetry; the central theme remains that of poetry, but coupled to it is a new emphasis on man, a shift of interest from the act itself to the agent of the action, and a concern for the real which intimates that, while Surrealism has value in its liberation of poetic materials, it may not contain all poetic supplies. The key to this 1934 edition lies in *Artine*.

Artine was first published in 1930, and, significantly, it is Char's first work published by the Editions surréalistes; [9] in 1934, *Artine* became the second section of the collection *Le Marteau sans maître*. Because it has remained textually intact since its first publication, *Artine* offers the best available poetic document for the assessment of Char's Surrealist experience.

Artine is a prose poem which consists of 13 paragraphs. On the surface, *Artine* appears to be a Surrealist rendering of a dream, a series of dreamlike events related to the physical act of love. However, *Artine* is not a dream recital, but a single poem. It is unified by one theme: the value of surreality.

Artine is written in the form of a dramatic monologue in which the poet is a man in the "real" world, a dreamer in the dream world, and a poet of both worlds. The "rêveur-poète" describes his relation with Artine, "la modèle" who visits him in the world of sleep. According to Georges Mounin, "Artine ...c'est

---

[9] *Ralentir travaux* was published by the Editions surréalistes six months earlier, but it is a work of collaboration by Breton, Eluard, and Char; *Artine* is Char's first individual volume published under the auspices of the Surrealist group.

la surréalité." [10] Mounin is not entirely incorrect, but his explanation seems too narrow. Artine is the surreal, but, in addition, she is the muse of inspiration and imagination, a muse who has existed throughout the history of poetic productivity. She represents the ageless poetical problem of divine fury, creative genius, and the Surrealist pure imagination in conflict with work, reflection, and engagement in a literary occupation. It is this conflict that Char treats in the poem *Artine*; in his character of Artine, he concretizes the abstract notion of the poetic muse of inspiration, intuition, and imagination.

Artine may be divided into four parts: 1) the first paragraph prepares the evocation of the dream world; 2) paragraphs II-VI announce the dreamer's descent in the world of sleep; 3) paragraphs VII-XII present the actual experience which occurs in this dream world; and, 4) paragraph XIII contains the poet's assessment of his experience.

Paragraph I is printed in italics in order to set it apart from the rest of the poem; this paragraph is one of preparation and designates the setting of *Artine*, "un lit," the object from which one enters the world of sleep and dreams. In this bed, 20 objects are enumerated; all are related to the familiar everyday world of man. What is unfamiliar is the relationship of each to the other and the idea of placing them in a bed, an unusual setting for each one. This anti-realistic detachment of the familiar objects from their accepted position and application, a Surrealist dislocation of objects, disrupts logical sequence and establishes the dreamlike atmosphere of the poem. By the compilation of this specific series of images, the setting ceases to be limited to a bed in the concrete sense; rather, the "lit" represents a concretization of the universe; it is the universe which the first paragraph evokes, and it is from this enlarged setting that the poem gains its universal quality.

In the second part of *Artine*, the dreamer descends into the world of sleep in order to free his subconscious from all rational control. He hopes to find a knowledge different from that of the real world and reason; this "ordre des rêves" [11] is to free him from the constraints and limits of logic and renovate the knowledge

---

[10] Mounin, p. 73.
[11] All quotations are from the 1930 edition of *Artine*.

of the mind. This experience is described in terms of physical love, for Artine comes of her own accord; she is neither invited nor sought; she is desired. The phrase "domaine de l'amour où l'activité dévorante" reinforces the concept of desire that Artine awakens. By its connotation, love is an exchange, a singleness formed from two opposites, and an effort at communication; above all, love carries with it a fusion of irreconcilables, for it is freedom and yet attachment, desire fulfilled and yet desire unfulfilled. This intimate union of opposites is one of demanding activity, vitality, and energy. It is the idea of doing, not of mere existing; it is the freeing of one's inner self from all controls and inhibitions asserted by the logical real world. Moreover, this action is "en dehors du temps sexuel," that is, it refutes temporality; it is even beyond man's memory in its timelessness. The destruction of human temporal limits extends further the dreamer's desire to surmount his human condition. In this isolation from chaos, from limits, from logic, the dreamer completes the first stage of his journey to find the "ordre des rêves qui hanteraient dorénavant son cerveau"; he falls asleep; he is now closed off from his known order of reality.

"Artine traverse sans difficulté le nom d'une ville" concretizes the movement into sleep and denotes the *a priori* existence of the real world. Even imagination has some contact with the real. The real world has an *a priori* existence to the dream world: the isolation of the dreamer or the absence of the concrete presence is a prerequisite for such a Surrealist experience. Although the world of dreams distorts the real, it does not abandon spatiality and temporality. On the contrary, it disrupts and alters the appearance of the real. The roots of the dream world and of the Surrealist experience are in the real world and complete elimination of this real world would result in a total loss of value in the Surrealist experience.

The sixth paragraph is a Surrealist effort to submerge the conscious in order to reach the depths of the subconscious where imagination and inspiration function freely and purely. "L'état de léthargie qui précédait Artine" confirms the Surrealist notion that one must attempt to render one's self into a passive physical and mental state, liberate one's self from all control, and enter a realm of sensory receptivity; this preparation is the preliminary requisite for the liberation of the creative thought processes of the imagination; it is necessary if one wishes the experience to occur properly within the subconscious where the logical sequence of the known is disrupted and the new vision attained: "Artine apportait les éléments indispensables à la projection d'impressions saisissantes sur l'écran de ruines flottantes." This passive condition is analogous to the "édredon" which recalls "lit," the concretized setting of the poem; but this state, passive externally, will be one of activity within the innermost depths of the wealth of the subconscious: "en perpétuel mouvement." The importance of paragraph six is to set aside rational control in order to reach the dream world, and it is an explicit announcement of the consuming activity in which the dreamer is to participate.

The third section of the poem describes the dream experience. Even though Artine enters through the real world, she maintains the ability to renew and revitalize with each visit the dreamer's experience. The reference to "la transparence absolue" signifies the surreal divination of the hidden meaning of the objects of the real world; Artine permits this new perspective of the real to be projected on the mind's screen; in crossing through the real, she frees the intuition and the imagination and permits the surreal to come into existence.

Artine's visits must precipitate the dreamer beyond mere sleep, for in that state the real and the dream conflict, each distorting the other in turn. In order that the imagination, freed within the dream world, may gain its proper ascendency over the real, there must be a more active destruction on the part of the dream:

> Les apparitions d'Artine dépassaient le cadre de ces contrées du sommeil, où le *pour* et le *pour* sont animés d'une égale et meurtrière violence.

These visits accomplish this necessary transformation through an all-consuming act; still in contact with the real, it distorts the real by giving it an unusual perspective. Although Artine effects an animated and new evolution, the real world continues to assert its presence: "il s'agissait d'accueillir ...la multitude des ennemis mortels d'Artine." As saltpeter attempts to subdue the sexual drive, the objects of the real world insist on resuming their usual position in their habitual setting. The odious appearance of the "visage de bois mort" implies a rupture in the action; a footnote to this phrase in the 1930 edition explains this image as referring to Jesus Christ, that is, to a crucifix made of wood, indicating the intrusion of the real world in one of its more restrictive aspects, organized religion. Omission of this footnote in subsequent editions reveals that no footnote is necessary to qualify the image; in fact, the deletion of the footnote widens the possibilities of interpretation.

In the eleventh paragraph the real world disrupts this journey for the second time; it returns the dreamer into contact with the concrete. "Une tête qui n'était pas la mienne" not only asserts an interruption of the experience or an intrusion from the outside, but it is also the dreamer's realization that it is his real physical condition and his reason, unlike his subconscious existence, that has threatened to dispell Artine. The appearance of this unknown head is the manifestation of the conscious self previously set aside. This second interruption is not overcome as quickly; it has a lingering quality as does the effect of sulpher on the olfactory senses. Moreover, in this second contact with the outside world, the real seems to have some significance in and of itself: "présence en soi et immobilité vibrante." [12] The real world has become more difficult to escape.

The return to the dream world in paragraph twelve completes the quest for the knowledge or truth that the dream world offers. It seems that this truth can only be understood within the dream world; the absence of light indicates the absence of a cipher to this truth in the real world, and, consequently, implies the lack of practical application of this knowledge in man's daily existence.

The twelfth paragraph seems to parody a filmed epic with a repetitious traditional portrayal of the human condition in a tragic

---

[12] It is possible that this phrase refers to André Breton's definition of beauty as expressed in *Nadja*: "La beauté sera CONVULSIVE ou ne sera pas." Like Breton, Char places a value on a vibrant quality that is neither static nor dynamic and which is formalized in his concept of "sérénité crispée" in 1950. Furthermore, *Nadja* was published in 1928, two years prior to the composition of *Artine*; there are definite similarities between the figures of Artine and Nadja, for both are free spirits in an urban setting and both incarnate a certain Surrealist attitude; however, there are more major differences than similarities so that Char's creative authenticity remains unimpaired by a suggested resemblance between his Artine and Breton's Nadja; this is also true of Char's "Madeleine qui veillait" (1949), who has a similarity with Artine and Nadja. The fact that Breton and Char were in close contact at this time cannot be contested because Char collaborated with Breton and Eluard on *Ralentir travaux*, published six months earlier.

world and emphasizes the shortcomings of dream knowledge. The truth gained from this experience is no more practical than the cinematic world and no more original than the classical concept of man. This lack of a new and profound truth to enlighten man's perspective of his reality and totality is further qualified by the notation that each truth offered by Artine has a correlation with a previously accepted concept. Because the imagination is unable to liberate itself from the *a priori* existence of the real world, it perpetuates unknowingly the prior imaginative creations of man. The dream world, in its attempt to transform the real through the liberation of the imagination and stimulation of the subconscious, is never able to break with the real world, and yet it loses contact with the real condition of man's everyday problems.

The last part of the poem announces the rupture with the dream world and the return to the real world; it is the triumph of the real world as the basis of a potential aesthetics; it is a choice in favor of a poetics that maintains definite and positive contact with reality against a poetics of pure imagination and intuition based within the subconscious. The "modèle" is Artine, the incarnation of the surreal who glides from the real into the subconscious dream world; she is eliminated ("tué") as the only possible source of poetic activity. The "rêveur" is now the "poète"; these terms are not synonymous; a dreamer can be a poet in the sense that a poet must have imagination, but this dreamer without a specified occupation will produce the same shallow "épopée," "héros," "livre." The poet is related to the dreamer, but unlike the dreamer, he must not abandon the real world. The term "poète" is a vocational term; the poet has an occupation, a need to work, to use his reason in order that he may judge which experiences or insights revealed by the imagination are to be communicated within the poem. There must be imagination before the poem comes into being, but there must also be work to realize and present the poem. There is no elimination of the role of imagination and inspiration; rather, it is an option to fuse imagination with reality, inspiration with control, emotion with conceptual thought. It is the addition of a conceptual value to the Surrealist notion of poetry as activity that *Artine* presents. It is what Char later formulates: "Le poème émerge d'une imposition subjective et d'un choix objectif." [13]

There is, therefore, only one theme in *Artine*, that of poetry, its activity, its domain, and the position of imagination, intuition, and inspiration within that domain. Artine impresses the poet by her singularity, but her visits satisfy only the dreamer, not the poet. It is important to note that at no time within the poems is Surrealism rejected; although its scope is expanded, Surrealism is affirmed as having value in poetic activity.

Artine is a tightly knit prose poem. The dominant characteristic of the vocabulary is the juxtaposition of concrete and abstract terms; the confrete terms refer to the real world, while the abstract ones reflect the dream world; they are constantly placed in juxtaposition in order to concretize the abstract dream world. Because of this juxtaposition, the vocabulary seems to be erudite, but all of the terms are familiar ones; there are no rare or unusual words. The concrete terms are commonplace, everyday words, but they are placed in unusual and unfamiliar combinations in order to attract attention, to express the impossible, and to materialize the abstract world of dreams. Combinations such as "Offrir ... un verre d'eau à un cavalier lancé" and "édredon en flammes" create new meanings out of familiar associations. The juxtaposition of terms also gives the vocabulary an emotional, rather than an intellectual, appeal.

Many of the terms are words expressing motion and activity; the persistence of a vocabulary of movement to describe a somewhat passive state is not contradictory, for there is much activity within this passivity. The terms of motion enhance this notion of activity and increase the emotional intensity of the poem. Above all, the vocabulary is condensed; there is much effort to express the maximum by the minimum in order to necessitate participation by the reader.

The syntax is highly controlled and rigorous. There are a few syntactical difficulties which arise through the suppression of transition words and connectives; this effort to suppress linking terms creates an effect of non-control and forces the reader to take part in the creation of the poem.

---

[13] *Partage formel*, XXIX, in *Seuls demeurent, Fureur et mystère* (Paris, 1948).

The main part of speech which carries the weight of the action are nouns; this is a Surrealist technique to enhance the visual quality of the poem. Nouns not only abound in their familiar subject-object usage, but they are also the basis for adjectival and adverbial clauses which are placed where a simple adjective or adverb would have sufficed. This method of qualification and clarification results in an effect of extension and accumulation; it dramatically reinforces the emotional intensity of the poem, and it permits greater freedom in the juxtaposition of concrete and abstract terms to create new images.

The verb tenses used in *Artine* are of particular interest; proportionately, the imperfect tense dominates, and it is used to denote description and repetition in the past of these escapes into the dream world and the encounters with pure imagination. Through the imperfect tense, the past is completely separated from the present, for these escapes no longer occur; they belong solely to the past. The present tense is used to express factual knowledge and it describes the properties of the objects and attributes of the personnages of the poem. It must be noted that the real world is associated with the present tenses and the dream world with the imperfect. The conflict between the two is thus reflected in the syntax.

The last line of the poem contains a "passé composé;" this is the only use made of this tense throughout the poem. The fact that the single appearance of the "passé composé" is in the final line separates this action from the rest of the poem; this separation, which indicates the completion of one single act in the past, completes the destruction of the time of the poem. The last line becomes the poem; the preceding twelve paragraphs cease to denote a narrative of a past event and become an explanatory extension of the only event that actually does occur in the poem: "Le poète a tué son modèle." Poetry gains its authenticity from the real world.

The vocabulary, syntax, and rhythm support the content of the poem and are in unity with it. The tone alone seems to present a contrast; the tone is pensive, reflective, cogitative in contrast with the poem which appeals to the imagination through its visual imagery and which emphasizes activity in its theme. However, this pensive tone does not break with the content and form; there is an inherent conceptual dimension to the poem, and it is this conceptual quality that the tone expresses.

In *Artine*, Char affirms what may be considered the Surrealist notion of poetry as activity. As a concretization of the dream world which distorts the real world, *Artine* is a Surrealist setting; there is expressed the idea of a new order of knowledge that might be gained from this dream level of existence and experience. The attempt to escape from the real world and man's reason in order to penetrate the domain of man's thought processes and find pure imagination is also a Surrealist trait. The emphasis placed on the participation of the subconscious, inspiration, intuition, imagination, and liberty within poetic action and the evocation of the involuntariness of the poetic state are directly related to orthodox Surrealism. Similarly, the personification of Artine as a woman, the allusions to the love act, and the subsequent importance of woman within the construction of the poem are Surrealist. The presence of the real world is Surrealist in its relation to the dream world, for the surreal has its cornerstone in the concrete.

Char has used many techniques advocated by the Surrealists. However, the presence of numerous Surrealist qualities in the form and content does not restrict *Artine* to being representative of Surrealism, for *Artine* seems to go beyond Surrealism. The last line of *Artine* is, without question, an affirmation of reality; it is such a strong affirmation that it nearly succeeds in negating the abundant Surrealist traits. With the disposal of Artine, the muse of inspiration and imagination, the poet negates the unique value of the dream world; this is not a refutation of Surrealism, but an implicit rejection of it as the ultimate solution for poetry. It is an option on Char's part to return to reality and to integrate imagination into the world of the concrete and to exercise rational choice in what is of value in inspiration. It is this decision which is foreshadowed in *Artine*.

Already in *Artine* in 1930, Char seems to recognize the failure of Surrealism to fuse imagination and reality, inspiration and work, poetic activity and exaltation of language and poetry. Yet, *Artine* affirms the Surrealist notion of poetry as activity, and this idea persists throughout Char's poetry. At the same time that Char affirms in *Artine* a greater value in the role of the real, previously implied in *Arsenal* and *Le Tombeau des secrets*, he adds a non-Surrealist conceptual quality to the notion of action in poetry.

The date of composition of *Artine* is given as 1930 by Pierre Berger: "En 1930 (c'est semble-t-il), l'année au cours de laquelle *Artine* fut écrite..." [14] This is the same year that Char "avait lu Lautréamont avec un sens très aigu de sa vision ... la pureté de la vie secrète des choses..." [15] An interest in the objects of the world and the desire to render them more benevolent within the world of man is first perceived in *Artine*; this tendency to humanize the world of the concrete is closely associated with Char's orientation towards the cause of man. These two aspects of his poetics are further developed in *L'Action de la justice est éteinte* and emerge as the dominant characteristics of *Poèmes militants*.

The title of *L'Action de la justice est éteinte* (1931) affirms the value of Surrealism; this movement opened the way for the future of poetry by ending the jurisdiction of past poetics which relied on restrictive rules. "L'action de la justice est éteinte là où brûle, où se tient la poésie, où s'est réchauffé quelques soirs le poète." [16]

L'Action de la justice est éteinte is of particular interest for its revisions; while few changes were made between the 1931 and 1934 editions, all but two poems, "Poème" and "L'Instituteur révoqué," were either revised or put in a different order for the 1945 edition of *Le Marteau sans maître*. Although the major revisions occurred after what is considered as Char's formal period of Surrealism, these revisions are directly connected to the attitude and interests expressed in the 1931 and 1934 editions.

The 1931 edition praises the Surrealist movement for its recognition that the role of the poet is to lead man to understand and accept reality. This edition also continues the exploration of certain aspects of Surrealism already examined in *Arsenal* and in *Artine*: the role and value of inspiration and imagination versus the role and value of the real. The 1934 edition maintains this Surrealist attitude, but in the 1945 edition, this attitude is further enlarged to include all that is new in poetry; Surrealism has been of inestimable service to poetry, but the new poetry is not the sole

---

[14] Pierre Berger, "René Char," *Poètes d'aujourd'hui*, (Paris, 1951), p. 21.
[15] *Ibid.*
[16] "Introduction," *Oeuvres d'Arthur Rimbaud* (Paris, 1957), p. x.

province of Surrealism. The 1945 version of *L'Action de la justice est éteinte* reveals that Char's poetics are indebted to certain theories which he first tested during his adherence to Surrealism. The 1945 edition places the importance of the Surrealist movement and its relation to Char in an overall framework, while the 1931 edition is more closely connected to the actual movement.

The 12 poems of *L'Action de la justice est éteinte* are centered around poetic theory, and themes treated earlier recur: the fusion of opposites ("Poème"); love as a condition for poetry ("Poème," "L'Amour"); the importance of the real ("La Manne de Lola Abba," "L'Esprit poétique" and "Le Climat de la chasse ou l'accomplissement de la poésie"). The role of the poet to discover and communicate his discoveries is the predominant theme. This is reflected in the titles: "L'Oracle du grand oranger," "Poètes," "L'Artisanat furieux," "Les Messagers de la poésie frénétique," "Soleils chanteurs," "L'Instituteur révoqué." Previously adopted concepts are more fully examined and are placed within a more definite framework of poetic activity. The form of this poetic framework is widened; as it becomes more and more integrated into Char's poetics, this framework is extended beyond Surrealism.

Although there seem to be no new poetic discoveries introduced in any of the editions, an important fusion of two concepts occurs for the first time. The Surrealist concepts of poetic activity and the importance of the physical act of love were examined separately by Char in earlier volumes of poetry; this is demonstrated by "Poème," which remains textually intact in the four publications of *L'Action de la justice est éteinte*. In "Poème," creativity is attained through activity; the sexual act is an act of living in which all men may participate; in its amalgamation of these two acts, "Poème" represents Char's earliest fusion of the act of poetry and an act of living:

> Dans le domaine irréconciliable de la surréalité, l'homme privilégié ne pouvant être que la proie gracieuse de sa dévorante raison de vivre: l'amour.

While the two individual concepts of this fusion are based in orthodox Surrealism, the fusion itself forms the core of Char's poetry. "Poème" may restrict the act of living to the physical act of love, but its significance lies in its positive fusion of poetry and life.

Of the 12 pieces in *L'Action de la justice est éteinte*, only one was omitted in 1945, "L'Esprit poétique." This text appeared in the 1931 and 1934 editions in the form of 14 aphorisms and one prose poem; nine of the 14 aphorisms (2, 3, 4, 6, 7, 9, 11, 13, 14) reappear in *Moulin premier* in 1945. "L'Esprit poétique" represents Char's second published attempt at aphoristic composition;[17] it emphasizes the fact that the discovery of poetic essence was his main concern during his adherence to Surrealism. The incorporation of a poem from *L'Action de la justice est éteinte* into *Moulin premier* links *Le Marteau sans maître* to *Moulin premier* and makes it likely that *Moulin premier* was appended to *Le Marteau sans maître* in 1945 in order to emphasize the independent character of Char's Surrealist adventure.

"L'Esprit poétique" is also important because it continues *Artine* in the prose poem "Chère Artine." This prose poem in the form of a letter addressed to Artine is concerned with the growing importance of the real, and it questions the values of inspiration and the dream world:

> J'ai l'impression que vos rêves majeurs ne m'atteignent plus comme par le passé.... Notre rencontre remonte à Octobre 1929. Depuis cette date les hippodromes ont cessé de m'être favorables.

The date, October 1929, is most likely a reference to Char's first trip to Paris and his introduction to the Surrealist group. In *Artine*, Char affirms the importance of the real; in "L'Esprit poétique," he rejects pure inspiration as being ineffectual in the real world; Artine has outlived her usefulness as a guide, for she stops short of the true source of poetic truth: "à la proximité de la Beauté." Inspiration is only of value if it begins in the real world, not in the sleep or dream world of Artine:

> une jeune fille ...égorge un coq, puis tombe dans le sommeil léthargique, tandis qu'à quelques mètres de son lit coule tout un fleuve et ses périls. Ambassade déportée.

The phrase "Ambassade déportée" added in 1934 reinforces the idea that the muse of pure inspiration and imagination, Artine, has

---

[17] The first is "Le Sujet" in the 1930 edition of *Arsenal*.

been sent back to her own realm by the poet; she fulfilled her post as the highest ranking agent of the dream world sent to represent this other possible state of knowledge, but her services are no longer required by the poet who has opted for the real world. The dismissal of Artine foreshadows Char's rejection of Surrealism; this is further maintained in "Le Climat de la chasse ou l'accomplissement de la poésie," which replaced "L'Esprit poétique" in the 1945 edition.

"Le Climat de la chasse ou l'accomplissement de la poésie" expands the scope of poetry which "L'Esprit poétique" presents and continues the fusion announced in "Poème." "Le Climat de la chasse" treats the conditions necessary for poetry; poetic activity requires courage, patience, skill, and industry, qualities not unlike those demanded in the hunt. There must be activity, reason, involvement, and physical love; physical love fuses opposites, occurs in a moment, and through its fulfillment offers a new perspective to the pursuit. It is in a climate of action and even violence that poetry is sought, but its accomplishment eternalizes an instant of truth, which is that poem continually coming into being. "Le Climat de la chasse" retains and yet expands the Surrealist concepts of activity and the importance of physical love as fulfillment. In this poem, as in "Poème," the act of poetry and an act of living are irrevocably fused.

Although the arrangement of "Le Climat de la chasse" occurred after 1934, it is significant to note that not a single phrase was composed after 1934. Each of the eight paragraphs is taken from poems in the 1934 edition of *Le Marteau sans maître*; paragraphs three and seven are from "L'Esprit poétique"; four poems from the 1934 version of *Poèmes militants* were condensed to form the remaining six paragraphs: "Le Cheval de corrida" (P1, P2), "Drames" (P4, P6), "L'Accomplissement de la poésie" (P5), and "La Mère du vinaigre" (P2, P8). Hence, discussion of "Le Climat de la chasse" belongs to Char's 1930-1934 Surrealist period. Its arrangement may postdate this period, but not its composition.

The 1931 and 1934 publications of "L'Esprit poétique" and its 1945 replacement, "Le Climat de la chasse ou l'accomplissement de la poésie," represent the main concern of *L'Action de la justice est éteinte*, as well as that of *Le Marteau sans maître*. "L'Esprit poétique" is a bridge from *Arsenal* and *Artine* to *Moulin premier*, while "Le Climat de la chasse" continues the orientation of Char's poetics and poetry towards the fusion of the act of poetry and an act of living and links *L'Action de la justice est éteinte* to *Poèmes militants*.

L'Action de la justice est éteinte completes *Arsenal* and *Artine* and it proclaims the end of the jurisdiction of the past. *Poèmes militants* offers a demonstration of this declaration.

Composed between 1931 and 1933, *Poèmes militants* was not published as a separate volume prior to its appearance in 1934 as the fourth section of *Le Marteau sans maître*. *Poèmes militants* aggressively asserts the victory of Surrealism in the enrichment and revitalization of poetry. In these poems, the new poetry is affirmed; these poems also warn that all that is new becomes old in turn, that while the triumph of the new wrought through the efforts of the Surrealists is permanent the spirit of the new must be continued beyond Surrealism.

The 1934 edition of *Poèmes militants* is more explicit in its affirmation of Surrealism than the 1945 edition. The textual revisions in the latter are mainly omissions. They tend to eliminate direct references to Surrealism, as the following three examples illustrate:

> A bas la pensée
> De confronter l'étagère avec le fruit [18]
>
> Comme la raison précieuse
> Vaincue dans son propre élément [19]
>
> Passagers du Rêve asymétrique [20]

Furthermore, five texts from the original group of 22 poems do not appear as distinct texts: "Le Cheval de corrida," "Drames," "L'Accomplissement de la poésie," "La Mère du vinaigre," and "Les Liaisons sentimentales de l'image." All five poems were condensed to their bare essentials and reappeared in the 1945 edition of *L'Action de la justice est éteinte* as follows: the first four poems were assimilated into "Le Climat de la chasse ou l'accomplissement

---

[18] "Vivante demain," *Poèmes militants* in *Le Marteau sans maître* (Paris, 1934).
[19] "Les Observateurs et les rêveurs."
[20] "Crésus."

de la poésie"; from the fifth poem, one line, "Chemin des sources ancien chemin des sables," was incorporated into a revised form of "Sommeil fatal." The revision of these five poems in 1945 is noteworthy because these texts evaluate poetic theory; they are not examples of this theory, as are the other 17 poems. Moreover, these five 1934 texts contain lines which were not incorporated into the 1945 edition, but lines which set forth Char's concept of poetry in 1934 and show what aspects of Surrealism appealed to Char. He praises the freedom of "le génie poétique/Sans bagages" [21] and the return to the original meanings of words: "L'Esprit croit au pied de la lettre originelle". [22] Char was interested in the cultivation of spontaneity ("Poème accidentel") [23] and in the possibility of attaining an absolute totality through the dream world: "Nous aurons en dormant/Encore surpeuplé l'espace entre la vie et la mort." [24] Above all, he exalts the new: "La jeunesse légitime aux opinions inavouables navigue sur les lacs des étables modernes." [25] Char describes his identification with the Surrealist poets in these lines from "L'Accomplissement de la poésie":

Chercheurs d'or des rendez-vous de minuit
La liberté dans la souffrance de jouir une fois créatrice
Bourreaux légistes passionnels
Nous avons lacéré l'odieuse cataracte sur les yeux de l'amour
Délivré le langage
Flambé les ferments.

In these lines which appear only in the 1934 edition, one sees an enthusiastic Surrealist poet, militant in his acclamation of Surrealism. On the other hand, the 1945 edition reveals a poet who no longer feels a need to struggle for the acceptance of the new literary spirit which he so strongly advocated in his youth.

The title changes between 1934 and 1945 reflect an effort to go beyond the limits that Surrealism imposes by generalizing the lessons learned from contact with Surrealism; this is expressed by the overall title *Poèmes militants*. "Les Asciens" is a 1945

---

[21] "Le Cheval de corrida."
[22] *Ibid.*
[23] "L'Accomplissement de la poésie."
[24] "Drames."
[25] "L'Accomplissement de la poésie."

change to the agent of the action from the 1934 implication of object, "Minerai." "La Plaine" in 1945 represents what the poet defies, whereas the 1934 title, "L'Accident dans la plaine," is an affirmative description, connoting a relativity which is limiting in scope. "A la faveur de la peau" is an active title which suggests the need to fuse opposites. The change of "Trianon" to "Pour Mamouque" is a change from object, a place, to agent, a man, Mamouque. The title changes in the poem of hommage to the Marquis de Sade for having been the first to attempt to restore to literature the role of physical love reveal the evolution of another general characteristic. The 1934 title "La Puma de D. A. F. Sade" evokes the sensual, while in the 1945 version the title is a summary of the poem: "Sade, l'amour enfin sauvé de la boue du ciel, cet héritage aux hommes contre la famine."[26] The progression from an erotically evocative title in 1934 to a more explicit and inclusive heading in 1945 marks the growing importance of the title throughout *Le Marteau sans maître* and in Char's poetic formation; the title becomes the poem, and all that is expressed within the poem refers to the title and is contained by the title.

Most of the poems of *Poèmes militants* defend the contributions of the Surrealist movement to poetry. "La Luxure" justifies the role of the dream world which distorts the real to present new perspectives which may lead to a new totality: "De déplacer sur des distances considérables / Les paysages habituels." "Métaux refroidis" also maintains the value of sleep and the need for inspiration, for the metals of poetic construction cannot be forged unless they are first heated by inspiration. In "Chaîne," there is a feeling of the continuity or totality of man's reality, for the view of one link of reality leads to another and eventually to a completed chain. Connected to this belief in an ultimate totality of existence is the dialectic of absence-presence that appears in much of Char's poetry. There can be no absence unless it be preceded by presence; because absence recalls presence, these two poles of reality cease to be irreconcilable: "Il n'y a pas d'absence irremplaçable." The new poets are hailed as the "Bourreaux de solitude," responsible for the rebirth of poetry as expressed in "Les Asciens"

---

[26] The title was changed again in the 1963 edition to a less complex one, "Sade"; however, this 1963 title is still an inclusive one, whereas the 1934 title was limited to one aspect of Sade.

("Envahisseurs du nouvel âge primitif") and in "Cruauté" ("Nous sommes les pieds d'une grandeur sans pareille"). The importance of physical love is again affirmed in "Vivante demain," "L'Historienne," and "Sade." In "Confronts," one of the most "militant" poems of this volume, the real and the dream are fused; imagination and love are both necessary to poetic activity, and the poets who have distorted old values to free poetry and lead man to his absolute reality are praised: "Les mondes en transformation appartiennent aux poètes carnassiers / Les distractions meurtrières aux rêveurs qui les imaginent."

Intermingled with the poems which praise Surrealism are those which demand that Surrealism be enlarged. "Les Observateurs et les rêveurs" defines a poet as one who observes the real, who dreams the unreal, and who combines rationally these two experiences:

> Demain commenceront les travaux poétiques
> Précédés du cycle de la mort volontaire
> Le règne de l'obscurité a coulé la raison
>   le diamant dans la mine.

"Crésus" emphasizes the value of action; the act is more important than its results. The agent must go into his innermost self to gain a new perspective for action. One lesson gained from immediate contact with the Surrealist movement is summarized in this line: "A présent je sais vivre." "Vivre" also means to exist, and, by extension, to exist by acting, acting being the key to creativity.

"Versant" is the most significant poem of the *Poèmes militants* group; Char properly places it as the last poem of this section, for it is a summary poem. Surrealism had value as a literary movement; although the new has triumphed, poets must not become complacent with this victory; they must continue to seek the new beyond Surrealism:

> A présent que décroit la portée d'exemple
> Quel carreau apparu en larmes
> Va nous river
> Coeurs partisans?

"Versant" closes *Poèmes militants* and, in so doing, closes the exploration, examination, and evaluation of Surrealism which the first four sections of *Le Marteau sans maître* undertake. "Versant" announces *Abondance viendra*, the final section of *Le Marteau sans maître*; this last section develops the warning implicit in "Versant" that Surrealism, though valuable, is inherently limited, that the future of poetry remains to be discovered.

Abondance viendra announces that poetry has a rich future because of the Surrealist liberation of literature from the limitations of rules, traditions, and conventions of the past. The title is an optimistic one which proclaims that the future of poetry is yet to come. While the new has been accepted, it is the task of the poet to continue to explore the possibilities of poetry.

"L'Eclaircie" is the opening poem of *Abondance viendra*, and, as its title suggests, it indicates that the Surrealist movement has made possible a clearing in the hazy skies of literature, an important beginning for the future, but only a starting point. In "L'Eclaircie," Char salutes Surrealism for having revitalized poetic imagination, but at the same time he emphasizes the need for conceptual activity on the part of poets in the future: "Le sort de l'imagination adhérant sans réserves au développement d'un monde en tout renouvelé ... pourra être déterminé ... à la suite de la brutale montée à l'intelligence non soumise." Although "Eaux-mères" is a Surrealist rendering of a dream experience, it exceeds the limits of Surrealism in its concern for the relation of poetry to the moral conduct of man:

> Il va falloir changer ma règle d'existence.
> Ma tâche est désormais de ...protéger [l'homme].
> Il est menacé.

It is significant to note that the desire to defend man, which has been suggested in earlier poems of *Le Marteau sans maître*, emerges more strongly at the end of *Le Marteau sans maître*. This confidence in life and in man is one of the dominant traits of *Abondance viendra*; it is a theme which points directly to *Placard pour un chemin des écoliers* and *Feuillets d'Hypnos*. In "Les Rapports entre parasites," Char rejects the despair of history and offers to "Bâtir une postérité sans amertume" through poetry.

"Migration," "Domaine," and "Intégration" continue the themes of *Poèmes militants*: creativity through action and the importance of love: "Mes songes, hors l'amour, étaient graves et distants."[27] Above all, *Abondance viendra* demands that the rich resources of poetry be tapped, for "La Sécurité est un parfum;"[28] poetic activity must go beyond what Surrealism demands: "Grand tronc en activité, crois-tu au dénouement par la lèpre?"[29] The importance of Surrealism is not denied, but for Char it belongs to the past, as the past definite tense of this line demonstrates: "Nous fûmes le théâtre d'étranges secousses."[30] Poetry has been renewed and has reached a "Midi réhabilité,"[31] but the poet's task is not over. "Devant soi," the final poem of this section, stresses the call to the future: "Equarrisseur, ta descente est éteinte." All is to be done in the immediate future.

Abondance viendra is the last section of *Le Marteau sans maître*, but it is the least autonomous of the sections, for it depends upon an examination of *Le Marteau sans maître* in general and of *Poèmes militants* in particular. *Abondance viendra* appears only in the collective editions of *Le Marteau sans maître*; none of its seven poems has appeared separately or in any of Char's later anthologies. *Abondance viendra* completes *Le Marteau sans maître*; it formally announces the end of Char's adherence to the Surrealist group through its further development of this theme from *Poèmes militants*: while poetry cannot be separated from action, it cannot be limited to the Surrealist concept of spontaneous activity.

Another connection between *Abondance viendra* and *Poèmes militants* is found in the dates of composition. *Poèmes militants* was composed between 1931 and 1933; *Abondance viendra*, written between 1932 and 1933, coincides with part of the period of composition of *Poèmes militants*. Char seems to have planned *Abondance viendra* to continue the themes of *Poèmes militants*. His idea to organize via a progressive thematic unity seems to have been formulated between 1932 and 1933. In this respect, *Poèmes militants* probably predates *Abondance viendra* in a general sense although the interdependence of the two is certain.

---

[27] "Domaine," *Abondance viendra* in *Le Marteau sans maître* (Paris, 1945).
[28] "Migration."
[29] "Intégration."
[30] *Ibid.*
[31] *Ibid.*

Char's decision to end his formal adherence to the Surrealist group was not a sudden decision, nor was it a decision to make an overt break with the movement; rather, it was a growing conviction that poetry must be free of all limits. Recognition of the limitations of Surrealism is reflected in the first three sections of *Le Marteau sans maître*; in *Poèmes militants*, the resolution to go beyond Surrealism is made, and it is fully expressed in *Abondance viendra*.

Furthermore, Char's poetics and poetry seem to take a more final form by early 1933. *Abondance viendra* is the most stable group of poems in *Le Marteau sans maître*,[32] for very few changes were made between the two publications, and, of these 13 changes, seven are minor ones.[33] Like the revisions made in *Arsenal*, *L'Action de la justice est éteinte*, and *Poèmes militants* between 1934 and 1945, the changes in *Abondance viendra* are those which tend to eliminate or minimize Surrealist traits in favor of more universal characteristics and those which reinforce the overall thematic unity of *Le Marteau sans maître* as a journey through and beyond Surrealism.

1935-1936: *Moulin premier*

The title of *Moulin premier* suggests that this volume has a dual purpose; "moulin" denotes a building which houses a machine capable of refining raw materials. It also refers to the agent who sets the machine in motion, that is the poet within the framework of creative activity. The mill represents the poet's first formal structure; it is "premier" in time and space. Although construction is now complete, it will serve as the foundation for future, but not Surrealist, creative activity. *Moulin premier* presents an expression of Char's poetics at the end of his first public period of development, and in retrospect, it announces Char's voluntary withdrawal from identification with the Surrealist movement.

---

[32] *Artine* is the only section of *Le Marteau sans maître* which remained textually intact, but it is a single poem, while the other four sections are groupings of poems. In this view, *Abondance viendra* may then be considered as the least revised group of poems of the *Marteau sans maître* collection.
[33] See Appendix III.

Moulin premier reviews Char's Surrealist adventure as expressed in *Le Marteau sans maître*; it incorporates the lessons gained from this experience through its development of the theme emphasized in *Abondance viendra*: the need to further the cause of poetry and develop its inherent possibilities. After publication as a separate volume in 1936, *Moulin premier* was appended to *Le Marteau sans maître* in 1945.

While critics generally give 1935-1936 as the date of composition, it seems probable that the design for this work was formed in 1933, or at least not later than 1934. This possibility is seen in the revisions made in *Arsenal* and *L'Action de la justice est éteinte* for the 1934 edition of *Le Marteau sans maître*, in the addition of *Poèmes militants* and *Abondance viendra* to the first three sections in this edition, and in the general organizational pattern of *Le Marteau sans maître*.

The 1936, 1945, and 1963 editions of *Moulin premier* consist of three parts: an introductory poem, "***," a central section of aphorisms, and a concluding poem, "Commune présence." The major difference between the editions is found in the number of aphorisms: 63 in 1936 and 70 in 1945 and 1963. Of the seven additions, six (XIV, XV, XLI, XLVIII, LIX, LX) are from "L'Esprit poétique" of the 1934 edition of *L'Action de la justice est éteinte*.

Although it is not publicly known when Char determined to republish *Le Marteau sans maître* and append *Moulin premier* to it, it is plausible to propose that this decision was not made earlier than 1936.

Moulin premier underwent little revision for the 1945 publication. The few textual changes that do occur are those which reduce specific references to Surrealism in order to relegate Surrealism to its historical position in the liberation of poetry. Connected to the textual changes are changes in the typographical form of several aphorisms. These revisions are in line with two general tendencies of the 1945 *Le Marteau sans maître*: an effort to concentrate what is being expressed by the elimination of transitional and qualifying phrases and yet retain continuity and fluidity through the titles or appearance on the printed page, and, in the second place, an effort to clarify what has been condensed through the use of punctuation. In the 1945 edition of *Moulin premier*, all footnotes are incorporated into the text of the aphorism itself, punctuation marks (commas and exclamation points in particular) are more frequent, the first line of several aphorisms appears in capital letters to attract attention to the focal point of interest, and long paragraphs are often broken into two short paragraphs.

The aphorisms of *Moulin premier* summarize Char's poetic position at the end of his second period of development and indicate the future direction of his poetry. Although these aphorisms are neither Char's first published ones nor his first efforts to express poetic essence through the aphoristic form, they do represent his first consistent efforts as a theoretician and reveal that he has mastered the aphoristic form. *Moulin premier* may be considered as Char's first formal declaration and definition of his concept of poetry.

Moulin premier is concerned with the domain of poetry and the role of the poet. The poet has a responsibility to use all sources which may permit the birth of a poem, but at the same time he must make certain that he communicates only what will have meaning in the real world: "Persévérons dans le réel..." (XVII). Reason and reflection must precede intuition and imagination, but intuition and imagination have a valid role in poetic activity:

> A l'expiration de la réflexion on se heurte à l'intuition...
> (IX)

> L'imagination jouit surtout de ce qui ne lui est pas accordé car elle seule possède l'éphémère en totalité.
> (XXX)

> Au désespoir de la raison le poète ne sait jamais 'rentrer'; quand par inadvertance il le fait, il réintègre son inspiration, sa division.
> (XXXV)

> un poème *fonctionne* dès lors que son composé se vérifie juste à l'application, et ce malgré l'inconnu de ses attenances.
> (LXIII)

The poet "devance l'homme d'action" (XXII) in his struggle to communicate the possibility of a better world through poetry:

"Qu'à toute réquisition un poème doive nécessairement *se démontrer* me pose le quantième épisodique de sa réalité" (LXVI). Within poetry lies the opportunity to conquer death: "Mort, tu nous étends sans nous diminuer ... je distingue déjà mes yeux nouveaux d'éternité" (LXX). Because death is a part of the life process, it is of service to the poet: "La pensée de la mort en nous contraignant à mesurer notre vitesse nous facilite et adoucit nos mutations" (LXIX).

The most significant aspect of *Moulin premier* is its anticipation of *Le Poème pulvérisé*, published in 1947. In *Moulin premier*, Char describes a poem as a fragment which explodes into being in one instant of time:

> L'étincelle dispose (VII).
>
> Qu'à toute réquisition un poème puisse efficacement en tout comme en fragments, parcours entier, *se confirmer* (LXV).

Moulin premier not only expresses what Char accepts in the poetic act, but also reveals what he rejects. He is against rules, organized religion (XVII), tradition (XX), illusion (XXIV); he criticizes those who write for financial remuneration only (XXXIII, LIV) and those who like the kind of poetry which is easily grasped (LV). The poet's role is a "tâche de naissance" (XXIII), and the role of the reader is to participate in the creation of the poem; the reader must grasp the images and their connections so that they will have meaning within his framework of existence: "A toi, lecteur, d'établir les rapports/ ... A toi, rêveur, d'aplanir les rapports" (XXVI).

The two poems which frame the aphorisms of *Moulin premier* demonstrate Char's poetic development. "***" serves as a transition between *Le Marteau sans maître* and *Moulin premier*; it is a poetic declaration which summarizes what Char affirms in *Le Marteau sans maître*, and it illustrates the poetic theories set forth by the aphorisms of *Moulin premier*.

In 1936, "***" appeared as one stanza; it was divided between lines 12 and 13 into two stanzas in 1945. This division is a thematic one, for it marks the two aspects of poetic activity. The first stanza is a general description of the role of poetry to make known the real, while the second is more specific in its establishment of the conditions necessary for poetic activity.

In "***," Char proclaims that the ultimate goal and unique value of poetry lie in its capacity to communicate "La connaissance productive du Réel." Throughout *Le Marteau sans maître*, Char explored various means to elucidate and express poetic essence, and, in this aim, poetry has evolved for him into a synonym of existence. Through the vehicle of the poem, the poet can enable man to understand the nature of reality and to perceive its ultimate totality. Poetic activity provides man with a means for realizing his possibilities within this reality and justifying his existence. The poet alone has the responsibility to discover and communicate man's reality and his potential. In *Le Marteau sans maître*, particularly in *Artine*, Char emphasizes the role of the real; poetic activity must permit contact with reality if it is to express and vindicate the human position. It is the "connaissance ... du Réel" that Char sought in *Le Marteau sans maître* and that he affirms as the cornerstone of his poetics in "***"; this "connaissance" must be "productive," that is, it must have meaning for man.

The means to attain the "connaissance productive du Réel" are clearly seen in "***." The formulas and rules of the past are useless in this quest: "...pas d'après une mesure compliquée..." Poetry comes into being through activity which has the concrete at its base: "une sorte de commotion ... /Extraits du grossier." Poetic activity never loses contact with the real ("Sous le gel,") but this activity is of such a nature that it upsets the apparent order of the real to permit a new and more meaningful perspective of the real to emerge. According to "L'imbattable ordonnance qui préside en géologie," new islands are formed through a volcanic explosion; poetic activity is a "commotion" like that of a volcano; beneath the surface, it erupts, and in the wake of its explosion there is the new formation of an archipelago: "La formation excentrique des îles." These islands may seem to be disconnected on the surface, but the phrase "en amour" implies that they are joined. These few lines announce the poetics and poetry later emphasized in *Le Poème pulvérisé* (1947) and *La Parole en archipel* (1961).

Reason must select which aspects of the new perspective of reality gained through activity are to be presented: "une tactique fructueuse" refers to the poet's labor to make his discoveries known. The real must control and direct the imagination; the poetic act is vain unless it has value in the real; only then can the "connaissance productive du Réel ...*sentimentalement* passer pour collectivement satisfaisante."

The second stanza evokes the conditions which precede the poetic activity already described. Love is the act of living which makes poetic activity possible. The phrase "formons un couple" contains the essence of Char's concept of poetry. The "couple" refers to the fusion of the act of living and the act of poetry. In the first place, the couple consists of the union of man and woman; this convergence is one of active human participation which results in an explosion and a fulfillment, "collectivement satisfaisante." In the second place, the couple represents the act of poetry, for the union is composed of word and desire, the poem and the poet. The two facets of the couple are linked through the poet, who participates as the male in the human union and who transposes this desire into the poetic act, which when combined with word results in a poem. The fusion of the act of living and the act of poetry represented by the formation of a couple and the two aspects of this couple foreshadow *Lettera amorosa* (1953) in which the written word and desire are the two key concepts.

Through the couple, human experience becomes the controlling factor in the discovery of the real, for significant poetic activity must maintain contact with human reality:

> ...formons un couple
> Tels nous serons introduits
> . . . .
> A la réception vécue écourtée de la réalité
> Où commande ...notre indifférence notre expérience.

"***" defines the theory of poetic activity that demands a fusion of life and poetry: "Commune présence" illustrates this theory. It is significant that Char chose the title of this poem as the comprehensive title for his 1964 anthology. "Commune" implies that which belongs to all men, that which can be achieved through a joint effort, that which is never individual nor unusual but that which is general and universal, even frequent, in its manifestation, its "présence," its state or being in the immediate vicinity. "Commune présence" is that which is known and accessible to all; life is the common denominator of mankind, and the means to discover the reality and its meaning are within the domain of the poet. It is the role and the responsibility of the poet to reveal to man his "commune présence," his present existence and his future through poetry.

The poem "Commune présence" has remained textually intact. In 1936, 1945, and 1963 it appears as a two-part poem; in 1957 and 1964 only the second part appears as "Tu es pressé d'écrire..." in 1957 and as "Commune présence" in 1964. The omission of the first part in 1957 and 1964 does not affect the significance of "Commune présence," for in the original version, it is the second part which evokes the "commune présence" while the first part expresses the problem and need for its exposure and revelation.

In part I of "Commune présence," the "éclaireur" represents the victory of the new poet whose creative activity has value for individual man's daily existence. This new poet is to replace those who stressed in the past the inhuman side of existence. The "inhumain" of Part I is the one who is non-poetic; he refused change: "Indiscernable il rôde sur le tracé des flaques/Et gouverne selon son rang/Gardien..." This "inhumain" has destroyed communication with nature: "L'arbre a châtié ... ses feuilles/La terre à bec-de-lièvre a bu le dévoué sourire"; instead of discovering the totality of reality, he has presented its mutilation and hostility. He, and those who resemble and follow him, have failed to maintain contact with reality:

> Sont-ils épris de leur propre mort
> Au point de ne pouvoir de leur vivant attribuant
> Se démettre déborder d'elle...

In Part II, the "tu" is the new poet who has maintained and affirmed contact with reality. "Tu es pressé d'écrire / Comme si tu étais en retard sur la vie" is the expression of the necessity to communicate his discovery to man. The lines "Hâte-toi de transmettre / Ta part de merveilleux de rébellion de bienfaisance" reinforce the urgency of this need; man has been given a pessimistic view of life, a view which only the poet of the real can contradict; man must be given the fruits of the poet's endeavor. "Effectivement tu es en retard..." suggests that the quest for the discovery of the truth of existence, although long and difficult, was successful: "La vie inexprimable / La seule en fin de compte à laquelle tu acceptes de t'unir." This "vie inexprimable" is the fusion of life and the poetic act which the poem concretizes. The path toward this goal has been one of many obstacles: "... est refusée chaque jour par les êtres et par les choses / Dont tu obtiens ... quelques fragments décharnés / Au bout de combats sans merci." Nevertheless, the "vie inexprimable" exonerates the poet's vocation: "Hors d'elle tout n'est qu'agonie soumise fin grossière." If the poet encounters death during his efforts to communicate his discovery, he is to resign himself to it: "Reçois-la... / Offre ta soumission / Jamais tes armes." Death is a part of life; the poet is mortal as is man and so he cannot hope to conquer death; his existence is his poetry; "Tu as été créé pour des moments peu communs." Man's world is one of finiteness, and the laws of nature include death: "la liquidation du monde se poursuit / Sans interruption / Sans égarement"; the poet cannot surmount death, but his poetry can: "Essaime ta poussière / Nul ne décèlera votre union." The union of the poet and his poem, of life and poetry, is a-temporal and a-spatial, universal and eternal.

The two poems and the group of aphorisms that compose *Moulin premier* conclude Char's second period of development and his quest for the nature of poetry. It is a journey that led him through and beyond Surrealism to the formation of a poetics and poetry based on contact with reality and on the fusion of life and poetry: "La poésie, c'est l'existence," [34] for only poetry can offer a new reality in which man can justify his existence.

Le Marteau sans maître (1934) and *Moulin premier* (1936) show Char's constant concern with poetry as creative activity. In these two volumes, Char includes his major Surrealist texts and expresses his assessment and modification of certain Surrealist themes and techniques. The 1945 and 1963 editions present Char's retrospective view of his Surrealist experience, for they were prepared when Char was no longer associated historically and aesthetically with the Surrealist movement:

---

[34] Char's definition as quoted by Pierre de Boisdeffre in "Poésie vivante — René Char," *Les Nouvelles littéraires* (12 février 1959), p. 7.

A Georgette Char [35] qui a convoyé la plupart des poèmes du *Marteau sans maître* et leur a permis d'atteindre la province de sécurité où je désirais les savoir. [36]

René Char was formally a Surrealist between 1930 and 1934, but his 1934 revisions indicate that his poetry was moving beyond Surrealism before 1934. In his revision of the 1930 edition of *Arsenal*, Char undertook an exploration of the materials, Surrealist and otherwise, available to the individual poet. In *Artine*, composed in 1930, he decided to opt for the real world; this early poetic document demonstrates at the height of his enthusiasm for Surrealism that Char's poetics and poetry are developing beyond the Surrealist movement. As early as the 1931 edition of *L'Action de la justice est éteinte*, Char acknowledges his participation in Surrealism and his acceptance of certain aspects of it, but his view of the movement has begun to evolve into a historical one. Surrealism has contributed significantly to the future of poetry; it was a needed literary force for the liberation of poetry from the constraints of the past and the struggle to gain acceptance for the new spirit of poetry, but the new poetry and its possible richness have been made known and recognized. It is the victory of the new, not the triumph of Surrealism, that Char proclaims. By 1932, he was beyond the movement. In *Poèmes militants* and *Abondance viendra*, completed in 1933, Char asserts that Surrealism must be rejected if poetic activity is to be meaningfully communicated to others.

Further evidence of Char's early rejection of Surrealism is found in his poem "Hommage à Paul Eluard," written in the summer of 1932. This text shows what Char had hoped to gain through formal contact with the Surrealist movement. He praises Eluard's interest in man's acceptance of the physical world through poetry and his efforts to grasp truth through images:

La subjectivité ...déséquilibre le poète.

A hauteur d'Eluard les nuages invisibles deviennent des fleuves visibles... la perfection du poète et l'humanité primitive.

---

[35] Char's wife, Georgette Goldstein, whom he married in 1932.
[36] Dedication to the 1945 and 1963 editions of *Le Marteau sans maître suivi de Moulin premier*.

Although all editions of *Le Marteau sans maître* represent Char's Surrealist experience, they also contain evidence that Char never fully adhered to Surrealism. By 1934, Char has matured into a poet whose task is to be the conscious instrument, "le marteau," of objective reality which can be discovered through creative activity. Identification with any group is a limitation which he must reject, for he must be free, "sans maître," in order to explore and reveal all means (Surrealist and non-Surrealist) to this reality in which alienation and contradiction are replaced by integration and fulfillment.

Moulin premier, written after *Le Marteau sans maître*, codifies the principles of Char's poetic structure in its emphasis on creative activity as a fusion of life and poetry; this fusion had been evolving throughout *Le Marteau sans maître*. However, *Moulin premier* presents this fusion as an emotional feeling and as an intellectual concept; the latter suggests that Char's poetry will ultimately replace philosophy as the means by which man acquires understanding of his world. By maintaining close contact with the real world, the poet can discover this truth, which will dignify man's acts of daily living. This discovery is now possible because of the poet's adaptation of the Surrealist notion of poetry as action. Fusion of this act of poetry with the act of living becomes the basis upon which Char sets out to justify man's existence.

CHAPTER III

1936-1947: A POETICS OF MORAL RESPONSIBILITY

The 1936 publication of *Moulin premier* marks René Char's voluntary rejection of Surrealism and initiates his orientation towards a poetics of responsibility which examines man's position in the world in order to establish human dignity. The fusion of the act of poetry and the act of living emphasized in *Le Marteau sans maître* suivi de *Moulin premier* forms the cornerstone of this third period of development. Achievement of this fusion is not an end in and of itself; it must have meaning for individual man and for the community of men. To live is to act, but every act appears menaced by the flux and destruction of the world. If man is to learn how to fuse poetry and life, he must first be shown the nature of the world, his own nature, and, above all, the nature of the menace which threatens both him and his world. It is this problem of definition and presentation which dominates Char's poetry from 1936 to 1947.

One may distinguish three stages in Char's third period of development: 1) the prewar years, 1936-1939, during which the poet emerges from an inner crisis and moves towards a greater involvement with the cosmos and the condition of individual man (*Placard pour un chemin des écoliers, Dehors la nuit est gouvernée,* and *Le Visage nuptial*); 2) the war years, 1939-1944, which reflect the growth of Char's humanism because of the experience of war and its resulting fraternity and need for communal action (*L'Avant-monde, Partage formel, Feuillets d'Hypnos,* and *Les Loyaux adversaires*); 3) the immediate postwar years, 1944-1947, which present an affirmation of faith in man's capacity to assert his dignity through the glorification of the menace (*Le Poème pulvérisé*, *La Fontaine narrative*, and *Recherche de la base et du sommet*). The role of love is directly associated with the role of destruction and parallels the same three stages of evolution: 1) the awareness of impending destruction and an emphasis on the possibility of strengthening man through union with woman; 2) definition of both the menace and of fraternal love; 3) exaltation of the menace and love as consummated action, the highest virtue.

1936-1939: Awareness of the Menace

From 1923 to 1935, Char had evolved a poetics based on the fusion of the act of poetry and the act of living, but he had restricted the act of life to the physical act of love shared by two individuals. The realization that he had somewhat limited the act of love to an erotic experience was precipitated by two events. One was the outbreak of the Spanish Civil War in 1936, the other his recovery from a serious illness (1936-1937). Together they led him to the crisis described in *Placard pour un chemin des écoliers* and *Dehors la nuit est gouvernée*.

Char's personal acquaintance with Spain and its people was the result of two visits prior to 1936. The Spanish Civil War and its ensuing atrocities made him aware of the universality of the struggle to survive. At about the same time, contracting an acute case of blood-poisoning (1936), Char came face to face with the vulnerability of his own being; this adversity affected Char the man, rather than Char the poet, and set him on a course of questioning the nature of man and the nature of his universe. The crisis that Char experienced from 1936 to 1937 was artistic as well as personal. His emergence from this inner turmoil is reflected in a more universal and more humanistic concept of poetry, that is, in an extension of the act of living which is to be fused to the act of poetry.

In the "Introduction" to the 1949 edition of *Dehors la nuit est gouvernée précédé par Placard pour un chemin des écoliers*, Char explains that these two works, originally published separately, are to be considered jointly as representative of his poetic crisis and emergence from it:

> les poèmes de 'Dehors la nuit est gouvernée' obéissaient dans mon esprit, quand ils furent écrits, à l'exigence d'une

> marche forcée dans l'indicible, avec ...les provisions hasardeuses du langage et la manne de l'observation et des pressentiments.
> J'étais parvenu à cette époque, avec mon tourment... Quand à 'Placard pour un chemin des écoliers', puis-je dire ...à son propos que *j'ai couru?*... Cependant la persécution et l'horreur mijotaient déjà leur branle-bas.
> On n'a pas craint de réunir 'Dehors la nuit est gouvernée' et 'Placard pour un chemin des écoliers'.

The two main themes of *Placard pour un chemin des écoliers* are the awareness of the universality of the harsh reality in which the individual must live and the acknowledgement of a possible reaction, through love, against this oppression. In *Dehors la nuit est gouvernée*, which continues the examination of these two themes, Char discovers that human frailty may be overcome through the recognition of an inner consciousness and an outer order common to all men. While *Placard pour un chemin des écoliers* depicts the act of awareness of the poet, *Dehors la nuit est gouvernée* marks his struggle to reverse the limits of his horizon.

The title of *Placard pour un chemin des écoliers* suggests a public warning against the barbarism of war. The phrase "le chemin des écoliers" is a common French expression which means the longest road. What Char seems to convey is that it has unfortunately and shamefully required knowledge of hate, exploitation, persecution, and murder to bring about a redefinition of "les valeurs morales et sentimentales."[1] In the "Dédicace," he deplores the present for having destroyed innocence and purity, the "école buissonnière"; this nostalgia for the past is later developed in *Les Matinaux* (1950). The brief and simple line "Les temps sont changés" emphasizes the specific anguish of the poet and his general horror that suffering knows no barriers of geography or age. While "Les temps sont changés" is external in its description and refers primarily to the poet's awareness, it also foreshadows Char's closer identification with others in *Dehors la nuit est gouvernée*.

Underlying the "Dédicace" and the seven poems which form *Placard pour un chemin des écoliers* is a tone of indignation and

---

[1] "Dédicace." *Dehors la nuit est gouvernée précédé par Placard pour un chemin des écoliers* (Paris, 1949).

revolt against the isolation of the individual. Where there is union, there is the possibility of strength, and the union most readily accessible to all is that of the couple, man and woman. The role of woman is to renew man, to arm him with the promise of fulfillment which can enable him to combat the perils of existence, enable him to survive, to act meaningfully:

> Nous avons ouvert le lit
> A la pierre creuse du jour en quête du sang
> De résistance. [2]

The function of love is no longer erotic; instead, love offers an immediate possibility for hope against the harshness of reality.

Between the 1937 and 1949 publications of *Placard pour un chemin des écoliers*, only two textual revisions were made.[3] In "Dédicace" (II, 3), an adjective, "autonome," originally modified "existence;" the 1949 deletion of this qualifier suggests that between 1936 and 1949, probably during World War II, existence and independence became synonymous for Char; that is, authentic existence is of necessity autonomous. However, the priority of freedom is stressed in 1937: "Tu nous as passé liberté tes courroies de sable."[4] One line was omitted in "Les Vivres du retour:" "Embellir ton haleine malmenée par la rixe." In 1937, this phrase reinforced the idea that love contains the possibility of strength; however, this line also had the negative connotation that love can be abused, perhaps weakened; deleting this line emphasized the positive aspect of the poem.

The stability of form and content in *Placard pour un chemin des écoliers* is significant, for it is a general characteristic of Char's publications between 1936 and 1949; only the 1945 edition of *Le Marteau sans maître* suivi de *Moulin premier* interrupts this third period of relative textual stability.

---

[2] "Les Vivres du retour."

[3] The possibility of a third revision is found in "Compagnie de l'écolière" (I, 7): "Est-ce vous que j'ai vu sourire." The past participle "vu" was changed to the feminine form "vue"; however, the 1937 form may have been a typographical error, and, if so, its change in 1949 would be a mechanical correction and not strictly a revision.

[4] "Quatre âges."

The 1938 edition of *Dehors la nuit est gouvernée* consisted of 22 poems. By 1949 two of them had been placed in other volumes; "Gravité" became part of *Le Visage nuptial* in *Seuls demeurent* (1945) and "Biens égaux" was included in *Le Poème pulvérisé* (1947). The relocation of these two poems produces a broad thematic unity in *Fureur et mystère* (1948). The relation of "Gravité" and "Biens égaux" to the general structure of *Dehors la nuit est gouvernée* and their contribution to the themes stressed in *Le Visage nuptial* and *Le Poème pulvérisé*, combined with their positions within these works, indicate that, in the first place, *Dehors la nuit est gouvernée* represents an important aspect of Char's development, for it contains the basic thought elaborated in later works. Secondly, Char disregards the chronology of composition in order to enhance the organic unity of his work. Additional evidence of Char's concern with structural homogeneity is seen in his decision to add "Dépendance de l'adieu" to the 1949 edition; it was originally published individually in 1936. Furthermore, the title of the last poem of the *Dehors la nuit est gouvernée* collection was changed from "Validité" to "Postface"; this revision indicates Char's retrospective view of the volume, for this title change is one that could have been effected only after the publications of *Seuls demeurent* and *Le Poème pulvérisé*, that is after the relocation of "Gravité" and "Biens égaux." The 1938 title, "Validité," reviews what the poet has established as authentic in *Dehors la nuit est gouvernée*, while the 1949 title is a specific announcement that the basic truth reached is to be continued and more fully probed. "Postface" relates the importance of Char's inner crisis to the whole body of his work, whereas "Validité" merely summarized this crisis.

A study of the eight lines deleted between the two editions reveals a stylistic condensation achieved through the elimination of superfluous elements; omission of all that tends to restrict interpretation of the poems [5] and everything that suggests the personality of the poet, as in "Le Temps du store" (II, 1; IV, 3-4), leads toward a more open-ended poetry. The most interesting change is the deletion from "A un fantôme de la réflexion surpris

---

[5] "Passerelle" (II, 4); "Confins" (III, 5); "Une Italienne de Corot" (IV, 3); "L'Essentiel intelligible" (IV, 1; X, 1).

chez les pleutres de la providence"; one line was deleted: "Le verbe et le désir interprètent l'espace." This sentence contains the most concise statement of Char's poetic theory, the fusion of life ("désir") and poetry ("verbe") in an act of communication ("interprètent") of limitless cosmic dimensions ("espace"). It recalls the odyssey undertaken in *Le Marteau sans maître,* summarizes the message of *Dehors la nuit est gouvernée,* and announces *Le Visage nuptial* and *Lettera amorosa.* There are two plausible explanations for the suppression of this line; first, the union of desire and the written word is the particular subject of *Le Visage nuptial,* which was not composed as a volume of five poems in 1938; secondly, *Partage formel,* a collection of aphorisms on the role of union as an essential part of the theory of poetry, had not been written at the time. In other words, Char no longer needed this line in 1949 because its implication had been fully developed.

The major innovation of *Dehors la nuit est gouvernée* is the expansion of the term "l'homme"; it denotes man in the abstract sense and man as the center of poetic activity. As "l'homme" replaces "le poète," Char's poetry becomes more cosmic in its mode of operation, more humanistic in its application, and more organic in its expression. The act of the poet merges with the act of the man. "Dehors" signifies that the poet has come out from his inner self and entered an expanded world. Moreover, this greater degree of involvement with others is an ordered one; it is "gouvernée." The discovery that there is an order to the universe occurs when the self joins in union with another. To confront the "nuit," to restore the harmony of existence for human and poetic action, only the order of love is effectual and efficacious: "Au sein de l'arbitraire le désir débardeur de chaume rentre l'ordre de l'amour." [6]

The fact that the term *man* has replaced the term *poet* in Char's style and thought does not mean that he is no longer concerned with the role of poetry in the modern world. On the contrary, the relationship of man and poet is essential to his poetics, as his use of the first person forms "je" and "nous" indicates. The "je" evokes the poet as a man whose unique task is that of a "Visionnaire adapté aux surprises de la terre/Malgré l'intimité mul-

---

[6] "Validité."

tiforme du néant"; [7] he alone has the verbal power, "Sauveur exténué ô langage," [8] to communicate the presence of a cosmic harmony and the importance of love. It is the responsibility of the poet, the "je," to lead others to recognize the value of revolt: "la rage ... est chaste." [9] The strength necessary to accept the "Maigre terre condamnée" [10] where each one (including man and poet) dwells can be acquired individually through love:

> O front de mon amour,
> Il est temps de sortir,
> De brutaliser la sottise. [11]

As expressed by "Tous compagnons de lit," this particular act of living provides a basis for unifying all men; "Notre langue commune dans l'éternité sous le toit gardien de nos luttes, c'est le sommeil, cet espéranto de raison."

The assimilation of "je" into "nous" offers a more general and yet more familiar frame of reference. The plural "nous" reflects the unity of man and poet against the common menace: "jamais solidaires en totalité." [12] It is to be noted that Char's stylistic distinction between "je" and "nous" is established as early as 1937 and that *Dehors la nuit est gouvernée* anticipates his exaltation of communal action in *Feuillets d'Hypnos*.

Significantly, the current of fraternal feeling in *Dehors la nuit est gouvernée* is accompanied by a realistic awareness of the baser side of human nature. Although Char knows that "La régie de l'homme est fragile" [13] because frequently in man "le mal surnage et le bien coule à pic," [14] he is consistently confident in the validity of the order of love to strengthen the individual against all adversity and insure man of a better future through action in the present: "Le désespoir n'est plus gothique." [15]

---

[7] "Dire aux miens."
[8] "A un fantôme de réflexion surpris chez les pleutres de la providence."
[9] "L'Essentiel intelligible."
[10] "Conséquences."
[11] *Ibid.*
[12] "A un fantôme de réflexion surpris chez les pleutres de la providence."
[13] "Prouver par la vie."
[14] "Tous compagnons de lit."
[15] "A un fantôme de réflexion surpris chez les pleutres de la providence."

While the function of union is emphasized as one part of the message of *Dehors la nuit est gouvernée*, it is the exclusive concern of *Le Visage nuptial*. In fact, this theme is so thoroughly presented in *Le Visage nuptial* that the work as a whole is apt to be treated as Char's concept of the role of sex, rather than being properly assessed as an extended clarification of *Dehors la nuit est gouvernée*.

It is possible that Char conceived the poem "Le Visage nuptial" [16] during the composition of *Dehors la nuit est gouvernée*, but it does not appear likely that the two works were written concurrently. "Le Visage nuptial" realizes the solution suggested in *Dehors la nuit est gouvernée*, namely that sexual union offers a moment of harmony with the universe and provides man with the condition necessary for poetic activity. The theme of union is continued and further defined in "Le Visage nuptial" in the recurrent description "l'homme debout." This image first appears in the final line of "Tous compagnons de lit" *(Dehors la nuit est gouvernée)*: "Nous ne nous avouons pas vaincu/quand dans l'homme debout le mal surnage et le bien coule à pic." "L'homme debout" refers to an individual roused from sleep; in the world of sleep or inactivity, he resembles all men; once he is awake, his baser side, "le mal," alienates him from others. The problem is to reverse the results of the awakened state so that "le bien" may prevail. "Le Visage nuptial" contains the solution. A sexual union with woman releases the individual man from the past and permits him to glimpse the possibilities of a better future; he is enriched by a sexual experience which revitalizes his strength in the present. Woman has ended his estrangement and isolation:

> Voici le sable mort, voici le corps sauvé :
> La Femme respire, l'Homme se tient debout.

The rebirth of man through woman is emphasized by the reflexive verb "se tient"; the individual can now act on his own initiative; he can hold himself erect and proud, for the celebration

---

[16] A distinction must be made between the poem and the volume. The 1938 edition is limited to the single poem "Le Visage nuptial," while all subsequent publications (1945, 1948, 1962) consist of five poems of which one is the specific poem. I have differentiated between the two by enclosing the title in quotation marks when it refers to the poem and by italicizing it when it refers to the volume of five poems.

of love ennobles man's human condition. What was considered a possibility in *Dehors la nuit est gouvernée* is accepted as an actuality in "Le Visage nuptial"; throughout Char's work, "l'homme debout" represents man's inherent majesty of being:

> Salut à celui qui marche en sûreté à mes côtés, au terme du poème. Il passera demain DEBOUT sous le vent.[17]

> Il y a un homme à présent debout, un homme dans un champ de seigle, un champ pareil à un choeur mitraillé, un champ sauvé.[18]

The poem "Le Visage nuptial" is situated in a cyclical framework, and the five poems which constitute the volume of *Le Visage nuptial* are arranged according to the progression of the theme. "Conduite" announces the direction of the work; woman ("Bien-aimée") is praised for the change ("alchimie") she can effect through union. "Gravité" emphasizes the seriousness of sexual union as a condition for action; desire for woman is desire for release from monotony and isolation; the satisfaction of the sexual desire places fulfillment immediately within human access, for it contains the promise of hope: "Un parfum d'insolation/protège ce qui va éclore." "Conduite" and "Gravité" function as overtures to the actual performance of the sexual union celebrated in "Le Visage nuptial." Sex is not an escape from the present; it is "un retour compact" which makes the present acceptable, even agreeable.

"Le Visage nuptial" is probably the most important text in the group because its title is also that of the volume. However, the true meaning of this poem can only be grasped through "Evadné," the poem which follows. Not only does "Evadné" place "Le Visage nuptial" within its proper context, but it also heightens the importance of "Conduite" and "Gravité," for these two introductory poems become more general in application than a first reading might suggest. "Evadné" presents the results of the couple's sexual alliance: "...au début d'adorables années/La terre nous aimait un peu je me souviens." In the moment of union, the participants

---

[17] "Fenaison," *Seuls demeurent* (Paris, 1945).
[18] "Louis Curel de la Sorgue."

attain harmony with the world, if only for a brief moment; time and space are conquered; there are no limits whatever to the cosmos in the consummation of love between a man and a woman. Through sexual union, man gains a glimpse of the eternal and infinite oneness of his universe, and this insight allows him to hope. This knowledge is achieved through the order of love; because of the celebration of "Le Visage nuptial," the world is in order: *Dehors la nuit est gouvernée.*

The "Post-scriptum" which ends *Le Visage nuptial* explains the poetic purpose served by sexual union and its accompanying insight into the unity of the world: "Le trèfle de la passion est de fer dans ma main." The sexual experience provides the poet with the condition necessary for creative activity; he fuses "désir" and "verbe," desire for union and the written word which communicates the resulting cosmic harmony.

Although there are no significant variants [19] for any of the editions of *Le Visage nuptial*, there is an interesting change in the order of appearance in the 1957 anthology, *Poèmes et prose choisis*, in which "Gravité" precedes "Conduite." Since both poems form the introduction and contribute to the expanded setting of "Le Visage nuptial," it is possible to reverse their order without interrupting the unity or the chronology of the basic theme. By placing "Gravité" in the initial position, the role of desire is emphasized. However, in the 1962 edition of *Fureur et mystère*, "Conduite" returns to its original position. While the provisional change in order reflects Char's concern for organizational unity and its inherent possibilities, "Conduite" is a somewhat more general text than "Gravité" and seems more appropriate as the introductory poem of *Le Visage nuptial*.

It is difficult to determine the dates of composition and organization of *Le Visage nuptial*; what is certain is that "Gravité" was written in 1937 and "Le Visage nuptial" in 1938. It is probable that Char wrote the other three poems and decided to relocate "Gravité" during World War II. In the 1945 edition, the

---

[19] One word change occurred between 1938 and 1945; in 1938, the line (IV, 6) was: "De voix vitreuses de départs lynchés." The last term was changed from "lynchés" (1938) to "lapidés" (1945); this revision does not alter the meaning of the line or stanza; rather, the term "lapidés" replaces "lynchés" in order to present a better contrast with "vitreuses."

subtitle "L'Emmuré" was added to "Gravité." "L'Emmuré" refers to the condition of the actor described in the poem; it also evokes *Feuillets d'Hypnos*, written during the war:

> La reproduction en couleurs du *Prisonnier* de Georges de la Tour ...semble ...réfléchir son sens dans notre condition.... La femme explique, l'emmuré écoute.... Le Verbe de la femme donne naissance à l'inespéré mieux que n'importe quelle aurore.
> Reconnaissance à Georges de la Tour qui maîtrisa les ténèbres hitlériennes avec un dialogue d'êtres humains.
> (178)

Moreover, in "Evadné," the turbulent landscape of the present is contrasted with the calm of the past; several similar descriptions are found in *L'Avant-monde*. In any case, the final form of *Le Visage nuptial* does not appear to have been undertaken before 1939, the year the war began.

The ballet *La Conjuration* (1946) is a representation of the theme of union as it is expressed in *Dehors la nuit est gouvernée* and *Le Visage nuptial*. The use of the dance form externalizes the emotions of the act of love; "Le poète rêve de donner un sens moins furtif à ses actes..." Man's contradictory feelings (apprehension, fear, boredom, defiance, hostility, independence, authority, desire, passion, frenzy) are fused into a beneficial union with woman; she renders possible that which seems impossible, the reconciliation of opposites.

> Adieu aux formes à jamais fixées dont le plaisir permanent se détourne. Quête du vertige. LE FRUIT NE PROVIENT PAS DE LA FLEUR. IL EST SON CONTRAIRE. Le fruit est le prolongement du soir. Il est le trait d'union entre le soir et le risque. La fleur se limite à n'être que le diamant diurne. [20]

La Conjuration was included as a part of the 1948, but not the 1962, edition of *Fureur et mystère*. While it is conceivable that *La Conjuration* was not finished until after the war, it seems to have been begun either immediately before the war or during the short period of respite between the initial German triumph and

---

[20] *La Conjuration* in *Fureur et mystère* (Paris, 1948), p. 174.

Char's activity in the Resistance. It is not certain that *La Conjuration* belongs chronologically to Char's prewar period; yet, its emphasis on the role of woman and the act of union places it closer thematically to *Dehors la nuit est gouvernée* and *Le Visage nuptial* than to later works, particularly closer to the *Seuls demeurent* section (which includes *Le Visage nuptial*) than to the other sections of *Fureur et mystère*.

1939-1944: FRATERNAL ACTION

Before World War II, Char's work was relatively unknown in France and elsewhere. His publication of *Seuls demeurent* (1945) and *Feuillets d'Hypnos* (1946) resulted in widespread acknowledgement of his poetic genius.

Because Char was not "discovered" by critics until these two works appeared, most studies about him fail to perceive that the war served as a catalyst, not as a cause, for his poetic development. The themes of humanism, fraternal love, optimism for the present and the immediate future, faith in man, the problem of existence, the necessity of freedom, and concern for a definition of the poet's responsibility in the face of the harshness of everyday reality had been part of Char's work for almost twenty years. These interests were perhaps not as fully emphasized in his earlier texts as in the war texts, but, nevertheless, they were already a part of his poetry. His personal involvement in the war provided the framework for the rapid maturation of these concerns; even if the war had not occurred, it is more than probable that Char's poetics and poetry would have taken the direction they did. It was not the war and Char's intimate association with it that effected his recognition of the poet's moral responsibility to others; rather, the war acted upon him as a catalyst and hastened this evolution.

Seuls demeurent consists of three sections: (1) *L'Avant-monde*, which contains 32 poems and is the section most often referred to as *Seuls demeurent*; (2) *Le Visage nuptial*, which complements the theme of union of *Dehors la nuit est gouvernée* and which appears here for the first time as a group of poems; and, (3) *Partage formel*, which is a group of aphorisms on poetic theory.

1936-1947: A POETICS OF MORAL RESPONSIBILITY

The texts of *L'Avant-monde* span six years of poetic activity, from the end of the author's inner crisis (1938) to the liberation of France (1944). The first 13 poems are prewar and have a similar theme: the role of the poet. In "Argument," dated 1938, the poet's task is to surmount the apparent contradictions of reality in order to enable man to develop through "...la transhumance du Verbe," for the poet is "L'homme qui s'épointe dans la prémonition, qui déboise son silence intérieur et le répartir en théâtres, ... c'est le faiseur de pain." In the examination of his rejection of Surrealism, Char acknowledges a debt to that movement. He finds satisfaction in having adhered, in his youth, to the Surrealist group, but feels that his rejection of it is justified: "Je sais que la conscience qui se risque n'a rien à redouter de la plane." [21] In his poetic independence, he has sought and found unity: "J'ai, captif, épousé le ralenti du lierre à l'assaut de la pierre de l'éternité." [22]

The fourteenth poem, "Le Loriot," ends the poetic quest of the prewar poems. Dated September 3, 1939, "Le Loriot" describes the advent of World War II as a moral catastrophe: "Tout à jamais prit fin." The remaining poems of *L'Avant-monde* are connected to the war, either directly or by allusions.

Char's participation in the war is reflected in a series of poems entitled "Neuf poèmes pour vaincre," [23] written between 1940 and 1944. These nine poems review and summarize his attitude during the war years. In "Chant du refus," subtitled "Début du partisan," the poet becomes a combatant, hopeful that "beauté et vérité fassent que vous soyez *présents* nombreux aux salves de la délivrance!" "Vivre avec de tels hommes" describes the poet's discovery that the end of his isolation from others is replaced by a greater desire for truth and beauty. "Ne s'entend pas" stresses the duty to act, while "Carte du 8 novembre" expresses a feeling of inadequacy in the face of so much suffering, "ce nouveau calvaire." "Louis Curel de la Sorgue" extols the virtue of freedom, in contrast to the despair and disgust evoked in "Le Bouge de

---
[21] "Calendrier."
[22] "Afin qu'il n'y soit rien changé."
[23] This title and the particular grouping of the nine poems have only appeared in *Poèmes et prose choisis* (1957). The texts were in no way altered for this new arrangement, and I find that this grouping provides a convenient framework for discussion.

l'historien." Knowledge that the war is ending ("le dégel ... de la nausée") is found in "Plissement," which also recognizes the necessity of action as the lesson of war: "Vers ta frontière, ô vie humiliée, je marche maintenant au pas des certitudes, averti que la vérité ne précède pas obligatoirement l'action." In "Hommage et famine," woman is praised for having caused man to hunger for love which gave him the inspiration to continue. The last poem of the group and of *L'Avant-monde* is "Liberté," which captures the instant of freedom, freedom not only from the German occupation, but also from all limits; freedom is a moral good, and its absence is evil.

L'Avant-monde is dominated by two major themes, the creative act of the poet and the poet in action. Underlying the texts is a consciousness of unity between man and woman, man and men, men and the world. The poet's very act of participation in the war reflects the fusion of poetry and of everyday living; his awareness of the inherent unity of the world becomes even more acute through his personal involvement with others, for he finds that all men are equally threatened by war and seek the same goal, liberty.

Partage formel, the last section of *Seuls demeurent*, demands that poetry be in direct contact with the experiences of life; only truth which has been gained through action, truth which has been actually lived, is the proper domain of poetry. *Partage formel* is a poetic declaration that experiences are universal and can be shared through language. While the prose poems of *L'Avant-monde* present the everyday action of the poet, the aphorisms of *Partage formel* explain the evolution of his poetic theories and their interdependency with experience.

Moulin premier (1936), as has been noted in Chapter II, represents Char's poetic development through and beyond Surrealism. *Partage formel* begins where *Moulin premier* ends. In fact, this work appears to be a direct continuation of *Moulin premier*, for it sets forth explicitly why Char rejected Surrealism:

> Le poète doit tenir la balance égale entre le monde physique de la veille et l'aisance redoutable du sommeil, les lignes de la connaissance dans lesquelles il couche le corps subtil du poème, allant indistinctement de l'un à l'autre de ces états différents de la vie (VII).

A l'âge d'homme j'ai vu s'élever et grandir sur le mur mitoyen de la vie et de la mort une échelle de plus en plus nue, investie d'un pouvoir d'évulsion unique: le rêve. Ses barreaux ...ne soutenaient plus les lisses épargnants du sommeil ... dont les figures chaotiques servirent de champ à l'inquisition d'hommes bien doués mais incapables de toiser l'universalité du drame, ... l'obscurité s'écarte et ...VIVRE devient ... la conquête des pouvoirs extraordinaires ... que nous n'exprimons qu'incomplètement faute de loyauté, de discernement cruel et de persévérance.

Compagnons..., allez la lampe éteinte et rendez les bijoux. Un mystère nouveau chante..., Développez votre étrangeté légitime (XXII).

The correspondence between *Moulin premier* and *Partage formel* is also seen in the arrangement of *Poèmes et prose choisis* (1957). Divided into two parts, the second division of this anthology contains a selection of Char's aphoristic writings. Significantly, none of the aphorisms of *Moulin premier* is included; this work is represented solely by "Tu es pressé d'écrire..." and is immediately followed by *Partage formel*. Char's decision to exclude *Moulin premier* and include *Partage formel* is a tacit announcement that *Partage formel* not only continues but supersedes *Moulin premier* in its representation of the first twenty years of his poetic development.

Additional continuity between the two works is found in the almost verbatim recurrence of one aphorism. In *Moulin premier* (LVII) one reads: "Il faut être l'homme de la pluie et enfant du beau temps." This thought is rephrased in *Partage formel* (XIX): "Homme de la pluie et enfant du beau temps, vos mains de défaite et de progrès me sont également nécessaires." The slight change of emphasis is actually one of chronology. In *Moulin premier*, this line refers to what he thinks the poet ought to be, while in *Partage formel* Char describes what he knows the poet has to be. It is to be noted that in *Partage formel* Char accepts much of what he only suggested in *Moulin premier*.

In *Partage formel*, as in his later aphorisms, Char uses the term "le poète." In *Dehors la nuit est gouvernée*, "l'homme" tended, at first, to replace "le poète"; this distinction was maintained in *L'Avant-monde*, and it prevails in Char's poetry after 1937; the term "poète" is reserved for the aphoristic form through which he expresses his poetics. In addition, it marks a general trend in Char's work: at the completion of each stage of his poetic development, Char publishes a collection of aphorisms as a summary of his evolution to that point. This was observed in *Moulin premier*, it is evident in *Partage formel*, and it will occur again in 1947, 1948, 1951, 1953, 1956, and 1966.

Partage formel examines the nature of poetry and redefines the role of the poet. Although the poet must maintain close contact with the physical reality of the world, he must also be constantly aware of the value of his imagination, which enables him to act against the apparent contradictions of the real in order to expose the original harmony of relationships:

> En poésie c'est seulement à partir de la communication et de la libre-disposition de la totalité des choses...
> (XXX)

> Le poète est l'homme de la stabilité unilatérale (XXVIII).

He is the "magicien de l'insécurité" who offers the immediate reconciliation of "le possible *diurne* et le possible *prohibé*." In his effort to communicate "l'inextinguible réel," all means, "toutes les clefs," are permitted. As in *Le Visage nuptial*, desire and sexual union provide the conditions necessary for poetic activity:

> Le poème est l'amour réalisé du désir demeuré désir (XXX).

> Le poète est la genèse d'un être qui projette et d'un être qui retient. A l'amant il emprunte le vide, à la bien-aimée, la lumière. Ce couple formel, cette double sentinelle lui donnent pathétiquement sa voix (XLV).

Although *Partage formel* seems to continue the poetics outlined in *Moulin premier*, it adds two important dimensions to the poet's role: moral responsibility and prophecy. Char had always entrusted the poet with the task of communicating the structure of reality and man's relationship to it. Now he finds that the poet's involvement with others has caused him to enter into a struggle against evil, "aux prises avec le Mal." To refute the "manque de justice" which he observes in the community of men, he must lead man to the recognition that there is a common human nature, for experiences are universal; the poet is to show man how to act creatively for the general welfare of mankind:

> Certaines époques de la condition de l'homme subissent l'assaut glacé d'un mal qui prend appui sur les points les plus déshonorés de la nature humaine. Au centre de cet ouragan, le poète complétera par le refus de soi le sens de son message, puis se joindra au parti de ceux qui, ayant ôté à la souffrance son masque de légitimité, assurent le retour éternel de l'entêté portefaix, passeur de justice (LI).

The need for the poet to accept moral responsibility arises from his knowledge of the superficiality of contradictions and of the universality of experience. This awareness of unity makes him accountable to others. The poet is no longer "le reflet d'un fait accompli"; he is the "grand Commenceur" of hope in the present: "A chaque effondrement des preuves le poète répond par une salve d'avenir" (LIX). The attainment of a better future is guaranteed by the poem which is more eternal than the poet and which insures the perpetuation of his optimistic prophecy:

> Il ne sort pas toujours indemne de sa page, mais comme le pauvre il sait tirer parti de l'éternité d'une olive. (XLVIII).

> ...le temps est venu de confier à son destin le vaisseau du poème.... Et nous allons, lutteurs à terre mais jamais mourants (XXIV).

> Ta réponse, connaissance, ce n'est plus la mort, université suspensive. [24]

In *Moulin premier*, the poet's responsibility was primarily intellectual, restricted to the communication of his discovery of the nature of reality. In *Partage formel*, the scope of artistic responsibility is extended beyond talent and intellect to include the total involvement of the personality.

The usual date ascribed to *Partage formel* is 1942 because this is the date printed below the title in *Poèmes et prose choisis* (1957).

---

[24] "Mission et révocation," *Partage formel* in *Seuls demeurent* (Paris, 1945).

However, in the 1945 edition of *Seuls demeurent*, Char dates the final paragraph, "Mission et révocation," 1938-1944. The fact that *Partage formel* continues the main themes of *Moulin premier* and *Le Visage nuptial* makes it reasonable to assume that it was begun in 1938; it does not appear to have been started earlier than that date because it contains no references to the crisis of 1936-1937. The emphasis placed on the conquest of death, the uniqueness of the poet's vision, and the moral responsibility of the artist indicates that at least part of the aphorisms were composed during the war; this validates the 1942 date, which is most likely the date of completion. The 1944 date probably indicates revisions. While the precise date is unknown to the historian, it is certain that *Partage formel* presents the evolution of Char's poetics between 1936 and 1942, from Surrealism to humanitarianism, from *Moulin premier* to *Feuillets d'Hypnos*.

Historically and thematically, *Feuillets d'Hypnos* directly succeeds *Partage formel*. On the one hand, the *Feuillets* were written between 1943 and 1944, immediately after *Partage formel* was completed. On the other, the aphorisms of *Partage formel* review Char's poetic development and project its future course as a reflection of the universality of experiences. The *Feuillets* present the poet engaged in action. This work actualizes Char's personal fusion of poetry and action and marks his adoption of a poetics based on moral responsibility.

The form of *Feuillets d'Hypnos* is curiously different from the three forms usually employed by Char, and yet it belongs to all three categories. Some of the *Feuillets* are aphorisms on the role of the poet and the nature of poetry:

>Le poète, conservateur des infinis visages du vivant (83).

>Le poème est ascension furieuse; la poésie, le jeu des berges arides (56).

Others (for example: 219 and 222) recall the prose poems of *L'Avant-monde* in their expression of Char's attitudes during the war. One (221) is a free verse poem and it even has a title, "La Carte du soir." The *Feuillets* present specific episodes and general observations in a singular mixture of prose and poetry. Although the "feuillets" are numbered, each appears to have been written

1936-1947: A POETICS OF MORAL RESPONSIBILITY   95

independently of the others in a moment of personal conviction. However, the impression of random composition and organization is superficial, for the *Feuillets* have an inherent pattern, arranged to contrast the pessimism of war with the optimism of human dignity. The unity of the work is found in a structure which consistently enhances man through a humanistic theme and a sincere tone:

> Ces notes marquent la résistance d'un humanisme conscient de ses devoirs, discret sur ses vertus, désirant réserver *l'inaccessible* champ libre à la fantaisie de ses soleils, et décidé à payer le *prix* pour cela.[25]

Moreover, the thematic unity of this work is not interrupted by the additions of two notes, 230 and 231, in the 1948 edition.[26]

The *Feuillets d'Hypnos* is a wartime notebook kept by Char "comme une ménagère consigne ses comptes sur un calepin."[27] The numerous direct references to people, places, and events situate the *Feuillets* in a definite period of time and even give them documentary value. Historical accuracy is emphasized by the precision of these references, as the two corrections in the 1962 edition demonstrate.[28] However, the poet transcends history through the universal representation and application of each detail observed. The tendency to generalize from a particular locale or person is first noticed in *L'Avant-monde*, specifically in "Louis Curel de la Sorgue," and it comes to the forefront in the *Feuillets*, where the reality of the Céreste region determines the poet's contacts with the world. This characteristic of extracting the universal from a given detail appears more and more frequently in Char's work from the *Feuillets d'Hypnos* on and emerges as a dominant trait of *Le Poème pulvérisé* and *Les Matinaux*.

More than a notebook, the *Feuillets* form a poetic diary of a human and highly personal adventure. This work blends the

---

[25] Introduction to *Feuillets d'Hypnos* in *Fureur et mystère* (Paris, 1948).
[26] Because these two additions cause a minor change in the numbering of the last few notes, the references in this study are from the 1948 edition.
[27] Pierre Berger, "Conversation avec René Char," *La Gazette des lettres* (15 juin 1952), p. 11.
[28] In 65, Marcel Grillet is changed to André Grillet; in 87, the footnote to LS is clarified: "Léon Zyngermain, alias Léon Saingermain."

historical person of Char and the a-historical artist that is also Char. In moments of despair, anguish, hate, it is the former whose voice is heard, whereas the lessons learned from such experiences are expressed by the latter. These two aspects of the voice of the *Feuillets* are also seen in the title of the work. During the war, Char was known as Capitaine Alexandre and Hypnos. The distinction between the two appellations seems to be one of organizational reference. Capitaine Alexandre is Char, the Maquis leader of a group of men in the area around Céreste; Hypnos is his code name within the general structure of the Resistance movement. Although both pseudonyms are used in this work, it is Hypnos which appears in the title. In Greek terminology, Hypnos is the god of sleep. In the *Feuillets*, sleep suggests the presence of peace and freedom which are absent from life in the Maquis: "Si la vie pouvait n'être que le sommeil désappointé..." (198). Sleep is also a refuge from the fatality of everyday living: "... aujourd'hui je m'endors pour vivre quelques heures" (224). As the god of sleep, Hypnos was active at night, and so was the Maquis; "la lune d'Hypnos" recalls the secret parachute landings that Char directed.[29] Hence, Hypnos refers to Char's personal participation with others in the war and to his poetic message that fraternal action "au service de la vérité" is a moral good.

The events of war brought Char into direct contact with the struggle for survival. For him, war is only a personification of the everyday menace of fatality and nothingness which threatens human existence. The poet recognizes that while each being has a distinct personality, each is also a member of the community of men who share a common destiny of suffering and death. Furthermore, he becomes aware that this community refuses to acquiesce to the overwhelming forces which try to overcome it; in order to live, it accepts the risk of destruction. In this common will to act, the poet discovers the inherent dignity of man: "L'acquiescence éclaire le visage. Le refus lui donne la beauté" (81). The role of action is the main theme of *Feuillets d'Hypnos*. Through action, revolt against existing conditions becomes possible.

Because "L'homme est capable de faire ce qu'il est incapable d'imaginer" (227), the poet must realistically appraise the nature

---

[29] A full description is found in "La Lune d'Hypnos," *Recherche de la base et du sommet* (Paris, 1955).

1936-1947: A POETICS OF MORAL RESPONSIBILITY

of man and help him recognize his own worth. To do this, the poet must commit himself to involvement in the common struggle; in fact, action becomes a moral necessity for poetry:

> Le poète ne peut pas longtemps demeurer dans la stratosphère du Verbe. Il doit se lever dans de nouvelles larmes et pousser plus avant dans son ordre (19).

> Le poète, susceptible d'exagération, évolue correctement dans le supplice (154).

The poet has a dual nature; he is "solitaire" in his particular task of communication, yet "multiple" in that his own existence is threatened with annihilation:

> Vie..., désigne-moi ma part si tant qu'elle existe, ma part justifiée dans le destin commun au centre duquel ma singularité fait tache mais retient l'amalgame (223).

He is morally obligated to point out to others that they share not only the same destiny and the same menace, but also the same will to act.

In the *Feuillets*, man remains vulnerable, but his desire to expose himself and risk his mortality for a better future justifies him. In the presence of life and love, there is death. This is the real risk, and man's conscious choice to accept it authenticates his existence. Love is no longer limited to a sexual union between man and woman; it is an exchange between men who know intimately the risk that life demands but who are willing to challenge the void of reality.

Feuillets d'Hypnos affirms the poet's faith in man and in the human fraternity. War may bring out the more perverse aspects of human nature, but the manifestation of inner courage restores to man his basic dignity and contains his moral redemption:

> Chacune des lettres qui compose ton nom, ô Beauté, au tableau d'honneur des supplices, épouse la plane simplicité du soleil, s'inscrit dans la phrase géante qui barre le ciel, et s'associe à l'homme acharné à tromper son destin avec son contraire indomptable: L'espérance.[30]

---

[30] "La Rose de chêne," *Feuillets d'Hypnos*.

The most significant result of Char's war experience is his discovery that human nobility lies in the courage and will to risk action against the "pessimisme atonique" of existence. In united action, he has found "la citadelle de l'amitié" (17). The lesson of the war is the knowledge that a better future has become possible because "Nous nous sommes épousés une fois pour toutes devant l'essentiel" (17). Now, the poet must show men how revolt can reconcile them with reality.

Les Loyaux adversaires was first published in *Fureur et mystère* (1948), and it appears in that collective edition as a transition section between the prewar and postwar years. This group of 13 poems is undated, but most of the texts seem to have been composed before the war or during "la drôle de guerre," especially "Chaume des Vosges." The prewar poems emphasize the important function of love as it was considered in *Dehors la nuit est gouvernée* and *Le Visage nuptial* and intimate that love is equally menaced by "l'absurde chagrin de vivre sans comprendre."[31] In the prewar and war poems, there is an expression of nostalgia, a feeling that before the war there was harmony between nature and man: "Dans le sentier aux herbes engourdies, la chimère d'un âge perdu..."[32] The memory of this previous unity, "J'étais l'égal des choses,"[33] is sufficient evidence that a return to this order is possible, just as nature is reborn each spring after the threat of winter's destruction; it is nature which binds together the whole of existence and from it men can regain communion with the world:

> Redonnez-leur ce qui n'est plus présent en eux,
> Ils reverront le grain de la moisson s'enfermer dans l'épi
> et s'agiter sur l'herbe.[34]

To be "Loyal avec la vie" demands that the poet "vise à transformer *vieux ennemis* en *loyaux adversaires*";[35] man has not always been estranged from the outside world, and poetry will end his present isolation.

---

[31] "Chaume des Vosges," *Les Loyaux adversaires* in *Fureur et mystère* (Paris, 1948).
[32] "Le Thor."
[33] "Pénombre."
[34] "Redonnez-leur...."
[35] *Feuillets d'Hypnos* (6) in *Fureur et mystère* (Paris, 1948).

1944-1947: Glorification of the Menace

The theme of *Les Loyaux adversaires* contrasts nostalgia for the harmony of the past with the anguish of the present. This theme is continued in *Le Poème pulvérisé* (1947), which is the most significant of all Char's works with regard to his poetic evolution. In *Le Poème pulvérisé*, Char acts on his World War II experiences by celebrating his observation that man and the world are threatened with destruction. There was and must be chaos before there is creation; this was true of the past creation of nature, and it is true of the present of man. Reconciliation between nature and man or restoration of harmony is possible through poetic "pulverization." A "poème pulvérisé" demonstrates the simultaneity of appearance and disappearance; a new order is created at the very moment that the old order is destroyed; this is a theory of fragmentation. The explosion displaces and disperses the original entity and a new structure emerges:

> Pourquoi *poème pulvérisé?* Parce qu'au terme de son voyage vers le Pays, après l'obscurité pré-natale et la dureté terrestre, la finitude du poème est lumière, apport de l'être à la vie. [36]

The poem is the creation of a new reality, a totality:

> *Né de l'appel du devenir et de l'angoisse de la rétention, le poème, s'élevant de son puits de boue et d'étoiles, témoignera presque silencieusement, qu'il n'était vraiment ailleurs, dans ce rebelle et solitaire monde des contradictions.* [37]

The absolute exists in the present instant, in the *hic et nunc* of existence; it is the poet's responsibility to communicate the necessity of menace for the fulfillment of human nobility in the present through poems evoking "la totalité illuminée, ... la résurrection insensée." [38]

---

[36] "La Bibliothèque est en feu," *La Bibliothèque est en feu et autres poèmes* in *La Parole en archipel* (Paris, 1961).
[37] "Argument," *Le Poème pulvérisé* in *Fureur et mystère* (Paris, 1948).
[38] "Argument," *Arrière-histoire du Poème pulvérisé* (Paris, 1953).

A singular aspect of *Le Poème pulvérisé* is found in the explanatory notes of *Arrière-histoire du Poème pulvérisé* (1953), written "quelques mois plus tard ... en regard de chaque poème..."[39] This "oeuvre d'entr'aide"[40] contains precise information about each poem and reveals that while each poem has an independent existence, each contributes to the overall structure of *Le Poème pulvérisé*: "marquer l'autonomie et la dépendance à la fois de chacun des poèmes à l'égard des autres."[41]

Le Poème pulvérisé is dated 1945-1947 in the 1948 edition, but these dates most likely refer to the preparation of the texts for the collective volume. Certainly, the inclusion of "Biens égaux" from *Dehors la nuit est gouvernée* (1938) is evidence that not all of *Le Poème pulvérisé* was written at that time. Also, some of the texts are prewar ("Argument" and "Marthe") while others ("Hymne à voix basse," "Pulvérin," "Le Bulletin des Baux," and "Le Requin et la mouette") are dated 1946. With the possible exception of "L'Extravagant" and "Donnerbach mühle," few of the texts seem to have been written during the war, for "Affres détonation silence" and "Le Muguet" refer to the war as a past event. Hence, the composition of *Le Poème pulvérisé* appears to have been undertaken at two different times, 1937-1940 and 1945-1947, and the texts are so arranged that they offer a general view of Char's third period of poetic development.

The earliest poem in this volume is "Biens égaux," which "fut commencé très tôt, en 1937, puis abandonné."[42] First written during a time of personal anguish (Char's crisis of 1936-1937), the 1938 published form of "Biens égaux" emphasizes the role of chance in life and nature; chance seems to direct the fusion of opposites. In the 1947 text, all references to chance are omitted, and what is retained is the possibility of fusion through poetic action. Chance, which connotes an accidental, fortuitous event, is rejected in favor of a conscious act of exposure to danger, the risk accepted in *Feuillets d'Hypnos*; risk implies choice and the possibility of control. The rejection of chance in 1947 represents

---

[39] Jean Hugues, "Introduction" to *Arrière-histoire du Poème pulvérisé* de René Char (Paris, 1953).
[40] *Ibid.*
[41] "Argument," *Arrière-histoire du Poème pulvérisé*.
[42] "Biens égaux."

Char's optimistic faith in human action as a form of creativity. According to Char, the basic difference between the two texts is one of orientation; in 1937, "Je cherchais ... dans les êtres non un écho de mon anxiété ou de ma ferveur mais ces contrastes et ces vertiges sans lesquels le regard souverain n'existerait pas." [43] The experience of fraternal action during the war changed Char's 1937 attitude to one which does echo the sentiments of others; "Avec le plaisir de m'y désaltérer" [44] suggests the new moral responsibility of the poet expressed in *Partage formel* and *Feuillets d'Hypnos*.

Both the 1938 and 1947 texts contain the idea that man needs to transcend his solitary existence; as a garden is nurtured by the natural elements and the clumsy attempts of man, the individual needs to be animated by someone or something other than his own efforts. However, the poet is more confident of the role of poetry and of the value of exchange in 1947 than in 1938, as the revision of this line indicates:

> Où germerai-je, *moi qui jouis du privilège de sentir tout ensemble accablement et confiance, défection et courage, et surtout, la reconnaissance olographe de deux avenirs? Je n'ai retenu personne, sinon l'angle fusant d'une Rencontre.*

The italics mark those phrases which remain intact between 1938 and 1947; the 1947 text deletes the question and doubts raised in 1938 and emphasizes that a poem must be an "angle fusant," that a "Rencontre" of contradictions and opposites does exist, for he has experienced it in the past; the change in the last paragraph from "disant" in 1938 to "prédisant" in 1947 stresses the prophetic vision of the poet's glimpse of unity, and implies that the future of the past has been realized by the present: j'affirme que tu vis."

Comparison of the 1938 and 1947 texts of "Biens égaux" reveals that the poem was not revised in the sense that it was rewritten; rather, it was considerably condensed. This is important, for it indicates that the basic thought expressed in 1938 is maintained

---

[43] *Biens égaux.*
[44] *Ibid.*

in 1947, that is, the change is definitely one of attitude, not of concept; the poet was aesthetically responsible in 1938 for the communication of cosmic harmony, but in 1947, after the war, this responsibility had become a moral obligation on the part of the poet.

In *Le Poème pulvérisé*, "Biens égaux" is placed between "Les Trois soeurs" and "Donnerbach mühle," two poems which were composed concurrently during "la drôle de guerre" and which express the tranquility of nature before the impending destruction of war:

> Glas d'un monde trop aimé, j'entends les monstres qui piétinent sur une terre sans sourire. Ma soeur vermeille est en sueur. Ma soeur furieuse appelle aux armes. [45]

In "Biens égaux," there is an explicit sense of harmony in nature and of a prior relationship between man and nature: "J'étais épris de ce morceau tendre de campagne, de son accoudoir de solitude au bord duquel les orages viennent se dénouer avec docilité..." The arrangement of *Le Poème pulvérisé* sets in relief this sensitive reaction to the outside world which the war violently erased.

The idea of a previous communion between man and nature persists in *Le Poème pulvérisé*, but its presentation differs from that of *Les Loyaux adversaires*. *Le Poème pulvérisé* stresses the fact that destruction must oppose unity at every turn, for destruction insures the formation of a new unity. The experience of war resulted in a unity of men and in the new knowledge that revolt, a force of destruction, alone can counteract destruction:

> Juxtapose à la fatalité la résistance à la fatalité.
> Tu connaîtras d'étranges hauteurs. [46]

> Faites que toute fin supposée soit une neuve innocence... [47]

Hope for a reintegrated world lies in the poet's affirmation of faith in man's will to revolt, to confront his destiny:

---

[45] "Donnerbach mühle," *Le Poème pulvérisé* in *Fureur et mystère* (Paris, 1948).
[46] "Le Bulletin des Baux."
[47] "Le Requin et la mouette."

1936-1947: A POETICS OF MORAL RESPONSIBILITY   103

> Orageuse liberté dans les linges de la foudre, sur la souveraineté du vide, aux petites mains de l'homme. [48]

The aggressive character of joint action during the war is to be maintained after the war, not to preserve harmony, but "pour assurer la continuité" [49] of life: "Rien ne m'obsède que la vie." [50] To direct the revolt which is not a rebellion of anger but of fraternal love, the poet offers to the community of men a poetic guide for creative action in "A la santé du serpent."

"A la santé du serpent" is a group of 27 aphorisms which propose a militant poetics; only the constant threat of disaster makes man risk his vulnerability in an effort to control his destiny. Creative action is consummated action, the highest virtue of life and of poetry:

> Ce qui vient au monde pour ne rien troubler ne mérite ni égards ni patience (VII).
>
> Combien durera ce manque de l'homme mourant au centre de la création parce que la création l'a congédié? (VIII).

The serpent represents the poet and his role to scorn the impossible and so make it possible; his efforts can reverse the limits of man's possibilities.

The fusion of contradictions and the importance of the couple or of sexual union are an integral part of *Le Poème pulvérisé*. In fact, the union formed in the act of love represents the individual's experience of poetic "pulverisation." In the "Rencontre" of man and woman, two opposites accept the risk of participating through an exchange of being in a joint explosion which terminates in another separation. But, the moment of union, of "angle fusant," has been a moment of fulfillment and totality of being. The consummation of love reflects the universal pattern of creation, the dialectic of being-destruction-being.

---

[48] "Le Météore du 13 août."
[49] "Le Muguet," *Arrière-histoire du Poème pulvérisé* (Paris, 1953).
[50] "Le Météore du 13 août," *Le Poème pulvérisé* in *Fureur et mystère* (Paris, 1948).

In *Le Poème pulvérisé*, the poet's course of revolt involves the whole of nature, man and things. Harmony in, of, and with the world and the community of men at large, a universal "Rencontre," can only be established through a poetics which transforms the threat of destruction into a constructive force. Hence, poetic pulverisation is not merely a stylistic technique, but above all an essential theme: "Poésie, la vie future à l'intérieur de l'homme requalifié." [51]

The theory and necessity of poetic pulverisation as a means to a meaningful life are maintained in *La Fontaine narrative*, as the title suggests. The "fontaine" is a source from which surges a continuous stream of water; as the water spurts upward, it is dispersed into fragments; the fountain externalizes the simultaneity of appearance and disappearance, union and explosion, creation and destruction. On the other hand, "narrative" implies the exposition or presentation of a story or chain of facts or an event, in this case of a jet of water. In *La Fontaine narrative*, Char recounts the history of menace in the world. The continuity of destruction is seen in the annals of ever-changing nature (sea, volcanoes, wind, storms) and it has been immortalized in art by men like Rimbaud and Georges de la Tour. Yet, nature and art also contain the remedy of revolt against an apparent fate of violence; like the river which never rests, man must constantly refuse acquiescence. The threat of annihilation is to be countered by a similar act of destruction; "une ferveur belliqueuse" is the only proper human attitude, for it demands action, continual revolt, "fontaine," against the permanency of despair, "narrative."

Char's assessment of his war experiences and the necessity of their application in the post-war years is contained in *Recherche de la base et du sommet* (1955), a collection of prose texts written between 1941 and 1948.

Char's evaluation is based on his intimate association with the Maquis, which externalized for him the two extremes of reality, namely that survival is a daily unrelenting struggle and that combined efforts of resistance result in a triumph over the threat of destruction. However, he feels that the victory gained through the anguish and suffering of individuals during the war will be

---

[51] "A la santé du serpent," (XXVI).

negated unless the lessons taught by that event are maintained in practice. Although the historical occurrence of World War II has ended, the combat of everyday life continues. Since man dwells on this earth, all human acts must be, can only be, performed in the *hic et nunc* circumstances of this world, the "base" of human reality. Individual participation in joint action during the war led to the establishment of an absolute, specifically liberty. This absolute is within immediate human reach; it is accessible through the same qualities which led to victory in the war: fraternal love and revolt:

> Nous avons appris entre-temps à nous méfier de nos nerfs, à nous entendre avec nos douleurs, à nous supporter, à nous épauler, enfin à nous estimer un peu les uns les autres. [52]

> Gardez-nous la révolte, l'éclair, l'accord illusoire, un rire pour le trophée glissé des mains, même l'entier et long fardeau qui succède, dont la difficulté nous mène à une révolte nouvelle. Gardez-nous la primevère et le destin. [53]

Char reaffirms the moral responsibility of the artist to show man the need to continue to act upon his innate impulse for truth and beauty, for "Tout est à recommencer." [54] The "base" and the "sommet" of poetry are truth and beauty; the two are linked by the poet's creative revolt:

> Je m'inquiète de ce qui s'accomplit sur cette terre, dans la paresse de ses nuits, sous son soleil que nous avons délaissé. Je m'associe à son bouillonnement. [55]

The poet must instill in man the confidence that by remaining "debout" and accepting the challenge to assert himself and prove his inner dignity over and over, he will reach the "sommet" of life, truth and beauty in this world. Only creative action connects

---

[52] "La Liberté passe en trombe," *Recherche de la base et du sommet suivi de Pauvreté et privilège* (Paris, 1955).
[53] "Prière rouge."
[54] "Dominique Corticchiato."
[55] "Base et sommet."

the "base" and the "sommet" of existence, and only poetry makes known the possibility of this interaction.

Char concludes that the spirit of fraternal love and the attitude of revolt provide the means, the "base", for the continuation of the highest moral good, the "sommet," consummated action.

Fureur et mystère (1948) brings together in a single volume most of the texts which represent Char's years of quest for the establishment of human dignity. Although this collective edition does not include either *Placard pour un chemin des écoliers* or *Dehors la nuit est gouvernée*, the problem of union and its subsequent resolution in these two works is directly continued in *Seuls demeurent. Le Visage nuptial* and *Partage formel* contain the means of defense against the common menace: love and language. These two aspects of life are further universalized in *Feuillets d'Hypnos* and *Les Loyaux adversaires*, which stress the idea of a common struggle through common measures against oppression. The change from defense to offense is of major importance, for the poet has found that human solidarity is dependent upon the continual presence of menace: man needs to be threatened, for only then is he willing to act and accept the risk of challenging his world. *Le Poème pulvérisé* glorifies the fact that human existence is one of impending annihilation, because the threat of destruction gives man the means of offensive action: revolt. The "fureur" of human acts, this "fureur" for living regardless of the risk involved, justifies man's existence and accords him his dignity of being, his "mystère."

The 1948 and 1962 publications of *Fureur et mystère* and the 1949 edition of *Dehors la nuit est gouvernée précédé par Placard pour un chemin des écoliers* are marked by textual consistency; few revisions were made in the texts composed between 1936 and 1947. On the other hand, the 1945 edition of *Le Marteau sans maître* contains numerous changes undertaken during this same period. The explanation may be found in the historical person of Char. His personal involvement with others is accompanied by a solidification of style and thought; he is no longer merely the poetic on-looker of *Le Marteau sans maître* and *Moulin premier*; he has become a participant, a member of the community of men, and he has committed his poetics to the service of his fellow men, that is to all men, not only to the other poets. The significant change from "le poète" to "l'homme" and the thematic shifts from chance to risk and from defense to offense reflect his experience and his growing conviction that poetry must not only be fused with life, but that it must also be lived by the poet before it can have value for others. The strengthening of this attitude is seen in the revisions of "A une ferveur belliqueuse" in the 1962 edition of *Fureur et mystère* (*La Fontaine narrative*);[56] the changes augment the militancy of the attitude deemed necessary for action, that is, the attitude of revolt is even more strongly affirmed as late as 1962. It is Char's experience, his ever-increasing personal fusion of the act of poetry and the act of living, that contributes to the textual stability of these editions; he is no longer concerned with knowing how inspiration may serve his poetry; rather, it is life and his contact and identification with others that his poetry evokes; he has shifted from texts based first on poetic theory and secondly on life to texts based first on life and secondly a poetics adapted to those experiences. It is not the fusion of poetry and life, but of life and poetry that is sought, for poetry must be lived before it can be expressed.

Between 1923 and 1936, Char's poetry had been based on three main themes: discovery of the nature of the real world, fusion of poetry and life, and the notion of creative activity. These three concerns continued to dominate his work between 1936 and 1947, but the scope of their application was expanded through the poet's evolution to a poetics of moral responsibility. Char's option for a poetics in the world of the real, the *hic et nunc* of human existence, is by 1947 the only frame of reference of his poetry. His adoption of the Surrealist desire for a poetic explosion at the forge of inspiration and creativity has matured into a structural and thematic necessity of poetic pulverization, of destruction as a part of creation. The fusion of life and poetry, that is a lived poetics, is not only accessible sexually on an individual level, but fraternally, including the whole of the community of men engaged in a joint effort. Only consummated united action which recognizes the process of pulverization can create a healthy

---

[56] See Appendix III.

moral order in the *hic et nunc* of human reality and offer the hope of a better future through a better present.

The poet's responsibility comes from his singular vision of fusion of "base et sommet," "fureur et mystère," life and poetry. He has discovered the nature of human dignity and the value of fraternal revolt; he has demonstrated that men are no longer isolated from each other because their experiences are universal. Now that man has been fused into a fraternity of men, it remains for the poet to end human alienation from the world, to fuse men and nature.

CHAPTER IV

1947-1952: A POETICS OF INTERDEPENDENCY

René Char's fourth period of poetic development dates from 1947 to 1952. This period includes no major thematic or stylistic innovations; rather, it is marked by a return to a theme already noted in *Les Loyaux adversaires* and *Le Poème pulvérisé* and to certain stylistic techniques of *Les Cloches sur le coeur* and *Le Marteau sans maître*. The application of earlier techniques to a previous theme leads, however, toward a solution of the problem of man's relationship with the world in which he lives and to the expansion of Char's concept of poetry.

Char's resolve to discover and communicate the organic unity of the universe through creative activity attained its first major goal in his collective edition of *Fureur et mystère* (1948). In this work, he successfully reveals that the universality of experience gives each individual immediate access to the means to end human isolation and to participate in an exchange of self-knowledge; the union of two individuals in the sexual act permits each to know personally the value of joint action. If human exchange can be established on one level, it can be projected to include united action by the community of men at large. With the rediscovery of human solidarity, Char returns to the second aspect of the problem he confronted in 1937: the reconciliation of man with nature.

Nature refers to man's terrestrial environment, to the *hic et nunc* world which daily surrounds each individual and the whole human community. Although Char seems to restrict nature to a rustic context, he does not differentiate between urban and rural problems; for him, the struggle for existence is the same in the country and in the city. The term "nature" represents all things as they are.

Char's choice of a predominantly rural vocabulary between 1947 and 1952 stems from three factors. In the first place, he is a provincial by birth, and, more importantly, he is one by choice, for he has continued to spend part of each year in his native region of Vaucluse. Secondly, he has intimate, first-hand knowledge of country-life; it is instinctive and realistic on his part to use the framework he knows best. Thirdly, rural life has retained a simplicity and order which cities have obscured, that is, the country permits the most accurate acquaintance possible with the original essence of the physical world of matter. Hence, Char uses the rural as a base for the observation of specific details which he finds reflect the general qualities of man's environment.

It has already been noted that a tendency to generalize from the particular, to establish the whole from a part, characterizes Char's work. This is especially true of his writings between 1947 and 1952, for during these years he fully assumes the poet's moral responsibility advocated in *Fureur et mystère* to become the individual and solitary representative of all men. In a sense, he takes up again a Surrealist technique used in *Le Marteau sans maître*; he turns inward in search of his innate self and innermost feelings towards the exterior world. What he discovers to be valid and authentic in his personal experience and self-examination is accepted by him as having meaning for the human community of which he forms a unique part:

> Le poète passe par tous les degrés solitaires d'une gloire collective ...il obtient le résultat que l'on connaît. [1]

The very discovery of human exchange and the poet's moral responsibility in *Fureur et mystère* provides him with the foundation necessary for the continuation of his prime objective: the communication of the totality of reality.

---

[1] "Bandeau de 'Fureur et mystère'," *Bandeaux, Pauvreté et privilège* in *Recherche de la base et du sommet suivi de Pauvreté et privilège* (Paris, 1955).

The return to this interest does not signify a return to Surrealism, as his letter to Breton in 1947 indicates:

> Je ne peux pas aimer deux fois le même objet. Je suis pour l'hétérogénéité la plus étendue. [2]

The term "hétérogénéité" refers to Char's demand in *Partage formel* that the poet utilize every means available to communicate his discoveries, even if it is a means associated with a specific orthodoxy. Moreover, it is to be recalled that while Char rejected Surrealism as a literary movement, he retained and modified certain aspects of it:

> Je puis dire ...mon affection durable pour ce grand moment de ma vie qui ne connut jamais d'adieu, seulement les mutations... [3]

This statement really gives the key to the overall unity of Char's poetry and explains his consistent returns to previous techniques and themes. His fourth period of development reflects most concisely this inherent thematic and stylistic continuity, as well as his general plan for attaining his ultimate poetic goal.

This fourth period, which is relatively brief, includes only two major works, *Les Matinaux* (1950) and *A une sérénité crispée* (1951), and it shows no important textual revisions. There is a concentration on the presentation of a single theme, one previously stressed but set aside while the poet wrestled with the problem of human exchange.

Study of the style, theme, and chronology of Char's composition between 1947 and 1952 shows this period to be relatively free from complexities. However, because these texts reveal the pattern of Char's poetics and poetry in general, this period must be seen as the most important one for the literary critic; yet it is the period to which critics have devoted the least attention.

Although most of the texts of this period are dated by the poet, they can best be grouped thematically rather than chronologically: 1) the return to the theme of nature and ascertainment of the

---

[2] *La Lettre hors commerce, Pauvreté et privilège.*
[3] *Ibid.*

poet's role in the contemporary world in *Fête des arbres et du chasseur* (1948), *Le Soleil des eaux* (1949), *Claire* (1949), and *Les Matinaux* (1950); 2) the poet's moral responsibility as man's representative to generalize his particular and personal rediscovery of man's original harmony with nature in *A une sérénité crispée* (1951) and *La Paroi et la prairie* (1952). One work, *Pauvreté et privilège* (1955) was written concurrently during these years; in fact, it was composed between 1948 and 1954. This edition of prose texts is a valuable summation of Char's personal attitude during this period, as well as a presentation of his definition of poetry. For this reason *Pauvreté et privilège* and its companion work, *Art bref* (1950), will be treated separately at the end of this chapter.

Nature and the Contemporary World

In the course of self-examination, Char finds that his feelings toward nature are contradictory. On the one hand, he is threatened by the forces of the external world; on the other, he longs to be in communion with it, and, more importantly, this yearning is nostalgic, indicating a desire to return to a state of existence known in the past. This feeling of nostalgia attests to man's original experience of harmony with nature, which Char seeks to make accessible in the present.

Throughout Char's poetry, experience has a significant role. The poet's personal experience was essential to the discovery of the value of creative activity in *Le Marteau sans maître*; the revelation of its universality provided the basis for the establishment of human solidarity in *Fureur et mystère*; and, finally, the recognition of poetic individual experience as the measure of this universality forms the basis for *Les Matinaux* and *A une sérénité crispée*. However, Char's concept of experience is not limited to accepted definitions of the term. He admits that experience is an authentic means to acquire practical knowledge and to demonstrate ideas; through experience, one assesses the results of conscious participation in a specific event or series of events. But, his skepticism toward experience causes him to qualify its application. For experience to be useful, it must be undeveloped; it must contain the possibilities of growth and evolution; it is not merely a sum total of the past, but the primordial source for present and future action:

> Il m'est arrivé un jour d'écrire: "La connaissance nourrit et l'expérience flétrit." Il faut se méfier de l'importance de l'expérience, car elle rend les êtres et les choses sans juvénilité, imperfectibles. [4]

Furthermore, examination of Char's concept of experience clarifies his interest in youth and frequent usage of terms associated with it. Youth suggests the period of growth which precedes maturation in all living organisms. Its original qualities of activity, vitality, alacrity, willingness to change are still unimpaired. Youth represents that state of existence closest to the original source of being.

Concern with the original experience and emphasis on youth are first combined in *Le Soleil des eaux* (1949). Written in dialogue form, [5] this work is characterized by a simple vocabulary, an everyday conversational style, and a reliance on historical, geographical, and sociological facts. These characteristics provide Char with an authentic situation and setting for the presentation of his theme: harmony with nature is necessary in order to continue and perpetuate the existence of both man and his world.

The action of *Le Soleil des eaux* centers on a village of hard-working simple fishermen. Char's admiration for these people is based on his personal observation that they are close to man's original experience of harmony with nature because their very existence is a daily struggle against nature:

> La menace quasi constante d'anéantissement qui pèse sur eux est leur plus sûre sauvegarde. L'Apprentissage du poète qui a lieu en pareille compagnie est un apprentissage privilégié. [6]

---

[4] Pierre Berger, "Conversation avec René Char," *La Gazette des lettres* (15 juin, 1952), pp. 13-14.

[5] *Le Soleil des eaux* was first presented to the public as a dramatic reading in a radio broadcast on April 29, 1948; the first printed edition did not appear until 1949.

[6] "Pourquoi du 'Soleil des eaux'," *Le Soleil des eaux* (Paris, 1951).

The fishermen represent the human fraternity, threatened by the physical world, laboring successfully in common necessity against it.

The equilibrium maintained by this struggle is disrupted by a man-made institution, a chemical factory whose deposits of poisonous wastes into the river threaten to destroy not only the fish supplied by nature but also the fishermen whose livelihood is dependent on fishing. The only way to reestablish justice is through communal action against the common menace. The demolition of the factory by the fishermen restores the balance necessary to existence:

> La rivière pour nous ...c'est un peu comme le ciel pour les dévots. Mais un ciel qui accorderait le pain et l'apaisement de chaque jour au lieu de promettre la vie future.... On ne peut guère s'attacher à plusieurs choses à la fois, mais il faut être soi tout entier pour une ou deux de ces choses essentielles. Hors de cela, on est broyé sans espoir et notre conscience se détourne de nous. [7]

Youth receives special attention in *Le Soleil des eaux* when the older fishermen decide to exclude the younger ones from participation in the murder of the spy, Drac:

> Il ne faut pas mêler la jeunesse à cela. Nous sommes des hommes à l'abri du remords et de la confidence.... Il faut laisser tout son possible devant [la chose] à la jeunesse. [8]

Le Soleil des eaux forms the transition between Char's third and fourth periods of poetic development. It continues *Fureur et mystère* in its stress on the immediacy of life, the constructive use of the threat of destruction, and the value of joint action against this threat. It also reaffirms Char's belief in the dignity of man to further the cause of justice and justify human existence:

> ...dans le pire couloir de l'enfer, il y a quand même quelque chose ou quelqu'un à sauver. [9]

---

[7] *Le Soleil des eaux*, XIX (Paris, 1951).
[8] *Ibid.*, XXVIII.
[9] *Ibid.*, XXXV.

> ...je sais que mon semblable, au milieu d'innombrables contradictions, possède de déchirantes ressources. [10]

It is important to note, however, that Char's concept of justice in *Fureur et mystère* is expanded in *Le Soleil des eaux* to include things as well as people. Man is threatened by nature, but at the same time nature is threatened by man.

Interdependency between man and things is the principal theme of *Fête des arbres et du chasseur* (1949), dated September 1948. In this work, the exaltation of nature is contrasted with the destructive force of man, represented by a hunter:

> Les deux guitares exaltent dans la personne du chasseur mélancolique (il tue les oiseaux "pour que l'arbre lui reste" cependant que sa cartouche met du même coup le feu à la forêt) L'exécutant d'une contradiction conforme à l'exigence de la création. [11]

Fête des arbres et du chasseur contains the simple moral that man's hostility to nature is the cause of his estrangement from it and that it is necessary to maintain a harmonious equilibrium between man and nature.

The expression of nature as a beneficent presence for man is continued in *Claire*. *Claire* (1949) was written between 1947 and 1948, after *Le Soleil des eaux* and *Fête des arbres et du chasseur* and prior to the composition of *Les Matinaux*. Unlike most of Char's works, *Claire* has a single publication, a fact which has led most critics to dismiss it as a repetition of *Le Visage nuptial*. Certainly, *Claire* is a direct continuation of the theme of the role of woman and man's need for sexual union expressed in *Le Visage nuptial*, but what distinguishes *Claire* is its emphasis on the similarities between human existence and the outside world of nature.

In the subtitle, Char describes *Claire* as a "théâtre de verdure"; that is, it is a dramatic representation of the natural forces of life, all life. Man can learn to better his existence through the examples found in nature.

---

[10] The text of Char's presentation of *Le Soleil des eaux* on the occasion of its 1948 radio broadcast as established in the 1951 edition of *Le Soleil des eaux*.

[11] *Fête des arbres et du chasseur* in *Les Matinaux* (Paris, 1950).

The main character is Claire, a multiple personnage, who represents the role of woman in all times, places, and societies. She is juxtaposed with "la rivière," the stream which flows through the countryside. In fact, Char makes Claire and the stream synonymous incarnations of the poetic image of harmonious fusion.

The stream is a manifestation of nature characterized by its continual movement of water. To the land around it, it is a source of nourishment in times of need and a means of drainage in times of plenty. It serves other parts of the whole of nature by maintaining the balance necessary for growth. In the same way, woman offers man the opportunity for exchange as a prerequisite to the realization of his possibilities.

Closer examination of "la rivière" discloses that service to the land is not its only virtue. The individual stream joins with others to form a river, "le fleuve," which is larger than each of its component parts and more capable of greater responsibilities. The river is a mightier force than the stream, but its strength is dependent upon its union with the stream. As the stream symbolizes woman, the river represents man. The union of man with woman is his most immediate source of strength for fulfillment, for the attainment of his growth.

Moreover, the stream is vital to the sea, which is merely the harmonious reservoir into which the rivers flow. The sea is another expression for the community of men, the exchange of individuals, whose capacity for strength has been nurtured by woman. The immensity of the sea is dependent upon its original source, the stream; similarly, if the human fraternity is to be as united as the sea, each individual must continue to renew his vitality at its source, woman:

> Bientôt, tu ne seras plus seule; une Claire bien vivante, jeune, passionnée, active, s'avancera et liera conversation avec toi. Telle est la rivière que je raconte. Elle est faite de beaucoup de Claires. Elles aiment, rêvent, attendent, souffrent, questionnent, espèrent, travaillent. Elles sont belles ou pâles, les deux souvent, solidaires du destin de chacun; avides de vivre.[12]

---

[12] "Bandeau de 'Claire'," *Bandeaux, Pauvreté et privilège*.

A distinctive trait common to *Claire, Fête des arbres et du chasseur* and *Le Soleil des eaux* is their appearance in dialogue form. Char had previously experimented with styles of narration (*Artine*, 1930) and conversation (*Dépendance de l'adieu*, 1936). *Fête des arbres et du chasseur* represents his first known effort to combine these two technical skills with the art of pantomime, already used in the ballet *La Conjuration* (1947). The exploration of graphic means of expression results in a more intense, concrete, and visual poetic medium. The physical characterization of experience and sense perception enables Char to objectify existence, to bring clearly before the consciousness of others examples of the completeness of things as they are. After *Claire*, he makes only one more attempt (*L'Abominable homme des neiges*, 1956) to simulate a portrayal of life through strictly dramatic means. With the publication of *Claire*, Char becomes confident that he can render the poetic image on the printed page more visibly, more physically, more audibly than it can be realized by the performing arts. His accomplishments in *Le Soleil des eaux, Fête des arbres et du chasseur*, and *Claire*, especially *Claire* where the poetic image is the main character, prepare for his contact with the primordial world in *Les Matinaux* and *La Paroi et la prairie*; things of the world can be adapted to human use through reproduction in the poem. The poem is the only form of expression which can utilize all means of communication (gesture, dialogue, action) and grasp simultaneously the real and the ideal; the poem is where all aspects of reality (physical, sensory, and emotional) meet and fuse.

The texts of *Les Matinaux* were composed between 1947 and 1949, concurrently with *Le Soleil des eaux, Fête des arbres et du chasseur*, and *Claire*. In *Les Matinaux* (1950), Char attains the second phase of his drive toward the fusion of life and poetry: the discovery of man's original harmony with nature. The discovery is possible at this point because of the four theses established prior to and during 1947: the universality of experience, the moral responsibility of the artist, harmony within nature, and the beneficence of nature. These ideas are incorporated into the main theme of *Les Matinaux*: the reconciliation of man and things as they are.

Les *Matinaux* consists of ten sections, connected by the underlying idea of rebirth and beginning expressed by the title. The "matinaux" are the discoverers:

> Premiers levés ...d'une inquisition insensée —qualifiée de connaissance— et d'une sensibilité exténuée, illustration de notre temps, qui occuperez tout le terrain au profit de la seule vérité poétique constamment aux prises ...avec l'imposture, et indéfiniment révolutionnaire... [13]

The rising of the sun each morning heralds the beginning of a new day and optimistically suggests that all is yet to be accomplished and enjoyed. Like the sun, the poet must awaken men to possibilities of a better existence; he must rouse them to the challenge of the new to revolt against illusion and fatality (night). Man is to continue through action what only the poet can begin:

> Combien souffre ce monde, pour devenir celui de l'homme, d'être façonné entre les quatre murs d'un livre! Qu'il soit ensuite remis aux mains de spéculateurs et d'extravagants qui le pressent d'avancer plus vite que son propre mouvement, comment ne pas voir là plus que de la malchance? Combattre vaille que vaille cette fatalité à l'aide de la route, de ce qui en tient lieu, d'insatiables randonnées, c'est la tâche des Matinaux. La mort n'est qu'un sommeil entier et pur avec le signe plus qui le pilote et l'aide à fendre le flot du devenir. Qu'as-tu à t'alarmer de ton état alluvial? Celle de prendre la branche pour le tronc et la racine pour le vide. C'est un petit commencement. [14]

Each of the ten sections of *Les Matinaux* presents the poet's activity and role in this world, the contemporary world.

The first section is *Fête des arbres et du chasseur*, originally published in 1948. This poem serves a fourfold function as the introductory section: 1) because it contains the themes of *Le Soleil des eaux* and *Claire*, it connects these two works to *Les Matinaux*; 2) it announces that the major concern of *Les Matinaux* is to be the relationship between man and nature; 3) its use of a traditional style and dramatic form emphasizes the idea that

---

[13] "Bandeau des 'Matinaux'."
[14] *Rougeur des Matinaux, VIII*, in *Les Matinaux* (Paris, 1950).

the importance of the subject is one of long-standing concern in the history of man; and, 4) it holds the significance of the poet's discovery of man's original experience of harmony with nature: "Merci simplement à un homme / S'il tient en échec le glas." [15]

In the 20 poems which form *La Sieste blanche*, the second and largest section of *Les Matinaux*, Char recalls his earlier contacts with and insights into the relationship of man and nature. He reaffirms his belief that the elemental and the human are not contradictory but complementary and that they can be revealed through the poet's activity. *La Sieste blanche* reviews and summarizes Char's previously expressed observations, and each text contains not only the result of his examination, but also suggests the direction taken in the remaining sections of *Les Matinaux*.

Within nature, there is homogeneity; the apparent contradictions of space, time, age, size, and function are actually varying aspects of an inner overall harmony: "arc-en-ciel / S'unifie dans la marguerite." [16] The peace and serenity of nature and its objects, its "transparents," are interrupted by man who fails to understand that the conflicting forces mask a beneficent presence. The poet has the unique vision to grasp simultaneously the overwhelming contradictions which threaten the underlying unity: "Je touche à chacun de vous"; [17] he must lead man to act, to revolt against what seems to be and accept what is. More importantly, it is Char's personal artistic role, as the poem "Jouvence des Névons" confirms. Névons is Char's home in Isle-sur-Sorgue, and the "enfant" described is the young Char. This child was alone but happy because he communicated with the world of nature, represented by his companionship with the "ruisseau." It is the search for his own past experience of harmony with nature that Char the poet undertakes:

>   Dans le parc des Névons
>   Un rebelle s'est joint
>   Au ruisseau, à l'enfant
>   A leur mirage enfin.

---

[15] *Fête des arbres et du chasseur* in *Les Matinaux* (Paris, 1950).
[16] "Complainte du lézard amoureux," *La Sieste blanche*, in *Les Matinaux* (Paris, 1950).
[17] "Le Carreau."

This personal note is unusual in most of Char's poetry, but it dominates *Les Matinaux* in general and *La Sieste blanche* in particular, for Char the man and Char the poet become frequently inseparable in the "je" which characterizes many of the texts. It is a return to self-examination as a means by which to discover the truth.

Truth is the poetic goal, but like coral, it is often invisible, lying submerged beneath the surface, found by accident, "dans l'inconnu surpris."[18] However, truth also has other qualities of coral; it is solid, continuous, durable, and complete. Because of his singular vision, the poet can reveal the presence of truth and chart it for others, for "La Vérité vous rendra libres."

Because the establishment of truth must precede freedom, freedom demands revolt against illusion and pessimism:

> Le jeu d'échecs, précurseur d'affliction est méprisé dans mon pays.[19]

> Bonjour à peine, est inconnu dans mon pays.[20]

Freedom is synonymous with action:

> Ah! crions au vent qui nous porte
> Que c'est nous qui le soulevons.[21]

It is action against the menace of destruction, against the permanence of death which only the poet negates: "...la mort que je contredis."[22] As in *Le Poème pulvérisé*, Char continues to celebrate the fact that the threat of annihilation is a constant force in the world: "L'ogre qui sert chacun de nous / Et n'est jamais remercié."[23] The recognition of finiteness and mortality is necessary for revolt and constructive action, for creative activity.

Truth, freedom, revolt, and menace are prerequisite elements of action. Each of these requirements has a parallel in nature which supplies the overall framework, for nature binds the whole.

---

[18] "Corail."
[19] "Qu'il vive!"
[20] *Ibid.*
[21] "Cet Amour nous a tous retiré."
[22] "Montagne déchirée."
[23] "Le Permissionnaire."

The poet finds in nature "les tendres preuves," [24] concrete examples of abstract goals and details which suggests an all-inclusive unity. Because "Le Tout ensemble" of nature is realized through poetry, harmony between man and nature can only be made known through a poem:

> Il y avait un précipice dans notre maison. C'est pourquoi nous sommes partis et nous sommes établis ici. [25]

The chasm between man and nature was caused by man's refusal in the past to act:

> Déjà là, printanier crépuscule!
> Nous n'étions qu'éveillés, nous n'avons pas agi. [26]

In *La Sieste blanche*, Char not only returns to previously explored ideas but also to earlier techniques. Although the fraternal "nous" of *Dehors la nuit est gouvernée* (1938) and *Fureur et mystère* (1948) is maintained, it is the personal "je" of Char the man and Char the poet which prevails. The use in *Les Matinaux* of the "je" of *Le Marteau sans maître* (1934) is concordant with Char's decision to resume the process of self-examination as a means of fusing man and his reality. Hence, the reappearance of the "je" in *La Sieste blanche* is pertinent to the dominant theme of *Les Matinaux*. Based on the universal application of the particular experience of the poet, Char now seeks to define the role of the poet in the world, and more specifically in the contemporary world, a role which can be determined only when the poet can offer evidence that man and nature (things as they are) share a harmonious and simultaneous existence.

In *Fête des arbres et du chasseur*, Char uses a conventional framework to imply that the problem of man's relationship with nature has persisted throughout history. In *La Sieste blanche*, he continues to enclose these thoughts in the set forms of expression that have been assigned to poetry in the past. Some of the texts follow the form of sixteenth-century quatrains ("Complainte du lézard amoureux" and "Cet Amour nous a tous retiré"); one, "Le

---

[24] "Qu'il vive!"
[25] "Sur les hauteurs."
[26] "Le Tout ensemble."

Permissionnaire," resembles a fable, while another, "Qu'il vive!" is reminiscent of a litany. "Corail" suggests the alexandrine line. Meter, rhyme, stanza division, alliteration, and assonance are found to some degree in each text. The style of *La Sieste blanche* establishes the historical importance of the problem. "Mise en garde" is the only prose poem in this group, and, significantly, it is the first text, for its contemporary form and its use of the plural "nous" indicate that *La Sieste blanche* is designed to review a problem that still challenges poetry.

The simplicity of the texts of *La Sieste blanche* recalls Char's first work, *Les Cloches sur le coeur* (1928). However, except for the fact that all of his work since 1923 has had one ultimate goal of fusion and totality, *La Sieste blanche* is neither a return to nor a continuation of the style of *Les Cloches sur le coeur*; on the contrary, it uses traditional forms and characteristics as a device to emphasize his singular discovery of harmony between man and nature.

As *La Sieste blanche* summarizes previously expressed themes and relates them to the main theme of *Les Matinaux*, *Un Adieu, un salut* reviews Char's aesthetic development. This third section consists of two poems, "Antonin Artaud" and "Georges Braque intro muros." [27]

Written in 1948 on the occasion of Artaud's death, Char salutes Artaud's contribution to contemporary literature. Artaud was a "bel orage" which destroyed the old traditional concepts of art and prepared the way for the success of new ones. It is interesting to note that Char considers Artaud as the representative of his own past, for Artaud was expelled from the Surrealist group before Char joined it. The poem "Antonin Artaud" is not only a text of hommage to Artaud; it is also Char's assessment of the poetics which he practiced in the past, namely in the early 1930's; he affirms his earlier declarations for the new, but he feels that his subsequent development beyond the destruction of the old was the correct decision.

---

[27] These two poems were omitted in the 1964 edition of *Les Matinaux* in order to include them in the 1965 edition of *Recherche de la base et du sommet*. They are discussed here because Char originally published them in the 1950 edition of *Les Matinaux*.

In "Georges Braque intro muros," composed in 1947, Char shows the direction of his poetic growth from 1934 to 1947. Char finds in Braque's work the same problems and theories that he recognizes for himself; concern with reality, with making life acceptable as it is, with the universal application and significance of particular details. Hence, Char's poem in praise of Braque represents his poetic interests in the present. By 1948, Char has fused creative activity, represented by Artaud, with the concern for making known the dignity of the present, represented by Braque.

While *Un Adieu, un salut* is Char's retrospective summation of his poetic evolution as of 1948, *Le Consentement tacite* views his concept of the role of the poet between 1948 and 1949. This section is the first one in *Les Matinaux* to represent his poetics and poetry during his fourth period of development.

The eight prose poems of *Le Consentement tacite* are concerned with the poet in the world. Unless the poet has certain experiences, his work cannot succeed in reconciling man and his reality. The purpose of this group of poems is to describe things as they are; it is a poetic guide to the understanding of the forces which operate in the everyday world.

The main theme of "L'Amoureuse en secret" is the inseparability of objects, the interdependency of one entity upon another for definition and fulfillment of being; as the individual "lac de montagne" is known by its relation to the mountain, the "lit" is necessary to the very existence of "l'amoureuse." The recognition of the interdependency of things is essential to the process of maturation, for things and people grow and are shaped through exposure to the forces of life. Only the intimate knowledge of despair, for example, can lead to an appreciation of its absence, an appreciation of the beauties of life:

> Il semblait que ce que la terre avait produit de plus noble et de plus persévérant, l'avait, en compensation, adopté. [28]

Man needs to participate in a variety of experiences in order to be strengthened, to become "plus fort," [29] because attainment

---

[28] "L'Adolescent souffleté," *Le Consentement tacite* in *Les Matinaux* (Paris, 1950).
[29] *Ibid.*

of that which is worthwhile demands risk. Meaningful life results from a joyous struggle; life is a celebration of creative activity:

> La Fête, c'est le ciel d'un bleu belliqueux et à la même seconde le temps au précipité orageux. C'est un risque... C'est le grand emportement contre un ordre avantageux pour en faire jaillir un amour.... Et sortir vainqueur de la Fête, c'est ...de se jeter dans l'irréalisable de la Fête.[30]

The poet must expose himself fully to life and its experiences in order that his poetry reflect the totality of existence: "mon antique richesse, notre richesse à tous";[31] in poetry merge the past, present, and future, for it alone can fuse the contradictions that abound:

> ...tu étais Anoukis l'Etreigneuse, aussi fantastiquement que tu étais Jeanne, la soeur de mon meilleur ami, et aussi inexplicablement que tu étais l'Etrangère dans l'esprit de ce misérable carillonneur dont le père répétait autrefois que Van Gogh était fou.[32]

Diversity masks the underlying unity of life, which only the poet can comprehend, but this understanding is of no value unless it has meaning for others:

> ...ils se sont appliqués à suivre mon mouvement. Ils ne concevaient pas ma construction.[33]

Having reached the summit of life, poetry, the poet must return to the base of life, the physical world, and work there to communicate his discovery of unity and beauty. This is his agreement, his "consentement tacite"; he will commit himself to the service of poetry by accepting the risk of the struggle of everyday living:

> Nous allions nous séparer. Tu demeurerais sur le plateau des aromes et je pénétrerais dans le jardin du vide. Là, sous la sauvegarde des rochers, dans la plénitude du vent,

---

[30] "Grége."
[31] "Anoukis et plus tard Jeanne."
[32] *Ibid.*
[33] "Recours au ruisseau."

je demanderais ...de disposer de mon sommeil pour accroître ton bonheur. Et tous les fruits t'appartiendraient. [34]

With the establishment of harmony between the poet and his artistic mission in *Le Consentement tacite*, Char turns in *Joue et dors* to the major concern of *Les Matinaux*: the relationship between man and the outside world. *Joue et dors* is a small group of five poems in which Char expresses satisfaction with the agreement made in *Le Consentement tacite*. The poet is to expose himself, "joue," and function in this world; yet he is to be aware that he must also turn inward, "dors," to maintain contact with his ideal, poetry.

To the question, "Dans l'immense, comment devenir?," [35] he responds, "Joue et dors, que je mesure bien nos chances." [36] The poet is the active agent who successfully reverses the limits of the world and its apparent contradictions; he is the "cible" of the poem "Centon," separating the true from the false in order to direct men:

Je n'ai ni chaud ni froid: je gouverne. [37]

J'aime, je capture et je rend à quelqu'un. Je suis dard et j'abreuve de lumière le prisonnier de la fleur. Tels sont mes contradictions, mes services. [38]

As the title, "Centon," suggests, this text is composed in fragments; that is, the diverse limits which threaten the poet are presented in a superficially disorganized manner. The six paragraphs of the poem resemble individual aphorisms on the poetic role. However, the theme of one service through contradictory parts binds the six divisions into a closely-knit structure; the technical form of "Centon" is physical proof of the fusion that the poet seeks to attain.

Hence, the poet's service to man is that of fusion. Through his own encounters with things as they are and his ability to see

---

[34] "Les Lichens."
[35] "Joue et dors," *Joue et dors* in *Les Matinaux* (Paris, 1950).
[36] *Ibid.*
[37] "Centon."
[38] *Ibid.*

their interdependency and organic unity, he can lead man into a harmonious contact with the physical world.

In *La Sieste blanche*, Char criticizes man for having failed to act in order to maintain his original harmony with nature, and "Les Inventeurs" continues the attack. The "nous" of this poem refers to the historical community of men who permitted the peace and order of the world to be disrupted, as these lines demonstrate:

> Ils sont venus ...les rebelles à nos usages.
>
> Nous avons levé le front et les avons encouragés.
> Certes, nous aurions pu les convaincre et les conquérir,
> Car l'angoisse de l'ouragan est émouvante.

The men who destroyed were incapable of building anew:

> Hommes d'arbres et de cognée, capables de tenir tête à quelque terreur mais inaptes à conduire l'eau, à aligner des bâtisses, à les enduire de couleurs plaisantes. Ils ignoraient le jardin d'hiver et l'économie de la joie.

This is a condemnation of destructive action that is not followed by new construction; it is an affirmation of Char's 1947 pulverization theory of the need to destroy in order to create.

"Les Inventeurs" not only explains that man feels estranged from nature because he fails to act creatively toward it, but it also continues the theme of *Fête des arbres et du chasseur* and *Le Soleil des eaux* that man threatens nature's existence as much as nature threatens to annihilate man. Thirdly, "Les Inventeurs" contains an implicit plea for revolt, for change, for the risk of action in the present:

> Mais cela valait-il la peine que l'on en parlât et que l'on dérangeât l'avenir?

Instead of concentrating on the future, man must exert his efforts in the present. It is action *hic et nunc* that Char demands, for the refusal to act in the past resulted in a worse future, in the present alienation of man from nature.

Further emphasis on the necessity of a creative revolt is found in "Les Seigneurs de Maussane," which shows that refusal in the past to be ruled by others resulted in the establishment of human liberty:

> Nous avons fait saigner notre amour exigeant,
> Lutter notre bonheur avec chaque caillou.

If it was right to challenge an existing order in the past, it is just in the present. All is yet to be accomplished through creative activity "dans un naissant consentement." [39] The idea of "becomingness," of acts to be performed is the optimistic tone of *Les Matinaux*, hymns in praise of the discoverers, of those who are awakened to act constructively as opposed to those who acquiesce and conform.

Rougeur des Matinaux is perhaps the most significant section of *Les Matinaux*, for this section contains the explanation and purpose of *Les Matinaux*. It is a collection of 27 aphorisms which describe Char's concept of the poet's role in the contemporary world.

Composed in 1948, *Rougeur des Matinaux* is a handbook for poets. It contains advice and admonitions to the poet as to how and where he is to begin his work, what he can expect to encounter and experience in the course of his endeavors, and how to react to any limits he may find imposed upon him. The subtitle "Enclave délébile" suggests that poetry reverses all limits, that exposure and defeat are necessary to the success of the poet's mission:

> Accolade à celui qui, émergeant de sa fatigue et de sa sueur, s'avancera et me dira: "Je suis venu pour te tromper." [40]

The poet's task is a great responsibility, for he is the sole agent of man:

> L'évidence et ses à-peu-près sont collectifs. La vérité est personnelle. [41]

---

[39] "Pleinement."
[40] Epigraph, *Rougeur des Matinaux* in *Les Matinaux* (Paris, 1950).
[41] *Ibid.*

Throughout the whole body of his work, Char is consistent in his use of the aphoristic form to express his aesthetic views, beliefs, and observations. Usually, each collection of aphorisms is organized only by the overall subject of poetry; there is no detectable inner arrangement among the individual aphorisms. The rare exception to this pattern is *Rougeur des Matinaux*, which resembles more a single prose poem in the manner of "Centon" than a group of aphorisms. This collection has a definite thematic evolution; there is continuity from aphorism to aphorism; the theme begins, is developed, and advances toward a conclusion.

The first seven aphorisms are general descriptions of the poet's role; because he has a "mission d'éveiller" (II), he must maintain "l'état de l'esprit du soleil levant ... malgré le jour cruel et le souvenir de la nuit" (I). The poetic task demands the acceptance of the risk of exposure, but faith and confidence in his mission will sustain him in the challenge: "Au plus fort de l'orage, il y a toujours un oiseau pour nous assurer" (IV). The poet will find what he is seeking "dans la création et dans la nature communes" (V) if he goes "à l'essentiel" (VI), to the elemental and primordial source of being.

The eighth aphorism describes the purpose of Char's title, *Les Matinaux*, in particular and invites all poets in general to make poetry the beginning of an acceptable existence for men. The idea of beginning is maintained in aphorisms IX-XXV, which discuss the efforts required of the poet. He must never conform, but always revolt in the name of progress: he is to build, "édifier" (XVIII), despite the fact that he must "vivre plus près de la mort que les mortels" (XIX). He is free to revolt only through the acceptance of his own mortality:

> Nous grandissons en révolte ouverte presque aussi furieusement contre ce qui nous entraîne que contre ce qui nous retient (XX).

The poet must disdain death in order to remain free and solitary, and yet he must retain close contact with reality. Although his stay in the world is temporary, it is fruitful if it enables others to break the habits of conformity and live more knowledgeably and more meaningfully:

> Nous sommes des passants *appliqués* à passer, donc à jeter le trouble, à infliger notre chaleur, à dire notre exubérance. Voilà pourquoi nous intervenons! Voilà pourquoi nous sommes intempestifs et insolites! (XXV).

The last two aphorisms differ from the preceding ones in style and thought. Most of *Rougeur des Matinaux* is written in the first person plural "nous" and addresses all poets. The twenty-sixth one is more personal: "Je puis désespérer de moi et garder mon espoir en Vous." The "je" is Char who feels that his poetic endeavors will be justified through the efforts of "Vous," those who follow him in time and mission. It is also the expression of his belief that art is more enduring than individual man, that the history of each man is continued through the artists who represent him.

The conclusion of *Rougeur des Matinaux* is a concise summary of Char's poetics from 1923 to 1948, and it is a precise statement of what determines the authenticity of an act of poetry and an act of living. It is a definition of creative activity:

> Enfin si tu détruis, que ce soit avec des outils nuptiaux (XXVII).

The dialectic of being-destruction-being is what he sought and failed to find in Surrealism; it is the underlying theme of *Moulin premier* (1936) and *Le Poème pulvérisé* (1947); the failure to adhere to this dictum caused man's isolation from humanity and his alienation from nature. This is the purpose of *Les Matinaux*: begin anew. This is the ultimate goal of Char's poetry: fusion of the fragments of existence into one harmonious universe.

The comments of *Rougeur des Matinaux* are dramatized in *L'Homme qui marchait dans un rayon de soleil*, first published in March 1949. This one-act work is not designed to be performed publicly in a theater; on the contrary, it is to take place in the reader's mind and imagination. The aesthetic distance usually attained by the physical space of the theater is negated so that the reader must participate intellectually and emotionally in the simulation of the drama. The reader is the director and the actor of the play; he establishes the veracity of the work:

> Dans le volume d'une tête qu'on appelerait pour la circonstance *théatre*, peut se jouer le drame de l'*Homme qui marchait dans un rayon de soleil.* [42]

The subject of this drama is the position of the poet in the contemporary world:

> Sa silhouette est entourée d'un rayon lumineux. Le cercle magique de soleil s'accorde à son pas. Aucune goutte de pluie n'y pénètre.... Il ne pleut pas dans son univers et il le sait.

Although his efforts to share "le bonheur de sa condition" are frequently refused, "colère et révolte le soulèvent." He seeks contact and communication with those outside his circle through union with "la jeune fille," through the formation of the couple. However, the poet is envied and scorned, misunderstood and often condemned by the community at large because he represents "la réalité qui menace la fiction," because he is aware that "le monde ... est étranglé et saigné par les contradictions" despite existing rules and systems. He has to rebel against authority in the hope of provoking men to act for a better existence. Even when the figure of the poet disappears, his work, "le rayon," remains to give the community of men the light of poetry, the means to discover "le soleil," the common core of being, the unity of human reality.

Although the poet's role is one of "solitude toujours incomprise," it is a privileged one; this is emphasized in the final three sections of *Les Matinaux*. Each of these three divisions consists of a single short poem, and each contains a brief review of Char's confidence in poetry. *Ils sont privilégiés...* praises the poets whose unique gifts of vision and talent permit them to recognize the basic and elemental forces of the world and to use these experiences to grasp the unity behind the contradictions and reverse the limits of existence. In *Pourquoi se rendre?*, Char demands that poets never relinquish their special role; if they cease to revolt against authority, their mission will fail.

---

[42] *L'Homme qui marchait dans un rayon de soleil* in *Les Matinaux* (Paris, 1950). This text is omitted in the 1964 edition.

The form of *Toute vie...*, the last poem in *Les Matinaux*, is unusual in Char's work;[43] it recalls *Calligrammes* in which Apollinaire attempted to visualize themes through the actual structure of the poem. In fact, *Toute vie...* has the particular typographical appearance of Apollinaire's "Photographie," and like it, it represents a physical characterization of a person as he might be seen in a photograph or mirror. Each one who reads Char's text is to find himself reflected in the poem.

The theme of *Toute vie...* summarizes *Les Matinaux* and provides transition from *Fureur et mystère* to *A une sérénité crispée*. All that begins must put an end to something already in existence and end in its turn. There is no defense against this process of destruction, for even "ce livre" and its readers will be effaced in time. However, the pessimistic tone is countermanded by the future tense, "deviendrez"; the enigma in life is that it is a continual cycle; destruction is a part of life, but so is construction. Char's examination of the natural forces in the world reveals that there is a consistency of initial action; nothing is ended unless something begins. The poet, because of his privileged vision and capacity for sustained revolt, must be matinal, a beginner, a discoverer of what is.

RECONCILIATION OF MAN WITH NATURE

In *Les Matinaux*, Char finds that an interdependent relationship prevails in nature, among things as they are, and that this harmony is based on a cyclical process of renewal, rebirth, resurgence, of continual beginning. The poet's multiple contacts with the physical world of matter result in his awareness that the human and the elemental share common experiences and needs, that they are actually one. All life follows the same pattern. Understanding of the inner order in nature despite apparent contradictory forces and nostalgia for man's original harmony with it lead to the discovery of the simultaneous existence and ultimate unity of man and the

---

[43] Char's only other text which is characterized by a specific typographical form is "Dansons aux Baronnies," *Retour amont* (Paris, 1966). "Dansons aux Baronnies" is arranged to reflect the dance movement, the idea of exchange in a creative life, which is the subject of the text.

world. Hence, the presence of nature is beneficent to man; its very homogeneity assures him of his nobility. It is this guarantee that Char reveals in *A une sérénité crispée*.

Chronologically and thematically, *A une sérénité crispée* (1951) is the immediate successor to *Le Poème pulvérisé* (1947) and *Les Matinaux* (1950). Composed between 1948 and 1950, it was begun soon after the completion of *Le Poème pulvérisé*, and part of it was written concurrently with *Les Matinaux*. Further evidence of its connection to these two works is found in the title. "Sérénité" suggests the peace and order of nature found in *Les Matinaux*, while "crispée" is a direct reference to Char's theory of pulverization. However, *A une sérénité crispée* is more than a mere outgrowth of two previous works. It not only fuses *Le Poème pulvérisé* and *Les Matinaux* into a new poetic revelation of man's relationship with nature, but it also brings the major themes of those two works to completion.

A une sérénité crispée is a collection of 109 aphorisms and one poem on poetry and the poet's responsibility. The aphorisms are divided into two groups of which the first 98 are entitled *A une sérénité crispée* and the second 11 are entitled *Post-merci*, indicating that these 11 were added after the first part was completed. However, because the *Post-merci* section is no more than a thematic and stylistic continuation of *A une sérénité crispée*, it is not necessary to treat it separately. [44] In fact, in the 1965 edition, the title, *Post-merci*, is omitted. [45]

Specifically designed as "une santé du malheur," *A une sérénité crispée* represents a desire for the constant presence of the threat of annihilation so that man will risk his being and act; this is the same idea expressed by "A la santé du serpent" in *Le Poème pulvérisé*. However, *A une sérénité crispée* does not contain the militancy of "A la santé du serpent," but the tenderness of *Les*

---

[44] All quotations in this chapter are from the 1951 edition of *A une sérénité crispée*, and no distinction is made between the *Post-merci* section and the main body of *A une sérénité crispée*.

[45] In 1965, *A une sérénité crispée* appeared as the fourth section of *Recherche de la base et du sommet*. In this edition, 20 aphorisms were omitted, nine phrases deleted, and one phrase added (see Appendix III). While the 1965 changes result in greater condensation of style and thought, they do not affect the substance and meaning of the 1951 edition on which this discussion is based.

Matinaux. This change of tone from combat to perseverance is significant, and it is a change possible only through the experiences described in *Les Matinaux.* Revolt remains a key concept, but this revolt is not directed against outward catastrophes in the world but against the inward circumstances of man. It is moral and intellectual, rather than physical or emotional. It is no longer a question of the poet's task or mission, but of his duty, "devoir," his utility, his remedial function to fuse contradictions. In addition, the poet is to serve people and nature, all life, and make no distinctions between the two. The acceptance of things as they are and of the identification of the human and elemental as one, expressed in *Les Matinaux,* is at the basis of Char's attitude in *A une sérénité crispée.*

Serenity suggests the cessation of previous agitation and the freedom to act undisturbed. It is a state of calmness which implies the absence of struggle. Specifically, Char is referring to the end of World War II, for he is concerned with man's belief that the end of this war means inevitable peace. Char wishes to reply to the time (1948-1950) in which he and others are living: "Je parle pour les hommes de mon temps..." [46] In an examination of his era, he finds that the end of war does not mean the end of the threat of annihilation: "Il ne s'agit pas d'un péril relatif, mais absolu..." [47] Man needs a new means of defense to meet the challenges of his present situation:

> Le contenu des livres varie selon les époques. Aujourd'hui, ce n'est pas un combat que nous soutenons, c'est bien davantage: une sorte de patience armée nous introduit à cet état de refus incroyable. Mais demeurer ouvert, demeurer présent, retenir le frisson, limiter le méchant.... Les *Feuillets d'Hypnos* correspondaient à leur temps, *A une sérénité crispée* correspond au nôtre. [48]

Serenity is the present state of being, but it also implies complacency, an inclination to neglect action. Serenity in and of itself is conducive to illusion:

---

[46] Berger, "Conversation avec René Char," p. 10.
[47] *Ibid.*
[48] *Ibid.,* p. 11.

> Ce qui est passé sous silence n'existe pas moins. Dualisme vigoureux.

In opposition to the illusion and falsehoods that tranquility fosters, Char demands "une sérénité crispée." He finds no justification for a promised Golden Age or Paradise in the future:

> Etrange exigence que celle d'un présent qui nous condamne à vivre entre la promesse et le passé...

If man is to live effectively and meaningfully in the present, he must be free from historical determinism:

> ...l'Histoire adore la modération, c'est pourquoi l'Histoire est trouble, non troublant.

Char's distinction between "trouble" and "troublant" is significant, for it contains part of the explanation of his choice of the adjective "crispée." "Trouble" refers to an unclear and inexplicable state of agitation, disorder, tumult, whereas "troublant" suggests the act of disturbing a situation which is calm in the hope of stirring it to action. Where History fails to enable man to develop freely, poetry succeeds. Only poetry offers man complete freedom to act because only poetry is concerned exclusively with the present. The poet, not the historian, not the philosopher, is "troublant," rather than "trouble."

By troubling the calm surface, the poet provokes and maintains order:

> Dans le tissu du poème doit se retrouver un nombre égal de tunnels dérobés, de chambres d'harmonie, en même temps que d'éléments futurs, de havres au soleil, de pistes captieuses et d'existants s'entr'appelant. Le poète est le passeur de tout cela qui forme un ordre. Et un ordre insurgé.

Order is possible because the poet constantly fuses opposing forces into a healthy unity similar to the cyclical process of beginning and becoming observed in nature.

Because the poet's goal is the establishment of truth, he must realistically appraise man and accept him as he is: "jovialement cruel et terrorisé," strong, yet weak and vulnerable. What Char respects most in man is his possibility of action:

> J'aime l'homme incertain de ses fins comme l'est, en avril, l'arbre fruitier.
>
> Nous sommes le fruit contracté d'un grand prélude inachevé.

Because man has the potential to become productive through creative action, his duality as destroyer and victim is a positive quality which forces him to respond to others. The poet must channel this quality into a constructive exchange of self-knowledge and mutual respect: "En poésie, devenir, c'est réconcilier." Poetry is man's opportunity for self-affirmation and unity with the world.

The poet's duty is to keep man constantly aware of his need to act constructively despite his "diabolique ... condition." Existence cannot be comfortable if it is to be in harmony with the outside world: "Les vrais, les purs bâtisseurs haïssent la léthargie des forteresses."

Nevertheless, the fulfillment of artistic responsibility is also dependent upon the poet's own sustained revolt against acquiescence to the status quo and existing authorities: "Echapper aux orthodoxies." As in *Rougeur des Matinaux*, he must expose himself to anguish, suffering, and inevitable death. However, in *A une sérénité crispée*, his duty is greater and more strenuous and exhausting than previous assessments of it:

> ...sans l'angoisse, tu n'es qu'élémentaire, ni ne corriges pour rendre unique, tu pourriras vivant.
>
> Il faut intarissablement se passionner, en dépit d'équivoques découragements et si minimes que soient les réparations.

To reinforce his concept of the intense degree of participation required of the poet in the contemporary world, Char uses his own experiences as a particular example of the efforts and sacrifices demanded of all poets who accept the challenge of this commitment:

> ...ne m'a encore qu'invectivé ou porté au pinacle! C'est la preuve que je vis. Mais quel effort pour m'en convaincre...!
>
> J'ai cherché dans mon encre ce qui ne pouvait être quêté: la tache pure au delà de l'écriture souillée.

It is interesting to note the use of "je" in those passages which describe the poet's role. In *A une sérénité crispée,* the "je" is most frequently assigned to the expression of knowledge acquired in past experiences by Char as a poet. He generalizes his "je" in the manner of an elder craftsman who counsels and consoles his apprentices, affectionately informing them that he knows intimately the disappointments and frustrations they face. Through the "je," Char speaks retrospectively, authoritatively, yet modestly. He is confident of his role, proud of his past, and certain of his present. He is no longer seeking unity, for he has discovered successfully the means to attain his ultimate goal; it only remains for him to reach it. His problem is not that of revelation, but of communication:

> Toute association de mots encourage son démenti, court le soupçon d'imposture. La tâche de la poésie ...est de faire disparaître cette aliénation en la prouvant dérisoire.

Authenticity of the discovery is dependent upon the validity of the form of expression, of the poem. The theme is that beauty is found in the present world, not in an ideal future. This beauty or truth is possible because of the union of man with others, namely through the couple, of nature and its parts, of man with nature:

> Cet instant où la Beauté, après s'être longtemps fait attendre, surgit des choses communes, traverse notre champ radieux, lie tout ce qui peut être lié...

If the fusion of contradictions is the revelation, this principle must also be applied to the communication. If the poet is to agitate the complacency which a serenity of surface harmony can initiate, he must also agitate his poetic form to create new unities. This is a refinement of Char's 1947 theory of pulverization; it is destructive construction through the process of crispation.

The use of the past participle "crispée" indicates that the calm surface, "sérénité," is to be tensed, that is distorted for the purpose of contraction into a state of imminent action. Instead of revealing the actual proportions of the perspective, "crispation" diminishes it and reduces its scope. It shrinks the surface by drawing it together, by combining it. Crispation is synonymous with concentration and condensation, terms which precisely describe Char's style, his suppression of connectives, antecedents, and explanatory clauses, his open-ended phraseology which admits several possibilities of meaning at one time. This style has been evolving in Char's poetry since 1923, and, more obviously, since the early 1930's when he first mastered the aphoristic form. In *A une sérénité crispée*, his abridged techniques reach maturity, as the use of the adjective in the following example demonstrates: "Epreuves qui montrez aberrante la récompense."

Through stylistic and thematic crispation, poetry forces man to act: "Quand nous sommes provoqués, c'est certain, que dans notre réponse nous dérivons..." Crispation makes man aware of the necessity of creative activity to achieve and maintain the unity inherent in the world:

> Ah! si chacun, noble naturellement et délié autant qu'il le peut, soulevait la sienne montagne en mettant en péril son bien et ses entrailles, alors passerait à nouveau l'homme terrestre, l'homme qui va, le garant qui élargit, les meilleurs semant le prodige.

A une sérénité crispée is the poet's pledge of responsibility to the service of others; it is his urgent and vital commitment to action, "crispée," in order to realize and perpetuate the ideal of Beauty, Truth, Poetry, "Sérénité," in this world.

A une sérénité crispée ends with an untitled love poem, "A****," which is addressed to "tu," Char's nameless but ever-constant companion, poetry. "A****" not only closes *A une sérénité crispée*, but it also summarizes Char's poetic development as of 1950 and explains why poetry contains man's only hope of self-affirmation.

Regardless of the obstacles encountered in the act of living, poetry has proved faithful; it has sustained the poet's revolt and struggle against the encroachments of time, change, and despair. Because of "tu," there is no flux, only solidarity and continuity.

It is the good fortune of men to have the richness of poetry to justify their existence. Poetry is fraternal Truth and Beauty, immediately available and accessible. It contains the possibilities of human fulfillment through its continual process of beginningness. Above all, poetry concentrates on the present of man, which is reinforced by the predominance of the present tenses and the juxtaposition of past and future tenses.

The vocabulary of "A****" recalls Char's previous poetics, assesses his development, and foreshadows the direction of his poetic endeavors after 1950. The temporal phrases "depuis tant d'années" and "devant tant d'attente" express his confidence in his poetic role and eventual attainment of his vision. He considers his efforts in the past valid. References to "vertige," "éclipses," and "retours" reflect his exploration of Surrealism. "Douleur qui vient d'ailleurs" refers to his crisis of 1936-1937, and its solution is recalled in the phrase "la chair de notre unité." World War II appears in the lines "attendait notre mort," "nous combattre," and "notre nuée," while the whole message of *Fureur et mystère* is summarized in three lines:

> Chacun de nous peut recevoir
> La part de mystère de l'autre
> Sans en répandre le secret.

Le Poème pulvérisé and *Les Matinaux* are recalled in the succession of two verbs: "déchire et recommence." Even Char's collection of prose texts, *Recherche de la base et du sommet*, not published until 1955, is foreshadowed in the sentence "Tu as élevé le sommet."

The interesting description of poetry as "ma martelée" spans 20 years of Char's poetry. It recalls his Surrealist texts collected in *Le Marteau sans maître* and the necessity of creative activity. Secondly, it refers to the poet's risk of exposure to the experiences of anguish and threat of destruction and his acceptance of moral responsibility. This is also seen in Char's use of the personal "je" to represent the poet's particular experience in contrast with the collective "nous" of fraternal and universal experience. Thirdly, "martelée" describes the poet's duty to "crisp" man's existence, as set forth in *A une sérénité crispée*.

Char's poetic goal is to communicate the organic unity of the universe. His ultimate attainment of this goal is indicated by 1950 in these three lines:

> Une extrême chance compacte
> Et notre chaîne de montagnes,
> Notre comprimante splendeur.

The image of the chain of mountains is a forerunner of his 1961 work, *La Parole en archipel*. In addition, the very appearance of "A****" as a love poem announces *Lettera amorosa* in which the union of man and woman and of the poet and word are synthesized.

"A****" is more than an aesthetic review. It is a reaffirmation of Char's dedication to the service of poetry and his belief in the useful contribution of that service.

La Paroi et la prairie (1952) is the last group of poems composed during Char's fourth stage of development. In this work, Char completes his examination of nature and things, undertaken in *Les Matinaux*, by observing the animal kingdom in nature. Man is not directly described; rather, each animal selected for scrutiny represents a specific fact of reality, more particularly of human existence. The principal poetic theory which underlies *La Paroi et la prairie* is the idea that knowledge of individual details reveals the totality and continuity in nature and the universe. The title emphasizes this technique of extension. "Paroi" signifies the separation of one part from another; by studying the parts, the whole, "la prairie," can be seen and made known. The prairie is the total structure which draws the whole together. Furthermore, prairie is a synonym for nature, and the partition represents specific things as they are. Hence, nature binds together the whole of existence.

The organization of *La Paroi et la prairie* reveals Char's non-chronological order, for the four sections are arranged in inverse order. The first group, *Lascaux*, was composed last, in 1952, while *Transir*, the second section was written in 1951. The last two parts, *Quatre fascinants* and *La Minutieuse*, were written at the same time as *A une sérénité crispée*, that is, between 1948 and 1950. However, the thematic arrangement is progressive.

Lascaux consists of four poems, each inspired by the prehistoric paintings of the Montignac grotto which Char visited. The validity of these primitive sketches is evidence of the continuity in nature and the world, for what the caveman experienced in the past is still being experienced in the present.

The present fate of man was prophesied by these ancestors: "Lui, danseur d'abîme, esprit, toujours à renaître." [49] The earliest recorded experiences of man show that he has always challenged the unknown, accepted the risk of his fragility, been threatened with destruction, and yet desired beauty. However, primitive man identified with certain qualities of the beasts he drew: the courage of the horse, the passionate actions of the deer, the helplessness against inevitable death of the unknown animal. The future depicted by the frescos in the past is the present. Man must still risk his existence for it to have meaning.

The prophetic tone of *Lascaux* is continued in the six aphorisms of *Transir*, where the idea of coldness expressed by the title is associated with the present, while references to warmth and comfort are connected to the future. The poet is aware that man and the objects in nature have a common bond because they participate in a struggle for existence and fulfillment:

> La lutte contre la cruauté profane, hélas, voeu de fourmi ailée. Sera-t-elle notre novation?

Resistance through the act of poetry is the only means to justify existence, to warm and strengthen man for his task of living: "Au soleil d'hiver quelques fagots noués et ma flamme au mur."

The poet's confidence in man's ability to act despite his fragility is seen in *Quatre fascinants*, which describes four animals. Each animal personifies a human characteristic which the poet finds noble: the courage to accept the risk of the struggle ("Le Taureau"), mortality and fragility ("L'Alouette"), freedom and the will to act ("La Truite"). "Le Serpent" is more complex than the other three texts. Praised as the "prince des contresens," Char appreciates the serpent because he is always "marginal," never a part of a system of authority, and because he always refuses

---

[49] "Homme-oiseau mort et bison mourant," *Lascaux* in *La Paroi et la prairie* (Paris, 1952).

to accept exile, "fais semblant de fuir." He is "débonnaire," good even to the point of weakness. Char is attracted to the serpent in the same way that he admires man. Like the serpent, man is destructive and yet against the existing order of destruction; he is "contresens." The snake is necessary to threaten, "unit la lumière à la peur," and this is the role of the poet so that man will continue to struggle creatively despite his own inclination for evil.

Man not only has counterparts in nature; he is also a part of nature. His existence is inextricably dependent upon the forces of the outside world which he cannot escape. This is the present in which he lives. He must recognize his kinship with the world around him and accept the fact that he too is a part of that whole. The continuity of nature is his guarantee of existence.

Placed at the end of *La Paroi et la prairie*, *La Minutieuse* emphasizes the value to be gained through the examination of details. The poet and his muse, "La Minutieuse," stroll through a region recently destroyed by a flood. He finds that because this catastrophe has distorted the usual perspective of the area, he gains new evidence of beauty where the casual eye would perceive ugliness. Each part of this damaged region reflects a whole Beauty, but to communicate this beauty the poet must rely upon the observation of details familiar to others.

La Minutieuse appears as a "récit de rêve," and it is superficially similar to *Artine* (1930). Both texts describe the poet's relationship with his poetic muse, and both emphasize the usefulness of a distorted order of details so that a new perspective may emerge. However, *Artine* begins with the basic premise that the poet must be concerned with the real world. The roles of intuition, inspiration, and imagination examined in *Artine* are not a part of *La Minutieuse*. Moreover, there is no attempt to explore the subconscious. On the contrary, it is an effort to establish through self-examination the means of revelation, not the revelation itself. In *La Minutieuse*, the method of observation of details is chosen, and this is the method upon which the first three sections of *La Paroi et la prairie* are based.

In *La Paroi et la prairie*, the "crisped" state advocated in *A une sérénité crispée* is applied to the examination of the interdependency within nature described in *Les Matinaux*. The contemporary poet is to study certain details of the whole and reveal their inherent unity. *La Paroi et la prairie* is Char's first example of concentration for the purpose of expansion.

Pauvreté et privilège and *Art bref*

Les Matinaux (1950) and *A une sérénité crispée* (1951) demand that the contemporary poet commit himself to the struggle of everyday life in order that his poetry be authentic in the present. Poetry is every noble ideal, Truth and Beauty, desired but usually unattained by man because he fails to grasp the unity inherent within the world. As a man, the poet experiences the human fears of destruction and hopelessness, but the poet is a singular individual who also experiences the simultaneity of life and poetry. This special knowledge imposes on him the responsibility of communicating to others that the misery and want of the human condition can be overcome through the unique privilege of Poetry. This is the message of *Pauvreté et privilège* (1955).

Pauvreté et privilège extends *Recherche de la base et du sommet* (1941-1948) and consequently extends the scope of Char's poetics and poetry.[50] It is a collection of prose texts and essays which define Char's artistic attitude, methods, and ultimate vision. Most of the writings included in the first edition of *Pauvreté et privilège* were composed between 1948 and 1952: only two texts, *La Conversation souveraine* and "*Nous resterons attachés*," were written between 1952 and 1954, although two others, "*Nous ne serons jamais attentifs*," and "Béant comme un volcan," may have been composed after 1952.

Pauvreté et privilège is one of Char's most significant collections; certainly, it is his most informative and most confidential work, for this volume of texts contains his most succinct definition of Poetry. Moreover, *Pauvreté et privilège* provides the transition between his fourth and fifth stages of development.

Pauvreté et privilège presents Char's evaluation of his own poetic evolution to the present and foreshadows its future development. He appraises his poetic affinities with certain nineteenth and

---

[50] The 1965 edition is entitled *Recherche de la base et du sommet* and presents *Pauvreté et privilège* as part one.

1947-1952: A POETICS OF INTERDEPENDENCY 143

twentieth-century poets and modern artists. From this examination of his own artistic roots and the work of his contemporaries comes his affirmation of his belief that totality is attainable exclusively through Poetry.

In *La Conversation souveraine*,[51] Char pays hommage to the poets to whom he feels his work and all contemporary poetry are the most indebted. While he briefly mentions Lautréamont, Saint-John Perse, Pierre-Jean Jouve, "Artaud détruit," Eluard, and others, he concentrates on Apollinaire, Reverdy, Baudelaire, Hugo, Heraclitus, and Rimbaud.

Char is more akin to Arthur Rimbaud than to any other poet. Char's admiration for Rimbaud comes from Rimbaud's efforts to reconcile the fragments of reality into a harmonious, almost primordial, universe. This vision of a unified world is Char's major goal: "La vraie vie, le colosse irrécusable, ne se forme que dans les flancs de la poésie." [52] Char maintains Rimbaud's notion that nature has an important function in the realization of this unity:

> ...la nature chez Rimbaud a une part prépondérante. Nature non statique, ...mais associée au courant du poème où elle intervient avec fréquence comme matière, fond lumineux, force créatrice, support de démarches inspirées ou pessimistes, grâce. De nouveau, elle agit... [53]

Char accepts Rimbaud's concept of risk; poetry demands the risk of being, for it must be lived, intimately known, and experienced in order to be authentic. Char also recognizes that his demand for action in the present was advocated by Rimbaud:

> Rimbaud s'évadant situe indifféremment son âge d'or dans le futur. Il ne s'établit pas. Il ne fait surgir un autre temps... que pour l'abattre aussitôt et revenir dans le présent... [54]

---

[51] In 1965, this section was considerably expanded, but it remains an hommage to other poets.
[52] "Introduction," *Oeuvres d'Arthur Rimbaud* (Paris, 1957), p. XII. (This introduction is reprinted as part of *La Conversation souveraine* in 1965).
[53] *Ibid.*, p. XIII.
[54] *Ibid.*, p. XVI.

Moreover, Char finds a relationship between his style and that of Rimbaud; both he and Rimbaud concentrate on the expression of the exact moment of discovery, aptly described by Char as "éclairs," rapid flashes of harmony between man and the cosmos:

>...la *diction* précède d'un adieu la *contradiction*.
>Sa découverte, sa date incendiaire, c'est la rapidité. [55]

Much of Char's admiration for Rimbaud comes from the similarity of their respective poetics. In fact, Char even credits Rimbaud with the origin of the need for "crispation":

>...le présent, cette cible au centre toujours affamé de projectiles, ce port naturel de tous les départs. Mais de l'en deça à l'au-delà, la crispation est extraordinaire. Rimbaud nous en fournit la relation. Dans le mouvement d'une dialectique ultra-rapide, mais si parfaite qu'elle n'engendre pas un *affolement*, mais un tourbillon ajusté et précis qui emporte toute chose avec lui, insérant dans un devenir sa charge de temps pur, il nous entraîne, il nous soumet, consentants. [56]

However, the striking poetic affinities between Char and Rimbaud in no way detract from Char's genius and originality. While it is evident that much of Char's theory is derived from Rimbaud's poetry, it is equally true, in fact more importantly true, that Char does not identify with Rimbaud as "l'enfant terrible" nor as "le voyant." Rimbaud's attempt to surpass the human domain through the power of verbal expression led him to abandon poetry. On the contrary, the very base of Char's poetry is man and his reality. Char praises the power of language, but only as a means of communicating truth and beauty; his goal is not that of Rimbaud, that is the exaltation of language; rather, Char seeks to dignify man through a verbal vehicle of social intercourse.

La Corde sensible is restricted to Char's appraisal of those poets whom he considers to have contributed the most to literature and to his own poetry. The writers evaluated are those with whom he feels an aesthetic kinship, a "corde sensible" to the past. When

---

[55] "Introduction," *Œuvres d'Arthur Rimbaud* (Paris, 1957), p. XVI.
[56] *Ibid.*

1947-1952: A POETICS OF INTERDEPENDENCY

Char turns to a discussion of his present poetics and poetry in *Alliés substantiels,* he describes them in relation to contemporary artists.

Char, like most of the writers of this century, has always been interested in all forms of expression. Most of his original editions are supplemented by engravings, sketches, and water-colors by leading artists. Even his first volume of poems, *Les Cloches sur le coeur* (1928) contained drawings by Louis Serrière. Char's interest in painting, sculpture, engraving, ballet, pantomime, theater, and music is a part of his feeling that the plastic arts and verbal expression are concordant and interdependent.

The only non-twentieth century artist for whom Char has expressed artistic affinity is Georges de La Tour. [57] Char finds in La Tour's paintings the intuition that the multiplicity of fragments masks the totality and reality of physical existence. For him, Georges de La Tour is the artistic or visual counterpart of Heraclitus:

> Avant lui [Rimbaud], Héraclite et un peintre, Georges de La Tour, avaient construit et montré quelle Maison entre toutes devait habiter l'homme: à la fois demeure pour le souffle et la méditation. [58]

In 1950, Char published *Art bref,* a collection of prefaces [59] written primarily between 1946 and 1949 for art exhibition catalogues. The title is self-explanatory; a painting immortalizes one instant of reality. The earliest text in *Art bref* is "Jean Villeri I," which was published first in *Les Cloches sur le coeur* (1928), revised in 1938, and subsequently included in *Premières alluvions* (1946). "Jean Villeri I" is evidence of Char's early interest in painting because the particular moment expressed is complete and appears to the eye in much the same way as a poem which communicates the instant of fusion. The two texts [60] on Jean Villeri

---

[57] Georges de La Tour (1593-1652) has been "discovered" as a major artist only in the twentieth century.

[58] "Introduction," *Oeuvres d'Arthur Rimbaud* (Paris, 1957), p. XIV.

[59] The 1950 edition of *Art bref* also contained two poems, "Huis de la mort salutaire" placed in *Recherche de la base et du sommet* (1955) and "Madeleine qui veillait" moved to *Pauvreté et privilège* (1955). The relocation of these two texts is connected with Char's unity of presentation and connects *Art bref* to *Recherche de la base et du sommet suivi de Pauvreté et privilège.*

[60] A third text, dated 1958, is included in the 1965 edition of *Recherche de la base et du sommet.*

praise this painter's observation of the energetic forces in the world, while Pierre Charbonnier "nous offre l'image de sa route intérieure." In Balthus' paintings, Char respects the expression of silence and "un mystérieux ordre humain," and he admires the treatment of detail in Ciska Grillet's canvases.

Art bref contains Char's first group of texts on forms of expression other than poetry, but this work is limited to painting. In the 1965 edition of *Recherche de la base et du sommet*, Char includes all eight texts from his 1950 *Art bref*. In *Pauvreté et privilège*, he extends his interest to include other forms of art. His dialogue *Sous la verrière* stresses the interdependency of poetry and the plastic arts, for all authentic art is concerned with "la vie réelle et les choses qui la composent." Although the artist seems to change the usual order of objects, he is actually engaged in proving the unity behind them. Char defends the possibility of poetry to judge painting in *Lèvres incorrigibles*, a written painting, a "toile du poète." In this text, which is also one of the rare occurrences of humor in his work, Char scorns traditional subjects which treat the exploits of the past and neglect the possibilities of the present.

In *Alliés substantiels*, Char expands his critical appreciation of art and its affinity with poetry through texts on sculpture (Alberto Giacometti) and wood engraving (Nicolas de Staël), as well as painting (Louis Fernandez, Victor Brauner, Wilfredo Lam). The final text of this section in 1955 is an essay on music, entitled "Entre la prairie et le laurier," in which he advocates "une nouvelle aventure terrestre," a union of poetry and music.[61] Char finds evidence of poetry in all of the arts, and it is poetry which enables man to understand their singularity and their universality. Poetry is the supreme art, which ends all diversity, political, economic, social,[62] artistic.

Of all the modern artists considered important by Char, Georges Braque is the one he admires most and the one to whom he is the closest artistically. Char has written several individual texts on Braque and a collection of five poems in his honor (*Cinq poésies en hommage à Georges Braque*, 1958), and Braque illus-

---

[61] This text was omitted in 1965.
[62] *Y A-t-il des incompatibilités?*, in *Pauvreté et privilège*.

1947-1952: A POETICS OF INTERDEPENDENCY

trated more of Char's texts than any other artist. Their earliest joint effort occurred in 1947 when Braque designed the stage set for Char's ballet *La Conjuration*. In that same year, Char composed his earliest written praise of Braque, a text later included in *Art bref* (1950). Char exalts Braque's lucid observation of detail, his omission of superfluous elements, and his concentration on harmonious composition:

> Braque pense que nous avons besoin de trop de choses pour nous satisfaire d'*une* chose, par conséquent il faut assurer, à tout prix, la continuité de la création.... Dans notre monde concret de résurrection et d'angoisse de non résurrection, Braque assume le perpétuel. Il n'a pas l'appréhension des quêtes futures bien qu'ayant le souci des formes à naître.

Also in 1947, Char wrote "Georges Braque intro muros" (*Les Matinaux*, 1950), in which he identified his own poetics since 1936 with Braque's art of intimacy, conscientiousness, and careful construction of particular details to reveal the interdependency of objects. In *Pauvreté et privilège*, Char includes a poem on Braque, *En vue de Georges Braque*,[63] and significantly, he separates this text from those which describe other artists. Braque has a place apart because "sa façon d'appeler l'inexplicable donne la survie à ce cristal spirite: l'Art."

Both Braque and Char detach individual objects from the whole and examine each one as a particular example of the general unity within the world. Their work is exclusively concerned with the present of man, and, no matter what the object chosen, it is viewed in its relationship to man's existence. Because Char and Braque are aware of a mystery of being that cannot be effaced or ignored, it is often impossible to distinguish feeling from understanding in their expression. In addition, Char and Braque concentrate on one theme, the communication of an acceptable reality and human self-affirmation, and their work is a series of variations on this theme.

An interesting proof of the artistic similarity between Char and Braque is found in their use of the aphorism to express artistic theory:

---

[63] The 1965 edition is expanded to include seven texts on Braque under this subtitle.

> I am concerned with attuning myself to nature far more than with copying it. [64]
>
> Those who go ahead turn their backs on imitators. That is only what the imitator deserves. [65].
>
> One must be content with discovering, and be on guard against explaining. [66]

Any of the above notations could have been written by Char, who expresses almost identical thoughts in *Moulin premier, Partage formel, Rougeur des Matinaux,* and *A une sérénité crispée.*

It seems impossible to know whether Braque and Char influenced one another's work. The artistic affinities between them can at least be established. It is reasonable to assume, moreover, that their agreement on aesthetic principles and their mutual admiration contributed to the maturation of their artistic growth to some degree. Certainly, Char's work shows increased accents of confidence in vision after 1947.

It is interesting that while Char finds value in former Surrealists and in those whom the Surrealists admired he never praises a Surrealist. His *Lettre hors commerce* (1947) to Breton contains his most precise acknowledgement of his early adherence to that movement, and, at the same time, it contains his refusal to be associated with it any longer other than in a historical sense: "Ma part la plus active est devenue... l'absence." [67]

As if to prove his position, Char composed "Madeleine qui veillait" in 1948, first published in *Art bref* (1950) and later included in *Pauvreté et privilège.* This text describes his chance encounter with a young girl, Madeleine, and its similarity with Breton's *Nadja* is striking. In both works, the poet wanders through an urban setting with a free spirit incarnated in a woman. Moreover, for both writers, Truth, Beauty, and Poetry are syno-

---

[64] Georges Braque, quoted by Jean Cassou in *Georges Braque* (New York, 1964), p. 22.
[65] *Ibid.*
[66] *Ibid.*
[67] Although Surrealism as an active literary movement had ended by 1939, Breton hoped to revitalize this movement after World War II. His first step was to hold a Surrealist exhibition in 1947. He invited Char to participate in this event, but Char refused.

nymous and attainable in the *hic et nunc* of existence. However, Nadja represents the surreal,[68] while Madeleine represents the real. For Char, it is always the real, never the surreal, that is beautiful and true, that serves poetry and man:

> La réalité noble ne se dérobe pas à qui la rencontre pour l'estimer et non pour l'insulter ou la faire prisonnière. Là est l'unique condition que nous ne sommes pas toujours assez purs pour remplir.

It is reality that Char seeks to define and communicate; there is no need for the surreality of Breton. It is the acquisition of knowledge which enables one to establish a positive position to confront life, not the assumption of an attitude towards life.

Although Char's "Madeleine qui veillait" appears as a description of a surreal experience, this text contradicts Surrealism, for this poem is an account of the confrontation of "le Réel." This description of the real is probably the reason that "Madeleine qui veillait" was first published in *Art bref*, a work which treats different perspectives of reality as viewed by representative painters. It is possible to assume that Char relocated this particular text in *Pauvreté et privilège* because *Pauvreté et privilège* is a collection of texts on the artistic communication of "la vie réelle." Also, *Pauvreté et privilège* is the only work in which Char offers an examination of his predecessors and contemporaries and an assessment of his place in literary history. He cannot deny his early association with Surrealism, but by including *La Lettre hors commerce* and "Madeleine qui veillait" in the same work, he minimizes the importance of Surrealism to his later poetic development.

Pauvreté et privilège is an appraisal of Char's poetics. The examination of his literary predecessors in *La Corde sensible* presents the major themes of his work between 1923 and 1952: fragmentation and reconciliation, cosmic destruction through contradictory forces, harmony within nature and between man and nature, restoration of unity through the power of poetry and the risk of the poet, beauty in evil and distortion, explosive unity,

---

[68] While Breton abandons Nadja and finds fulfillment with a "real" woman, he, nevertheless, continues to favor Nadja's incarnation of the surreal.

beauty in contemporary reality, the need to struggle, formation of the couple and fraternal exchange. All of these themes have been explored to Char's satisfaction by 1952. His methods are similar to that of the plastic arts described in *Art bref* and *Alliés substantiels*: observation of the real, examination of details, generalization of the particular, safeguarding of the mystery of being, exposure of the physical continuity of existence, rearrangement of individual entities to reveal a hidden unity, suggestion of the whole through a selection of essential objects.

All of the artists discussed in *Pauvreté et privilège* share in Char's vision of unity and totality and serve to affirm his confidence in the supremacy of the creative activity of poetry. However, poetry and art are not valid synonyms for Char. It is true that he considers art as any expression, written or plastic, of Truth and Beauty, and in this sense his poems are a form of art. However, poetry, that is, the ideal of Poetry, is above and beyond the physical confines of the poem. Poetry is the only omnipresent and omnipotent force that operates in this world. Poetry has the same position in Char's universe as Christianity assigns to God:

> Si par extraordinaire, la mort ne mettait pas le point final à tout, c'est probablement devant autre chose que ce Dieu inventé par les hommes, à leur mesure, et ajusté (plutôt mal que bien) à leurs contradictions, que nous nous trouverions. [69]

The "autre chose" to which Char refers is Poetry, for only in Poetry can man find immortality.

Poetry includes all the forms of its representation. It is the collective term for art. Therefore, poet and artist are synonymous in all of Char's aphorisms and texts which depict and assess poetry and indicate how it is to be served. A poem and a painting can be equal in their portrayal of life and reality. But all poems, all paintings, all forms of art, are united by a common goal, Poetry. Poetry is Truth and it is Beauty, but, more importantly, the privilege of knowing Poetry is within the reach of every mortal being through a "partage formel" of the vision and creative ac-

---

[69] "A la question: 'Pourquoi ne croyez-vous pas en Dieu?'," *La Corde sensible* in *Pauvreté et privilège*.

tivity of those who accept the risk to serve it. It is not a question of raising man from the "base" to the "sommet" of life, but of bringing the privilege of Poetry (Truth and Beauty) into the poverty of existence. This is the task to which Char devoted himself between 1952 and 1961.

CHAPTER V

1952-1961: A POETICS OF FUSION

René Char's ultimate poetic vision is a fusion of all the parts, elements and individuals, into a perfect organic whole characterized by the unity of its diverse parts. The aggregate of this fusion depends upon the interdependency of its various parts. Although the parts remain distinct, their reciprocal relations form a homogeneous macrocosm, which is the cosmos. However, the macrocosm which is the universe or superstructure of all existence cannot be viewed in its entirety except through its constituent parts.

Between 1923 and 1952, Char concentrated on the particular attributes of the whole, and his examination revealed three major spheres of activity: Humanity, Nature, and Art. Each of these three spheres manifests an interdependency of its component parts for identity of purpose (art), solidarity of strength (humanity), and oneness of function (nature). However, these three spheres of activity are equally dependent one upon the other; Man (Humanity) needs to be threatened by Nature in order to maintain a state of response, of activity. By provoking man, Nature guarantees human continuity. Nature is the framework for human action. On the other hand, Nature is incomplete without man, who brings new possibilities of operation and fulfillment through his response to it. Hence, Nature and Humanity are mutually interdependent.

Above Nature and Man is Art, whose very existence is dependent upon the relationships between man and the human community, between nature and its objects, between Humanity and

Nature. But behind the microcosm of Art is an all-inclusive unity, Poetry. Poetry is both microcostic and macrocostic; it observes each part in its particular operation and in its overall contribution, and it views the inherent harmony of all the parts and strives to maintain their separate and generic integrity. Like the universe, Poetry represents a fusion of all the distinct parts into a whole, but unlike the universe, Poetry is accessible, immediate, and comprehensible within its unity and totality.

Because Poetry reveals the unity of the universe, each individual must produce an act of poetry at the same time as he performs an act of living in order to know this unity, this harmonious universe in which he lives. This fusion is the principal theme of Char's work composed between 1952 and 1961.

The communication of the theme of fusion has been the main objective of all of Char's work since 1923. However, it is a revelation which could only be indicated and not crystallized until 1952, by which time the roles of exchange, mutual interdependency, and privilege of poetry were made manifest. For this reason, Char's fifth period of development (1952-1961) necessarily recalls his previous works; it is a period of thematic renewal, stylistic continuity and condensation, and textual compactness. Moreover, the significance of this period is dependent upon his previous successes, for it represents the victory of Char's poetics and poetry; he leads man to recognize, accept, and participate in the totality of the universe through a fusion of poetry and life.

Char's fifth stage of development is characterized by an accumulative process which has two thematic steps of evolution: 1) the act of living and the act of poetry coincide in the union of man and woman, poet and word (the three versions of *Lettera amorosa* 1953, 1961, 1964); and, 2) Poetry is necessary to reveal and perpetuate this unity (*Les Poèmes des deux années 1953-1954*, 1955, *La Bibliothèque est en feu et autres poèmes*, 1957, *Poèmes et prose choisis*, 1957, and *La Parole en archipel*, 1961).

The Synthesis of *Lettera amorosa*

Lettera amorosa is a work of synthesis in which Char advances to a conclusion on the role of union from principles established in previous works, notably *Le Visage nuptial* (1938). In fact, the significance of *Lettera amorosa* depends upon comprehension of all of Char's poetry written before 1952, for this work is the product of his poetic evolution in a historical sense; its thematic and stylistic composition is the direct result of all his literary efforts since 1923. *Lettera amorosa* represents Char's first successful fusion of the act of living and the act of poetry.

Lettera amorosa spans the nine years, 1952-1961, of Char's fifth period of development, which is primarily characterized by its communication of the inherent unity of the universe, the basic theme of *Lettera amorosa*. Examination of the three editions of this work (1953, 1961, 1964) confirms the important thematic and stylistic synthesis of *Lettera amorosa*.

The original edition was composed in 1952 and published in January 1953. The "deuxième version" appears in *La Parole en archipel* (1961), the second most important work published during this period, and the "version définitive" forms the central section of *Commune présence* (1964). Through the three versions of *Lettera amorosa*, Char reveals the cohesiveness of his poetics and poetry, a fusion of theme and style into the very unity he seeks to present.

Lettera amorosa begins with an introductory quotation by Claudio Monteverdi, a "Dédicace," and an epigraph. The main body of the poem consists of individual paragraphs or notations, and the variants between the three editions are found in this section of the work. The notations are not numbered by Char, but in my discussion of the changes, I rely on a numerical system of reference.[1]

---

[1] I have numbered consecutively the original edition (1953), and all references to the 1961 and 1964 editions are within the original framework. My choice of Arabic numbers is based on Char's use of numbering. His only work numbered in Arabic numerals is *Feuillets d'Hypnos* (1946). Prior to 1951, all of Char's collections of aphorisms (*Moulin premier, Partage formel,* "A la santé du serpent," and *Rougeur des Matinaux*) are subdivided by Roman numerals, including "Le Sujet" (*Arsenal*, 1930), Char's first published aphoristic work. *A une sérénité crispée* (1951) is the first exception to this system, and its noticeable lack of numbers indicates a technical change on Char's part, a change which is maintained in his fifth period of development in *Le Rempart de brindilles* (1953) and *La Bibliothèque est en feu* (1956). It is probable that Char omits numbering as he attains the fusion of life and poetry, a fusion known to him as he composed *A une sérénité crispée* and a fusion first realized in *Lettera amorosa* (1953), a non-aphoristic work which initiates complete thematic and stylistic unity.

The 1953 text of *Lettera amorosa* has 40 notations, the 1961 edition has 31, and the 1964 publication has 38. These statistics show two patterns: reduction and expansion. In the deletions of the 1961 edition, Char suppresses all restrictive details, while in the additions to the 1964 edition he emphasizes the universality of the details retained. There are no major variants between the 1961 and 1964 editions; all phrase, line, and word deletions, that is all significant changes occur between 1953 and 1961. Between 1961 and 1964, Char makes no textual changes in the strict sense; he adds new notations in order to reinforce the general scope of the work.

The changes between the 1953 and 1961 editions of *Lettera amorosa* are found in the omission of nine entire notes and in the deletion of lines and phrases in ten other notes. There were some phrase and word changes,[2] but no additions. Study of each deletion and revision reveals a unity of purpose: the elimination of any detail which might restrict the possibilities of meaning of the work. These changes may be divided into four general categories.

In the first place, Char omits all personal details which might be considered more indicative of his own experience than of every individual's experience. An example is found in the omission of note 13 which describes a trip to the dentist for a tooth extraction as opposed by the retention of note 3 which expresses a more typical experience, that of the "avant-sommeil d'écolier." The state of "écolier" is more familiar in the general sense than the removal of a tooth.

Secondly, Char omits all details which tend to be limited to a sexual reference, demonstrated in the deletion of notes 23 and 37. The elimination of strictly erotic implications emphasizes the intellectuality of the union rather than the performance of the sexual act for mere physical pleasure.

Thirdly, all words and phrases which restrict the overall generality of a notation are either deleted or changed in order to insure the expression of the greatest range of meaning. In note 9, for example, Char changes the adverb of time "quelquefois" to "parfois" because the latter has a more general connotation.

---

[2] See Appendix III.

Similarly, he suppresses in note 18 the adverb "arbitrairement" because it is subject to restriction.

Fourthly, all details which impede the brevity of expression are replaced or omitted, particularly repetitive and explanatory phrases, demonstrated by the deletion of "les uns les autres" in note 8 and of "réciproquement" in note 19. The preservation of brevity is reinforced by the omission of the subject and verb, seen in the final line of note 25: "Il est déjà mi-fleur, mi-liquide." The 1961 deletion of "il est" sets the final nouns in relief and expands the meaning of "déjà" by giving it verbal, temporal, and spatial applications.

The four categories of revision made between 1953 and 1961 contribute to the overall characteristic of condensation which marks all three editions of the work. Char condenses his expression in order to disperse its meaning in all possible directions; it is what Poulet describes as from "la constriction à la dissémination." [3]

The 1964 edition of *Lettera amorosa* reinforces and augments this "disseminating" quality of Char's style. To the 1961 reduced version of the 1953 text, he added six new notes [4] and one reconstructed note (37). The six new notes emphasized the fusion achieved in union and its renewal through their exposure to totality: "Absent partout où on fête un absent." All six notes are characterized by a noticeable lack of personal, erotic, and particular details, as well as by brevity and generality. In his 1964 additions, Char follows the precepts of condensation for universality that guided his revision of the original edition between 1953 and 1961. This tendency is best demonstrated in his 1964 revision of note 37, entirely omitted in 1961. The 1964 form deletes the one particularizing detail, "opaque," and the two lines which have erotic implications, specifically the final line: "Anéantis par mon irruption luxurieuse." This line is replaced by a more general one, which retains the expression of intimacy but which is not restricted to a physical or emotional interpretation: "Blasons, durcis, ce matin, comme du miel de cerisier." Sexual

---

[3] Georges Poulet, "René Char: de la constriction à la dissémination," *Arc* (été 1963), pp. 33-45.

[4] See Appendix III.

union is suggested, but the emphasis is placed on its beneficial effects of union beyond the physical and emotional.

The revisions of *Lettera amorosa* reveal an aspect of Char's conclusion on the role of union. In his early poems (*Les Cloches sur le coeur* and *Le Marteau sans maître*), he sought to minimize erotic expressions, sensing that the sexual act was a condition for something beyond the physical. In *Le Visage nuptial*, he recognized that union with woman is beneficial to man in his daily struggle for existence; this was reinforced by his discovery in *Fureur et mystère* that man is justified by creative activity, the poet's vocation. Exploration of nature in *Les Matinaux* resulted in the knowledge that the human and the elemental are one, that all objects and individuals are interdependent in their existence and express the unity of the universe. In *Lettera amorosa*, he fuses all of these discoveries into a totality grasped through the sexual union; this fusion is necessarily dependent upon the poetic vision of a basic human act, immediate and common to all men. Char "constricts" this unity to "disseminate" it through the consummation of an act of poetry as the perfection of an act of living. *Lettera amorosa* is the fruition of *Partage formel*, for it is an expression of exchange through a formal vehicle, the poem:

Le poème est l'amour réalisé du désir demeuré désir. [5]

The title of *Lettera amorosa* reflects accurately and succinctly the character of the synthesis Char achieves. In the first place, the title is in Italian, and it is Char's only work given a title in this language. [6] The choice of Italian seems to come from a work by Claudio Monteverdi, because the introductory line is a quotation in Italian [7] attributed to Monteverdi. Char's use of this quotation in order to introduce the work gives *Lettera amorosa* historical veracity and universal application. It presents *Lettera amorosa* as the final product of a literary problem which has concerned artists of all times, places, and genres. In the second place, the love letter

---

[5] XXX, *Partage formel* in *Fureur et mystère* (Paris, 1948).

[6] Char has given Latin titles to two other works: "Cur secessiti?" in *Fureur et mystère* and *Homo poeticus*. *Lettera amorosa* is his only work entitled in a modern foreign language.

[7] The quotation appears in French in the 1953 edition but in Italian in the 1961 and 1964 editions.

is a traditional form of literary expression which can be rendered in either verse or prose and which can be set to music. In fact, one of the earliest known functions of a poet was to compose amatory poetry for others. The form of the love letter is an essential part of literary history. In the third place, a love letter has a precise connotation familiar to the general public.

Char's title, *Lettera amorosa*, refers to an established and familiar literary vehicle for the communication of the sentiment of love. This is precisely what the reader who is unfamiliar with Char's work and vision would find in this work. However, Char's *Lettera amorosa* is a written communication on love, but on love that is neither passionate nor sexual. It is a written description of the poet's relation with Poetry, a relation which is analogous to that which is established between a man and a woman in the act of love. It is a union in which the poet and the written word are fused into Poetry in the same way that man and woman form a couple. Love is the human expression of Poetry; it is the only means that the individual has to know and attain the Ideal; it is every man's particular representation of the Ideal and his particular participation in the totality which characterizes his existence.

The sexual union is a fusion of man and woman, into a single entity, the couple, which brings new solidarity, new fulfillment, and new possibilities of development to the participants. It requires the action of both individuals, and this activity is creative; from their joint efforts, a new perspective comes into being in one instant of time. Although this discovery is momentary in its revelation, it is enduring in its significance. The knowledge of this experience of total exchange and fusion suffices to strengthen the participants against any obstacles they may encounter and to inspire them to continue to act consciously for a renewal of the experience and for a discovery of other experiences with similar remedial effects. It is the individual discovery and communication of the act of Poetry. On the other hand, the act of poetry is the universal revelation and communication of the particular act of living which represents it, the union of opposites into one totality. It is the synthesis of poet and man with word and woman, of Life and Poetry.

It is significant that the words poet, poem and poetry never occur in *Lettera amorosa*, but these terms are suggested in the "Dédicace" where Char speaks of "l'Ouvrage de tous les temps admiré."[8] The term "ouvrage" refers to literary production; by capitalizing the word, Char applies it to the two levels of *Lettera amorosa*; it is love as the product of individuals and love as a literary object. Char's work is a combination of the two; poetic inception or literature is expressed by "lettera" and human love by its qualifier "amorosa." "L'Ouvrage" represents this combination and permits Char to omit literary terminology. Poet and man have become synonyms. However, this evolution is different from the one noted in *Dehors la nuit est gouvernée* (1938), where Char, by replacing the term poet by man, humanized the poet. In *Lettera amorosa* he "poeticizes" man; every man is a poet in his participation in the fusion of life and poetry.

Although *Lettera amorosa* is a love letter, it is not written in epistolary form. In fact, it follows no prescribed form, other than the use of prose sentences and paragraphs. The work appears as a collection of notes taken at random from a diary or journal written on various and distinct occasions over a long but unspecified period of time. Superficially, it resembles *Feuillets d'Hypnos*, for there seems to have been a selection of those notations which the agent or main speaker considers the most informative. However, *Lettera amorosa* is a single poem, which evolves through the sum of the individual notations.

Furthermore, *Lettera amorosa* is a dialogue between two actors, "je" and "tu"; however, the only speaker is "je." It is the art of the dialogue as opposed to the art of the monologue which is limited to a single speaker who soliloquizes alone as if he were alone. The one speaker of *Lettera amorosa* is not alone; there is someone else with him, and he is always aware of this second existence. The "tu" to whom "je" speaks is even more present than "je" through its physical absence. *Lettera amorosa* is a definite exchange between the present "je" and the absent "tu," an exchange reinforced by the "nous," which recalls the union in the past of "je" and "tu," a union which makes possible the present discourse.

---

[8] Unless otherwise indicated, all quotations in this chapter are from the 1964 edition

Throughout Char's poetry, there is increasing interest in the notion of absence-presence; he considers the state of absence to be stronger than the actual physical immediacy of an object or individual. Totality is recognized by the absence of diverse and contradictory parts. Some emotions, anguish for example, are known only through their cessation, through their absence; the same is true of basic human drives, hunger and thirst. The absence of liberty was the motivation for the resistance of World War II. The physical absence of "tu" in *Lettera amorosa* directs "je" and prevails: "Absent partout où on fête un absent."

"Tu" supplies unity to the work. Before 1952, Char's work is unified in general through the agent, through the voice of the poet, although there are several individual poems in which he achieves unity through the thematic and stylistic evocation of "tu." *Lettera amorosa* is his first example of an entire work which is unified through its object of address rather than its speaker.

Despite the dominance of "tu," the "je" is one of the more important features of *Lettera amorosa*, for it is the cumulative figure of the first person singular which marks Char's poetry. The "je" of *Lettera amorosa* is every man, artist and non-artist, individually and collectively. The use of the first person singular preserves each man's identity. The word "individual" is essential, for Char consistently repudiates any suggestion of "mass man." He advocates a collectivity of men formed by the bond of experience similar but not identical in requirements, effort, and results. Each man participates on an individual level in his act of union.

The synthesis of Char's use of "je" is seen in the temporal element which distinguishes the two actors of *Lettera amorosa*. "Je" is more historical than "tu." When "je" appears by itself, it is restricted to a description of past events and present feelings. Moreover, these events and sentiments are strictly physical or human. "Je" is associated with the history of man; his thoughts and actions occur within the concrete and everyday world ("ville," "pays," "terre," "sentier," "choses," "fenêtre," "chambre," "table," "boulevard"). On the contrary, "tu" is associated with those forces and objects which are more enduring than the average man or generation of men ("vent," "forêt," "soleil," "lune," "air," "mer," "arbre"). By itself, "tu" is connected to the past and present, but it is also an element of the future. "Je" is never used in conjunction with the future except in "nous," the couple of "je" and "tu." The future of "je" is completely dependent upon union: "tu es la Continuelle."

"Tu" is described in terms of love as man would describe a woman, and "tu" has a role similar to that of woman, while "je" represents individual man. The presence of "tu" in the past was beneficial to him; it strengthened him and permitted him to grasp totality in the present. Union with "mon amour" gives the poet and man the opportunity for self-affirmation and for the attainment of his nobility: "Je ris merveilleusement avec toi. Voilà ta chance unique." Through woman, man receives strength and the dignity of being, which make him free to act. Woman is necessary to justify his existence. Each time man and woman meet in union, they rediscover and recreate this unity, dignity, and freedom.

"Tu" is woman and the written word or poem: "je" is man and poet. Their unions result in the same discoveries and each subsequent exchange is a renewal of this revelation. Man and woman recreate poetry as the poet and his poem recreate life. Life and Poetry coincide. They are joined through creative activity which fuses all opposites and demands the dependency of one upon the other for meaning and authenticity.

The coincidence of Life and Poetry is accurately reflected by the arrangement of the paragraphs which form *Lettera amorosa*. The individual notations seem to be in random order with no obvious connection between the various parts except through the agent "je" and its object of address "tu." This apparent lack of harmonious organization is necessary, for each expression offers a different perspective of the relationship of the couple; behind each notation is "tu." In other words, Char's *Lettera amorosa* is written in fragments which appear disconnected and contradictory but which are no more than varying manifestations of one prevailing unity. The arrangement of *Lettera amorosa* is the realization of his pulverization theory (*Le Poème pulvérisé*, 1947), and its cohesive structure evolves from a multiplication of the fragments. The organization represents graphically human existence; life may seem fragmented, but it is not.

This process of multiplication is an important trait of the structure. Each encounter or union is illuminated by previous ones until the diverse experiences are multiplied into one meaningful existence, that of totality. Man justifies his existence through his contacts with woman, for only in the renewal of these unions does he discover the continuity that characterizes his existence:

> Tu es plaisir avec chaque vague séparée de ses suivantes. Enfin toutes à la fois chargent. C'est la mer qui se fonde, qui s'invente. Tu es plaisir, corail de spasmes.

"Tu" not only multiplies, it constricts so that "je" may view the totality as well as the continuity of existence. Char fuses his theory of poetic pulverization or fragmentation with his concept of crispation (*A une sérénité crispée*, 1951) in order to reveal the unity of the world. "Tu" is absent more than she is present because her absence "crisps" man's existence. It maintains him in a constant state of willingness to risk exposure and act. In most of the passages of *Lettera amorosa*, "tu" is absent, indicating that most of man's existence takes place without her, but her absence is so powerful and noticeable that she forces man to remain in a state of ready response; her absence permits him to perceive the unity that her presence offers.

The synthesis of Char's pulverization and crispation theories results in a more contracted view of unity. The "iris" image demonstrates the singleness and multiplicity of totality. In "Sur le Franc-bord," the appendix to *Lettera amorosa*, Char explains the various definitions of the word "iris." It belongs to nature (plant and animal) and at the same time to the cosmos (planet and rainbow); it includes literature, particularly poetry, and the physical anatomy of man (eye). It is the proper name of woman, specifically in her role of "femme aimée." Iris is a single term with multiple meaning;[9] it is all-inclusive and summarizes the totality of existence: "...IRIS. Iris plural, iris d'Eros, iris de *Lettera amorosa*." Iris represents the fusion of life and poetry:

---

[9] It is also interesting to note that there is no change in spelling in French between the singular and plural forms of iris, and that it can be either feminine or masculine, depending upon its application.

Merci d'être, sans jamais te casser, iris, ma fleur de gravité. Tu élèves au bord des eaux des affections miraculeuses, tu ne pèses pas sur les mourants que tu veilles, tu éteins des plaies sur lesquelles le temps n'a pas d'action, tu ne conduis pas à une maison consternante, tu permets que toutes les fenêtres reflétées ne fassent qu'un seul visage de passion, tu accompagnes le retour du jour sur les vertes avenues libres.

The role of union expressed in *Lettera amorosa* is the central point of emphasis of all of Char's poetry. As early as *Les Cloches sur le coeur* (1928), he announced that his poetic goal was to discover and communicate the inherent homogeneity of existence, human and elemental, terrestrial and cosmic. He achieves the fusion of the parts through the role of union, in which he includes a fusion of basic human opposites, man and woman, as well as one of the most apparently contradictory phenomena: presence and absence, the real and the ideal ("base et sommet"), the possible and the impossible ("pauvreté et privilège"). It is a fusion which negates all limits, especially those of spatiality and temporality.

Char's concepts of space and time are essential to his discovery of fusion (theme) and its revelation (style). He finds that man's past reluctance to act was based on a fear of destruction, a fear not unjustified by man's mortality, which seems an irreversible limit, a threat beyond human control. However, union solidified individuals into a joint force against a common menace and gave each individual the strength necessary to revolt, to expose his finiteness to the danger of death; in this act he became free and rediscovered his dignity (*Fureur et mystère*). Union with another is the essential source of human nobility. This nobility comes precisely from the acceptance of the risk to act. Confrontation of the present in the present fuses the three usual divisions of time: past, present, and future. The present is not only the realization of the future of the past (*Lascaux*), but also a merging of past and future, for knowledge of the value of union in the past gives rise to renewal and creative action in the present, and this action makes the future possible in the present. There is no temporal limit; there is only the present in which to act; no other time is accessible. The present tense prevails in all of Char's poetry in order that the present dominate the continuum of existence which is the present.

However, the negation of the possibility of future action is not Char's unique means of conquering time. Char associates this concept with two earlier ones: a denial of history (*A une sérénité crispée*) and immortality through art. Char's line, "Tu es la Continuelle," describes the eternal character of his concept of Poetry. Significantly, the noun "continuelle" is feminine, capitalized, and follows a present tense. The primordial source of human dignity is union with woman (*Claire*); it is immediate to all men; it was known in the past and it will be known to those to be born. Woman persistently reinforces the continuance of man against any influences or forces which might tend to weaken him; in this condition of endurance, the role of woman and the union she offers remain unchanged in their essential state. Poetry is equally continual and lasting; there is no break or interruption in its existence; its duration cannot be measured; it is beyond time, a-temporal. The present tense of the verb "être," the verb of existence, reinforces the unceasing, constant succession of existence that identifies Poetry. Char conquers time through the fusion of life and poetry, for this eternal "Tu" is the synthesis of man and woman and poet and the written word, the act of living and the act of poetry. Poetry overcomes human mortality and consequently time, all time, through the authenticity of its coincidence with life, through creative activity as expressed by union.

Poetry is a-spatial in the same way that it is a-temporal. It cannot be measured. It is "continuelle" in that it is the universe; it has the three dimensions usually assigned to space, but they can be seen only in the particular parts. The individual person or element and its contribution to existence can be gauged, but not the whole because of the process of multiplication which occurs within union. The individual self is multiplied in each union; it is increased through exchange. Each renewal augments the self and the number of unions enacted increases as its value becomes known. This is the concept of universal experience based on the idea of a common multiplier or intensifier, the act of Poetry. Poetry cannot be reduced beyond its single unit; it is first and it is last; it is the beginning and it is the sum. There is no end beyond it, of it, or within it. It is the universe; it is all there is. Poetry conquers space by replacing it:

Je ne puis être et ne veux vivre que dans l'espace et dans la liberté de mon amour.

Participation is significantly synonymous with creative activity; this is emphasized by the role of union in *Lettera amorosa*. Each individual may know the oneness which characterizes the universe through his own participation in that totality. Individual experience, known and universalized by the poet, reveals the humanized character of Char's cosmos. All objects, forces, elements are seen only in a human context; even the things which threaten to destroy man serve him because man must be menaced to maintain the necessary state of response. Because Char's poetry is oriented towards man, it is neither transcendent nor transcendental. For Char, the oneness of all existence is not only realizable in human experience; it is discoverable through empirical means. In fact, Char's overall poetic vision is one which denies all transcendency; it is one of direct apprehension of reality because of an ordinary and common experience. The absolute is no longer the ideal but the real. This is the synthesis presented in *Lettera amorosa*, a crystallization of Char's poetry in general.

1953-1961: The Necessity of Poetry

In *Lettera amorosa*, Char negates the limits of space and time through Poetry and the role of union without elaborating a systematic philosophy. Char does not make technical investigations of being, the structure of the universe, theories of knowledge, ethics, the phenomena of nature or theology. Nevertheless, these branches of knowledge, of philosophical learning, are incorporated into his concept of Poetry and are necessary to it.

Traditionally, philosophy has been the study of the truths or principles which are thought to underlie all knowledge and being or reality. In this sense of the term, Char's poetry is philosophical, for it is consistently and continuously concerned with the discovery and communication of the totality which he finds underlying all reality. For Char, unity is the governing principle of existence; what appears heterogeneous is merely a derivative of this unity. However, Char does not establish this unity through a systematic study; he believes in it, accepts it, and finds no reason to reject it. He begins with the idea of totality, and all of his poems are directed at revealing this totality. Char is a philosopher only in his interest in discovering the unity which characterizes the universe, but he never speculates on metaphysical problems. Man is as he is, physically and mentally, and he is accepted as he is, not as he ought to be. Things are as they are, and there is no need to know why or how the world evolved; it is. The problem is not one of metaphysical philosophy, and it is not one of natural philosophy, for things in nature are viewed only in their relation to man, never apart from him.

How man is to act is always at the center of Char's poetics and poetry. In this sense, one might attempt to detect evidence of a moral philosophy in Char's work. Certainly, Char is concerned with ethical principles, but he does not distinguish between evil and virtue, good and bad, moral and immoral (or even amoral) conduct. For him, creative activity is the only moral or ethical rule to guide man in his behavior. When man revolts constructively, he acts in the name of liberty, dignity, justice, truth. What Char views as evil, primarily the absence of freedom, arises through the failure to act. Hence, truth is ethical because it demands a specific mode of behavior; but there is no hierarchy of values, of good and right; there is only one principle of action.

Char's concept of Poetry contains philosophy, but it is not restricted to any single system of thought. Moreover, it goes beyond philosophy because it excludes no branch of learning, no phenomenon, no event. It attacks each and every dogma because any orthodoxy or even any science necessarily excludes others. In Char's universe, all is possible because all is included; each part belongs to the oneness which is the world, and in this unity the only mode of behavior is to respond to that unity, to act, to participate. Woman is necessary to justify man's existence because union with her permits him to participate in Poetry. Poetry is man's only means for self-knowledge and self-affirmation; Poetry replaces philosophy. This is the major theme of Char's work between 1953 and 1961.

Published in 1955, *Poèmes des deux années 1953-1954* was begun probably soon after the first edition of *Lettera amorosa* was completed. The fusion of life and poetry attained in *Lettera amorosa* is an integral element of *Poèmes des deux années,* although this work tends to stress the union of the poet and his poem or the written word. Because the poet bridges the two poles of existence ("base et sommet"), his responsibility is to lead others to the totality of reality; because he alone knows that Poetry is necessary to justify existence, his role and its importance must be made known. However, underlying Char's concentration on the poet in *Poèmes des deux années* is an implicit metamorphosis of man and poet; that is, Char's poetization of man in *Lettera amorosa* is maintained. The term "poet" in *Poèmes des deux années* refers to every man as well as every artist, for the authenticity of the poet's acts demands a fusion of poetry and life. The poet is the guide; he precedes other men only in marking the course which man is to take. By following the poet's direction, others can attain the poet's vision and knowledge of totality. Char's assessment of the poet's role in *Poèmes des deux années* is equally applicable to every human being.

Poèmes des deux années consists of three parts: *Le Rempart de brindilles*, *L'Amie qui ne restait pas*, and *Pourquoi la journée vole*. All three sections are thematically unified by Char's review of his previous works in the light of the fusion attained in *Lettera amorosa*, and they are stylistically unified through the figure of the poet.

Le Rempart de brindilles was written between January and March 1953, and it was originally published as a separate work in 1953. It is Char's first important publication after *Lettera amorosa*; this observation suggests the correlation of these two works. *Le Rempart de brindilles* consists of a group of 16 aphorisms entitled "Le Rempart de brindilles" and four poems which illustrate these aphorisms. Literally, the title refers to a defense established by fragile twigs; fragile or easily destructible objects become strong through the solidarity of union. "Le Rempart" refers to Poetry, while "brindilles" refer to the whole of humanity.

Poetry is man's weapon to confront life:

> Le dessein de la poésie étant de nous rendre souverains en nous impersonnalisant, nous touchons, grâce au poème, à la plénitude...
> Les poèmes sont les bouts d'existence incorruptibles que nous lançons à la gueule de la mort, mais assez haut

> pour que, ricochant sur elle, ils tombent dans le monde nominateur de l'unité.[10]

The "nous" of this aphorism is fraternal and applies to all men, individually and collectively; there is no distinction made between poet and man, for both are fulfilled and able to conquer time and space through creative activity, represented by the term "poèmes." The term "poem" is no longer restricted to a literary production. Char expands his use of this term to refer to any creative act or fusion of life and poetry. The union of man and woman generates a poem.

Perception of the totality of reality that Poetry offers demands action. Char affirms the positive role of destruction in maintaining man in the state of readiness for action:

> Echapper à la honteuse contrainte du choix entre l'obéissance et la démence, esquiver l'abat de la hache sans cesse revenante du despote contre laquelle nous sommes sans moyens de protection, quoique étant aux prises sans trêve, voilà notre rôle, notre destination, et notre dandinement justifiés. Il nous faut franchir la clôture du pire, faire la course périlleuse, encore chasser au delà, tailler en pièces l'inique, enfin disparaître sans trop de pacotilles sur soi. Un faible remerciement donné ou entendu, et rien d'autre.[11]

Man needs to be menaced in order to accept his mortality and act. It is action in the present and the constant desire to act in the future which enable man to confront life. The realization of his desire projects him into the future:

> Tout l'embasement ...est à réinventer. La vie bousillée est à ressaisir, avec tout le doré du couchant et la promesse d'éveil, successivement.[12]

Man is "le mortel partenaire" aroused to desire by woman, whose offer of immediate fulfillment renews this desire for action and assures man of his right to exist. By showing man his continuity

---

[10] "Le Rempart de brindilles," *Le Rempart de brindilles* in *Poèmes des deux années 1953-1954* (Paris, 1955).
[11] *Ibid.*
[12] *Ibid.*

and his possibility of present and future self-affirmation through union, woman makes man divine:

> La quête d'un grand Etre, n'est-ce qu'une pression de doigt du présent entravé sur l'avenir en liberté? [13]

> ...l'avenir ... ainsi éveillé d'un murmure, les devinant, les crée. O dédale de l'extrême amour! [14]

Figuratively, man dies in woman to be reborn through union with her:

> Nous sommes une fois encore sans expérience antérieure, nouveau-venus, épris.... Le désir vit... [15]

Without union, man is vulnerable to destruction; through union, he is strengthened, renewed, and aroused to act, for he is certain that his being has meaning now and in the future.

The responsibility of the poet is to show man that the development of his dignity is dependent upon constant action directed toward a purposeful object of creativity, Poetry. The poet must concern himself with man and his possibilities; his work must be directed to all men. Because he knows that man's only means of justification is found in a union of love, the human expression of poetry, the poet should restrict himself to this theme: "Prends garde... aux mots que tu écris..." [16] The poet is to reveal to man the acceptability of his condition so that he will assume the responsibility of his life and destiny.

Le Rempart de brindilles expresses Char's faith in man to act creatively for the realization of a better world. The responsibility of enlightenment and communication belongs to the poet, but the final responsibility of human destiny is placed on man. This is why the poet must concentrate on Poetry. Poetry gives man the dignity, strength, and freedom to confront life and make it meaningful.

---

[13] "Le Rempart de brindilles."
[14] "Le Mortel partenaire."
[15] "Le Front de la rose."
[16] "Le Rempart de brindilles."

The second section of *Poèmes des deux années* is *L'Amie qui ne restait pas*. Composed between September 1953 and January 1954, this section of 15 poems emphasizes the necessity of creative activity. In its hommage to a relationship whose past presence proves beneficial even in its present absence, this title is a direct reference to the concept of absence and presence expressed in *Lettera amorosa*. It is interesting to note that the word "amie" appears only in this section; it is not used in any earlier or later work.[17] However, the significance of this feminine noun is not in its rare appearance, but in its expansion of Char's representation of woman. Woman makes possible man's first exchange; this experience prepares him to enter into meaningful relationships with others. "L'Amie" refers to the fraternal union that woman offers through her primary sexual role. *Lettera amorosa* is limited to the fusion of life and poetry through the couple; this fusion is generalized in *L'Amie qui ne restait pas* to include a fusion of life and poetry by the human fraternity at large. In the same way that Char ended human isolation by proceeding from the communication of the exchange of self-knowledge accessible with woman in *Le Visage nuptial* (1938) to the establishment of the solidarity of the human community in *Fureur et mystère* (1938-1947), he proceeds from the revelation of man's fusion of poetry and life with woman to its attainment among all men. This process of generalizing from the particular is not only characteristic of the main body of Char's work, but it also reveals Char's adaptation of a logical methodology to his poetics and poetry.

Char builds in the same manner as an architect or mathematician. He began in 1923 with a theory of totality based on the fusion of opposites, and every poem since 1923 contributes to the elucidation and realization of this original plan. He announces his view of the structure of reality and presents it through a series of calculated reasonings and data, his poems. Thoroughness, caution, and prudence mark his investigation and demonstration of the unity and totality of existence. One typical manifestation of Char's orderly procedure to ensure the validity of his vision is

---

[17] Char does refer to "un Ami" in "Exploit du cylindre à vapeur," *Placard pour un chemin des écoliers* (1937), but the title of the second section of *Poèmes des deux années* is his first use of the feminine form, "amie," and the second occurrence is in the poem, "Victoire éclair," of this section.

represented by the term "Amie" to designate the fusion of life and poetry through fraternal creative activity.

The first poem of *L'Amie qui ne restait pas* is "La Double tresse," a double poem ("Chaume des Vosges" and "Sur la paume de Dabo") which expresses the two aspects of woman and union, presence and obscene. This double theme explains the constructive quality of the negative "ne... pas" of the section title. The dates 1939 and Summer 1953 are an essential part of the poem because they indicate the linear development of Char's poetics and poetry with regard to *Lettera amorosa* and its expansion initiated in *Le Rempart de brindilles*. In fact, the juxtaposition of 1939 and 1953 emphasizes the historical importance of *Lettera amorosa* in Char's work in general and in his fifth period of development in particular.

Furthermore, the double nature of this poem and the juxtaposition of its dates announce the twofold organization and purpose of the remaining 14 poems of *L'Amie qui ne restait pas*. The first seven poems form a thematic review of Char's concept of exchange prior to *Lettera amorosa*. The specific point of departure for this review is *Le Rempart de brindilles*, for it is undertaken retrospectively in the knowledge of the synthesis attained in *Lettera amorosa* and in the awareness that this synthesis can be expanded to a fraternal level. The second group of poems (the last seven) projects *Lettera amorosa* and Char's works prior to it into the realization of a fraternal fusion of life and poetry; "La Femme" becomes "L'Amie."

"La Double tresse" forms the transition between the first two sections of *Poèmes des deux années* by introducing the theme and structure of *L'Amie qui ne restait pas*. The first part of this poem is "Chaume des Vosges," which was originally published as a separate poem entitled "Sur une table de mairie" in the 1946 edition of *Premières alluvions*; in 1948, this text became "Chaume des Vosges" in *Les Loyaux adversaires* (*Fureur et mystère*). The 1948 title and the date 1939 refer directly to "la drôle de guerre" of 1939-1940, during which Char was mobilized and stationed in Alsace. This text was revised [18] and juxtaposed in 1955 to "Sur la

---

[18] The only major textual changes in *L'Amie qui ne restait pas* are found in "Chaume des Vosges."

paume de Dabo" to form "La double tresse," and its textual revisions reveal the continuity of Char's work.

The significant change between the 1946-1948 text and its 1955 form in *L'Amie qui ne restait pas* is found in the last two lines. Moreover, this revision indicates the importance of the synthesis of *Lettera amorosa*. The 1946 and 1948 poem was as follows:

> Beauté ma toute-droite par les rouges d'étoiles [19]
> A l'étape des lampes et du courage clos
> Dans l'absurde chagrin de vivre sans comprendre
> Ecroule-moi et sois ma femme de décembre.

The third line was deleted in 1955 doubtless because Char's discoveries after 1948 invalidated this line. Comprehension is possible because man can participate in the totality of the universe through woman; woman has ceased to be merely a refuge from the threat of destruction, "l'absurde chagrin"; she has become a source of strength for the acceptance and confrontation of that threat. The fourth line was revised to replace the third line: "Que je me glace et que tu sois ma femme de décembre." This change develops an idea merely suggested in the 1946 and 1948 text; woman is man's prime source for renewal. The new fourth line, added in 1955, recalls *Le Visage nuptial* and relates it to the themes of *Lettera amorosa* and *Le Rempart de brindilles*: "Ma vie future, c'est ton visage quand tu dors." Woman projects man into the future through her arousal of his desire for creative activity.

"Chaume des Vosges" evokes the value of presence, while "Sur la paume de Dabo" emphasizes absence. In this text, woman is represented by "un bouleau," a tree noted for its beauty in winter when it has no foliage. Permanence or the conquest of time and mortality is possible through the totality of absence based on a past experience of fulfillment: "Ton amour est trouvé."

The two parts of "La double tresse" are continued in the main body of *L'Amie qui ne restait pas*. The review suggested by "Chaume des Vosges" characterizes the first group of poems. Char begins his reexamination with another direct reference to his partic-

---

[19] The last phrase, "par les rouges d'étoiles," was changed in 1955 to "par des routes si ladres"; this revision indicates Char's stress on rendering the real world acceptable as it is; there is beauty even in the ugly (*La Minutieuse* in *La Paroi et la prairie*, 1952).

ipation in "la drôle de guerre" in "Fièvre de la petite pierre d'Alsace." This poem specifically recalls "Donnerbach mühle" (*Le Poème pulvérisé*, 1947) in its expression of the interruption of the harmony of nature:

> Nous avancions sur l'étendue embrasée des forêts... maintenant livrée à la solidarité de l'éclatement et la destruction.

Yet, unlike "Donnerbach mühle," this text evinces faith in man to persist and endure with the obstinacy of nature: "Bonds obstinés, marche prospère, nous sommes..." *Les Matinaux* is shown to be the successor to *Le Poème pulvérisé*. Similarly, Char links his interest in the plastic arts, expressed in *Art bref* and *Pauvreté et privilège*, to *Lettera amorosa* through "La Lisière du trouble." This poem describes a piece of Rodin's [20] sculpture which portrays the instant of fusion of life and poetry in the sexual union.

By its title, "Le Vipéreau" recalls "A la santé du serpent" [21] (*Le Poème pulvérisé*) and "Le Serpent" (*Quatre fascinants* in *La Paroi et la prairie*) and connects them to *Lettera amorosa*. Man resembles the viper in his need for union and in his condition to direct his destiny in the knowledge of past union. "Il est meurtrier devant toutes" because his daily existence is dependent upon renewal: "Son vis-à-vis, son adversaire, c'est le petit matin..." Like the snake, man's curse is that the realization of his desire projects his desire; "n'étant d'aucune paroisse" indicates the impossibility of sanctuary from desire.

The key term in "Vermillon" is "la source," which suggests *La Fontaine narrative* (*Fureur et mystère*) and *Les Matinaux*. The cessation of the actual moment of union or its absence increases rather than diminishes the value attained in presence; "notre endroit" remains intact. This idea of continuity is further clarified by the last poem of the first group, "Marmonnement." The

---

[20] A minor change occurs in the 1961 publication of this text (*La Parole en archipel*). Char clarifies the designation of his point of inspiration from the address, "77 rue de Varenne," to "Musée Rodin," which is located at 77 rue de Varenne.

[21] It is interesting to note that "A la santé du serpent" was published as a separate collection of aphorisms in 1954, during Char's composition and organization of *Poème des deux années*.

emphasis on the constructive function of absence presented in *Lettera amorosa* is summarized in this text: "Continue, va, nous durons ensemble bien que séparés..."

The second group of poems of *L'Amie qui ne restait pas* expands the review of the first group by concentrating on the value of the experience of past union. "Le Risque et le pendule" initiates the cycle of expansion with a demand for the risk of action. Man resembles the bee which must expose its fragility in order to gather pollen for honey, the creative function which justifies the bee's existence. In the same way, the poet and man must risk the exposure of their vulnerability to destruction and act. Man's highest act of living is the act of Poetry, creative activity, which justifies his existence. His only moral standard is this poetic act. However great the risk, it must be and is accepted: "Sans plus choisir entre oublier et bien apprendre." Creative activity is neither an escape or refuge nor a means of defense against the fragility of man. On the contrary, its risk is his only means of self-affirmation.

Acceptance of the risk to act leads man to his dignity of being and enables him to confront life:

> Jeter bas l'existence laidement accumulée et retrouver le regard qui l'aima assez à son début pour en étaler le fondement. Ce qui me reste à vivre est dans cet assaut... [22]

The poem or creative act, "ce frisson," [23] is necessary to man in the present, for it "me poussa dans l'avenir;" [24] it "reconstruit l'Amie" [25] and makes possible "une existence si forte." [26]

Significantly, "Invitation," the last poem of this group and of *L'Amie qui ne restait pas*, explains concisely Char's use of the fraternal term of "L'Amie" in the section title. In addition, this poem is based on the process of multiplication noted in *Lettera amorosa*. Participation in the sexual union is man's expression of Poetry, of creative activity as his only code of behavior. Universal practice of this code of Poetry is the means to unite all men in a better world:

---

[22] "Pour renouer," *L'Amie qui ne restait pas* in *Poèmes des deux années 1953-1954* (Paris, 1955).
[23] *Ibid.*
[24] "Le Bois de l'Epte."
[25] "Victoire éclair."
[26] *Ibid.*

1952-1961: A POETICS OF FUSION

Il n'y a plus de cauchemar ...Il n'y a plus d'aversion.
Que la pause d'un bal dont l'entrée est partout...

For the universal establishment and perpetuation of freedom, dignity, truth, righteousness, and justice, "J'appelle les amants." It is an invitation to all men to know the continuity and totality of the universe and to act upon this knowledge for the realization of the future in the present through creative activity. "L'Amie" represents Char's humanization of cosmic unity.

The last section of *Poèmes des deux années* is entitled *Pourquoi la journée vole* and consists of a single prose poem. In the 1961 edition of *La Parole en archipel*, this text appears as the last poem of *L'Amie qui ne restait pas* and not as a separate section of *Poèmes des deux années*. The importance of this change is found in the textual revisions of the poem.

In 1955, *Pourquoi la journée vole* consisted of four paragraphs which defended the poet's role in contemporary society. The first paragraph was deleted in 1961 probably because its negation of the geographical setting for poetic activity is not necessary in a text which stresses universality. The 1961 poem begins with the positive assessment of the poet's role as expressed in the first line of the second paragraph in 1955. The deletion of the second line of the second paragraph further demonstrates Char's concern to emphasize the universality of the poet's activity; the 1955 line, "La double nature de la douleur lui donne l'essor," was replaced in 1961 by this line: "Il n'est pas soudé à l'égarement d'autrui." It is a change from a description of the character of the poet to one which stresses his action. This stress on activity is also seen in the third line where Char changed "son étreinte" to "son saisir," a more active term, and in the fourth line where "il doit répondre" was changed to "il répond."

The communication of the moral truth of creative activity is the poet's contribution to society, and this ethical principle is universalized through the poet's ability to communicate it "dans tous les lieux où il n'est pas allé, où jamais il n'ira, chez les étrangers qu'il ne connaîtra pas." Poetry, the product of his union with the written work, is more eternal than the poet; it is a-temporal and a-spatial. The poet is "du pays d'*à côté*" because he renders the ideal into the real. The poet "brusque les adieux pour être là quand le pain sort du four" because he "vivifie puis court au dénouement."

He grasps the essential staple of human existence, animates it, that is, makes it known and accessible, and he reveals its possibilities by freeing it from all restraints. The poet concentrates on the present and its realization, not on the past.

The title, *Pourquoi la journée vole*, emphasizes the universality of the poet's activity in the present. His historical existence, "journée," is one of unceasing movement, "vole." This activity is not restricted to a single physical area; it circulates quickly, freely, and globally. *Pourquoi la journée vole* explains why only the poet is able to issue an "Invitation" for fraternal unity; his revelation is universal because its object, Poetry, is the universe.

Poèmes des deux années reexamines the fusion of life and poetry attained in *Lettera amorosa* and expands this synthesis into the possibility of realizing the ideal of a better world. The final text, *Pourquoi la journée vole*, emphasizes the universality of the poet's role to communicate to others the necessity of Poetry in order to direct man's conduct and justify human existence individually and collectively. This theme of the poet's duty to guide others is continued in *La Bibliothèque est en feu et autres poèmes*. In this work, Char moves confidently toward the replacement of philosophy by Poetry.

La Bibliothèque est en feu et autres poèmes (1957) is a collective work consisting of four major sections: *La Bibliothèque est en feu*, *Les Compagnons dans le jardin* (which in turn consists of four parts), *Autres poèmes*, and *Sur une nuit sans ornement*. Most of the texts were published separately before they were gathered into this edition. The only important text which appears for the first time is *Sur une nuit sans ornement*.

The second general characteristic of *La Bibliothèque est en feu et autres poèmes* is the predominance of aphorisms. Each of the three major texts (*La Bibliothèque est en feu*, *Les Compagnons dans le jardin*, and *Sur une nuit sans ornement*) is a collection of aphorisms; the emphasis of the work is on the examination of Poetry and the poet's role with regard to the human community.

Originally published in 1956, *La Bibliothèque est en feu* is dated by the author July-August 1955. It represents Char's second major step in his presentation of the moral necessity of Poetry. The aphorisms of *La Bibliothèque est en feu* concern creative activity.

The poet's work, "la bibliothèque," is written for and accessible to the public. His work is "en feu" because it is discovered in an intense moment of contact between disparate elements. Moreover, fire is an image for the terrestrial and celestial sources of energy; it is not confined to the physical world. The poet's energetic passion and work agitate others to respond to his act of ignited communication.

Furthermore, fire is destructive; it permits new perspectives to emerge into view. This aspect of fire recalls Char's earlier theory of constructive destruction; as fire connects earth and sky, the "pulverized" poem "crisps" man and brings him into contact with the totality of the universe. Poetic combustion, not philosophy, enlightens man.

Historically, the two main figurative meanings of fire have been passion and inspiration, and both are suggested in *La Bibliothèque est en feu*. For Char, passion refers to a strong amorous feeling, and it is usually associated with the desire for sexual union. Participation in the sexual act is a means for unity through fulfillment in the present and for continuity through projection into the future:

> ...le courant de notre existence est peu saisissable ...mais le facile mouvement des bras et des jambes qui nous ferait aller là où nous serions heureux d'aller ...à la rencontre d'amours dont les différences nous enrichiraient, ce mouvement demeure inaccompli... Désir, désir qui sait, nous ne tirons avantage de nos ténèbres qu'à partir de quelques souverainetés véritables assorties d'invisibles chaînes, qui, se révélant, pas après pas, nous font briller.[27]

The role of desire (passion) is necessary on an individual level for self-knowledge and on a general level for fraternal exchange. Desire is "une vérité amoureuse." Fire as desire refers to the poet and all men; the "nous" of *La Bibliothèque est en feu* is all-inclusive and fraternal.

On the other hand, fire as inspiration refers to the poet as the sole representative of mankind, expressed by third person singular

---

[27] "La Bibliothèque est en feu," *La Bibliothèque est en feu et autres poèmes* in *La Parole en archipel* (Paris, 1961). All the quotations are from the 1961 edition.

nouns and pronouns and by an equally impersonal first person singular "je". Inspiration is important, for the poet remains "matinal"; he is not the creator of that which could be, but the discoverer of what is:

> Celui qui invente, au contraire de celui qui découvre, n'ajoute aux choses, n'apporte aux êtres que des masques...

In order to have meaning, the poet's discovery must occur in this world: "sous les arbres reparle la fontaine." His discoveries enrich those whom he represents, while their communication frees him to continue risking his being in creative activity:

> Le poète ne retient pas ce qu'il découvre; l'ayant transcrit, le perd bientôt. En cela, réside sa nouveauté, son infini et son péril.

Although the poet is "la graine qui va tant risquer," he is able to conquer death through his creative activity. In fact, *La Bibliothèque est en feu* contains Char's most explicit affirmation of immortality through Poetry; this is reinforced by two of the three aphorisms added to this work in 1957: [28]

> L'éclair me dure.

> La poésie me volera ma mort.

The third addition to the work is: "On naît avec les hommes, on meurt inconsolé parmi les dieux." It refers to the poet's "métier de pointe"; his task is never comfortable; it does not bring relief. It troubles his existence, for he is born or gains meaning only through communication; without contact with others, he dies. Hence, the poet's most difficult task is not discovery, but communication. It is fire as inspiration for others. The poet must concentrate on written expression:

> Dans le poème, chaque mot ou presque doit être employé dans son sens originel.

---

[28] There are no important textual revisions or deletions between the 1956 edition and its subsequent publications in 1957, 1961, and 1964, other than these three additions.

Otherwise, his discovery of unity, "frais soleil," is not accessible to others. "La bibliothèque est en feu" is the poet's contribution to the human fraternity.

The presence of fire means the absence of that cold which numbs feeling and response. Fire as warmth suggests animation, enthusiastic interest, kindly attachment to others, and strong intimacy. Fire destroys the isolation of coldness; it generates outwardly towards others. Fire is fraternal; this feeling of kinship is the main theme of *Les Compagnons dans le jardin*, the second section of *La Bibliothèque est en feu et autres poèmes*.

The organization of the four parts of *Les Compagnons dans le jardin* reflects Char's pattern of publication which emerges during this fifth period of development. Before 1952, Char published separate small volumes of poems which he subsequently combined to form collective editions. The best examples of this organizational method are *Le Marteau sans maître* (1934) and *Fureur et mystère* (1948). This pattern of combining previously published sections to form a collective edition characterizes Char's publications in general. In 1952, this pattern changes in that it is particularized even further. Instead of publishing individual volumes, Char begins to publish individual poems as "plaquettes" and "minuscules."[29] Most of these special editions are accompanied by drawings or photographs. In fact, it is reasonable to assume that one of Char's main purposes in publishing "minuscules" is based on his interest in the plastic arts,[30] for he has even illustrated seven of his works.[31] It is interesting to note that 35 "minuscules" appeared between 1952 and 1961;[32] this observation indicates that this pattern of "pla-

---

[29] Most of Char's "plaquettes" and "minuscules" are published by his close friend, P. A. Benoît, and these special editions go to a very limited group of collectors. Nevertheless, the appearance of these "plaquettes" and "minuscules" after 1952 is of interest to the literary critic because these special editions reflect Char's interest in the plastic arts as well as his flexible pattern of organization.

[30] Only 11 of a total of 45 "minuscules" are not supplemented by artists' designs.

[31] The works which Char has illustrated are: *En trente-trois morceaux* (1956), *Le Pas de René Crevel* (1956), *L'Une et l'autre* (1957), *Elisabeth petite fille* (1958), *Traverse* (1958), *La Faux relevée* (1959), *Eros suspendu* (1960), and *L'Issue* (1961).

[32] The only two "minuscules" which predate Char's fifth period of development are *Amitié cachetée* (1951) and *La Lettre I du dictionnaire* (1951).

quettes" and "minuscules" is a major characteristic of his fifth stage of development.

Furthermore, these "minuscules" reveal Char's pattern of poetic unity. While each small edition has meaning in and of itself, its full significance does not emerge until it is placed within the superstructure of the whole body of Char's work. In other words, each "minuscule" is a fragment. Fusion of the fragments into a larger framework shows that Char's organizational pattern parallels his poetic vision of unity. This is accurately demonstrated by the arrangement of *Les Compagnons dans le jardin,* for seven of its 14 poems appeared first as "minuscules."

The first part of *Les Compagnons dans le jardin* is a collection of 32 aphorisms entitled "Les Compagnons dans le jardin." [33] It was written and published in 1957. The title of this group of aphorisms recalls an earlier poem, "Tous compagnons du lit" (*Dehors la nuit est gouvernée,* 1938), in which Char first proposed to establish the human fraternity on the basis of a common experience. The bed of the 1938 poem is replaced in 1957 by "le jardin," a broader term. The garden represents the physical world in which the human community acts. Moreover, this world is fertile, that is, it can be improved and developed through labor and attention, the poet's method.

Man resembles a flower which must be cultivated in order to develop its possibilities and flourish. The poet is man's prime gardener: "A une rose je me lie"; his act of cultivation occurs in the present, but it is not restricted to the present. That which is under cultivation is always in a state of growth, of coming into being. Man is projected into the future because he is in this state of activity, of growth, of becoming.

Man's highest act of living is an act of poetry; hence, all men must continually act creatively as does the poet, and in turn each individual must be a cultivator of his fellowmen. He is "rose," the one who is developed, and he is "éclair," a flash of energy and resplendency whose duration is momentary but whose mark remains to help others grow:

---

[33] In order to distinguish between the title of the group of aphorisms and that of the second section of *La Bibliothèque est en feu et autres poèmes,* I have used quotation marks to refer to the first and italicized the title of the latter.

Un poète doit laisser des traces de son passage, non des preuves. Seules les traces font rêver.

A poet is a man who acts creatively and acquires a measure of artistic immortality through his creative acts, his poems:

Ce qui me console, lorsque je serai mort, c'est que je serai là ...pour me voir poème.

As the garden of men cultivated by reciprocal acts of Poetry increases in its growth, it becomes stronger and more unified: "Dans nos jardins se préparent des forêts." A forest is more extensive than a garden; it rises higher above the ground, and it usually preserves some of its primordial character (*Les Matinaux*). It is thicker and more permanent than a garden. The future of man depends on man; the poet has shown him the way to live and act "dans le jardin." Now, all men must join in responsible creative activity in the present to guarantee the solidarity of mankind in the future: "O survie encore, toujours meilleure!" A better future depends on a creative present.

Bonne grâce d'un temps d'avril forms the second part of *Les Compagnons dans le jardin*, and each of the four poems of this group has appeared as a "minuscule." The first poem, "A une enfant," was published in 1955; in the 1961 edition of *La Bibliothèque est en feu et autres poèmes* (published in *La Parole en archipel*), this text becomes the second part of a double poem entitled "A deux enfants"; the first part of this 1961 text is actually "Elisabeth petite fille," published as a "plaquette" in 1958. Both parts of "A deux enfants" praise the maturation process of woman whose role is love and union, a theme continued in "La Passante de Sceaux," which was originally published in 1955 as "Bonne grâce d'un temps d'avril." Woman's functions, summarized in "Epitaphe" (1954), is "un travail d'amour." It is her task to oppose man, "L'Arbre frappé." This last text was published separately in 1961, but it was added to this group of poems in the 1957 edition of *Poèmes et prose choisis*; this indicates that "L'Arbre frappé" was probably written in 1957 immediately after the publication of the 1957 edition of *La Bibliothèque est en feu et autres poèmes*.

As *Bonne grâce d'un temps d'avril* stresses the growth process of woman, her "becomingness" to help man attain fulfillment,

Neuf merci, the third part of *Les Compagnons dans le jardin*, emphasizes man. Only two texts of *Neuf merci* appeared as "minuscules": "Berceuse pour chaque jour jusqu'au dernier" (1956) and "La Fauvette des roseaux" (1955). The poems of *Neuf merci* praise terrestrial man's mystery of being. Because he has many occasions to live but only one to die ("Berceuse pour chaque jour jusqu'au dernier"), these texts concentrate on man's acts of living which necessitate risk. He must be threatened ("Aux miens") to be free to act ("La Fauvette des roseaux"); union with woman ("Artine dans l'écho") gives him this freedom by fusing his earthly limited nature ("Les Palais et les maisons") into the a-temporal and a-spatial cosmos ("Dans l'espace"). *Neuf merci* praises human mortality, freedom, solitude, suffering, and the couple because they enable man to act and become noble through his acts.

The organization of the texts of *Bonne grâce d'un temps d'avril* may be contrasted with that of *Neuf merci*. The first group is arranged according to the chronology of the theme; the four poems trace the growth process of woman from birth and childhood to full maturity. On the contrary, the texts of *Neuf merci* follow no thematic pattern of organization. Each of the nine texts of *Neuf merci* appears as a fragment of man's reality, and the figure of man provides unity between the poems. This arrangement reveals Char's flexible pattern of organization, for it is possible to read *Neuf merci* in reverse order (from "Les Fauvettes des roseaux" to "Les Palais et les maisons") and grasp the underlying unity. For Char, it is more important to give the reader an impression of order than to impose on him a formal arrangement of the parts. The impression of order necessitates the reader's participation in the realization of cosmic unity; it makes Char's concept of the oneness of the universe more accessible and more authentic than a declaration of order and unity might attain.

Another example of Char's flexibility is found in the location of the text "Débris mortels et Mozart." In the 1957 edition of *La Bibliothèque est en feu et autres poèmes*, this prose poem formed the last part of *Les Compagnons dans le jardin*, but in the 1961 publication, it appears as the first poem of *Autres poèmes*. In 1957, "Débris mortels et Mozart" summarized *Bonne grâce d'un temps d'avril* and *Neuf merci* and linked them to "Les Compagnons dans le jardin," that is the companions consist of men and women. By moving the text to *Autres poèmes*, Char shows that it actually links the section of *Les Compagnons dans le jardin* to *La Bibliothèque est en feu* and announces the texts of *Autres poèmes*, the third section.

"Débris mortels et Mozart" expresses the totality and immortality attainable through creative activity; Mozart's creative acts endure beyond his death: "le Temps n'a pas d'endroit." Individual men and women, "débris mortels," may go "à travers Mozart" and end their fragmented mortality through union, the human act of Poetry: "tendre vainqueur de nos frayeurs conjuguées."

Affirmation of the possibility of a-spatial and a-temporal totality for all men in "Débris mortels et Mozart" underlies the other three texts of *Autres poèmes*. These texts were originally published as "minuscules" and seem to predate "Débris mortels et Mozart," as seen in this line from "Débris mortels et Mozart" which summarizes the theme of the passage of time of the other three texts:

> Sur la longueur de ses deux lèvres, en terre commune ...vers la totalité des hommes et femmes en deuil de patrie intérieure...

"Débris mortels et Mozart" presents the immortality known by the poet, while the other three texts present the human view of mortality.

The most interesting of these three texts is "Le Deuil des Névons" (1954). Its title recalls an earlier poem, "Jouvence des Névons" (*La Sieste blanche* in *Les Matinaux*, 1950); in fact, the line "Dans le parc des Névons" appears in both texts. Additional similarity between the two is found in their evocation of the past in general and of Char's historical past in particular. Névons is the name of Char's childhood home in Isle-sur-Sorgue, and, as the child of the 1950 text refers to him and his personal relationship with nature in the past, the 1954 text emphasizes this relationship in Char's present. The most autobiographical line in all of Char's poetry is found in "Le Deuil des Névons":

> Que d'années à grandir,
> Sans père pour mon bras!

This line is a direct reference to Char's fatherless childhood, for his father died in 1918. Moreover, this text was written shortly after his mother's death, which occurred in 1952.

In "Le Deuil des Névons," Char compares autumn and the approach of winter to man's life cycle; spring and summer are identified with childhood and youth. However, this is not a melancholy text despite the predominance of past tenses. On the contrary, it is an affirmation of the present and of the need to act in the present in order to insure the future of human existence:

> ...Il faut renoncer
> A ce qu'on ne peut retenir,
> Qui devient autre chose
> Contre ou avec le coeur,
> L'oublier rondement,
>
> Puis battre les buissons
> Pour chercher sans trouver
> Ce qui doit nous guérir.

The present is all that man has. He must refute the past and confront the present; he must act.

The last section of *La Bibliothèque est en feu et autres poèmes* is *Sur une nuit sans ornement*,[34] a group of 14 aphorisms which summarizes the importance of the poetic method to justify man's daily existence. This work also realizes the cosmic harmony first proposed in *Dehors la nuit est gouvernée* (1938).

The title of *Sur une nuit sans ornement* contains a cosmic metaphor, "nuit," to describe the physical world of man. It is usually at night that the poet as well as all men are revitalized for the risk and struggle of everyday life:

> La nuit porte nourriture, le soleil affine la partie nourrie.

Night has no measurable limits; it is an a-spatial phenomenon familiar to all. It diminishes the distance between earth and sky by eliminating the horizon which separates the world of nature and man from the rest of the universe. Only at night may one experience "une terre céleste," a feeling of absolute totality:

---

[34] In 1961, this text appears as the last one in *Autres poèmes*, not as a separate section. However, this change is minor, for *Sur une nuit sans ornement* still retains its final position in *La Bibliothèque est en feu et autres poèmes*.

> Dans la nuit, le poète, le drame et la nature ne font qu'un, mais en montée et s'aspirant.

Although night seems to have a temporal dimension as the time of darkness between sunset and sunrise, it is a constant temporal phenomenon. Night is always present at some point on the globe. It never ends; it is universal in its duration: "La nuit ne succède qu'à elle."

The a-temporality and a-spatiality of night represents, for Char, the continuity of human existence. There are no limits to man's acts; there are only the possibilities of his actions:

> La nuit déniaise notre passé d'homme, incline sa psyché devant le présent, met de l'indécision dans notre avenir.

Night is neither obscurity nor misfortune. On the contrary, it is the guarantee of man's oneness and harmony of being with the universe. Moreover, this guarantee is "sans ornement," without illusions as to human fragility and vulnerability:

> La reconduction de notre mystère, c'est la nuit qui en prend soin; la toilette des élus, c'est la nuit qui l'exécute.

Sur une nuit sans ornement affirms man and the act of Poetry, set forth in *La Bibliothèque est en feu* and "Les Compagnons dans le jardin." It is a call to the present and future of man through love:

> Dans la nuit se tiennent nos apprentissages en état de servir à d'autres, après nous. Fertile est la fraîcheur de cette gardienne!

La Bibliothèque est en feu et autres poèmes emphasizes the moral relationship that Char finds between life and poetry. Poetry is man's only guide for action to justify the present and assure him of a better future. The poet's duty is moral in that he alone is responsible for the communication of his discoveries of unity and continuity to help man realize his possibilities and become confident to act. Through the concurrence of an act of living and an act of Poetry, man accomplishes himself.

Char's concern for the moral necessity of Poetry to affirm man's dignity of being is reflected in his arrangement of the anthology *Poèmes et prose choisis* (1957). This work is divided into two parts; the first part consists of poems in verse and prose published between 1937 and 1957; [35] the second part includes aphorisms from 1936 to 1957 [36] as well as two prose texts from *Recherche de la base et du sommet suivi de Pauvreté et privilège* (1955). The poems represent the results of the poet's discoveries; they are the poet's creative acts. The aphorisms, on the other hand, represent the poet's method; they form a guide for others to act creatively and experience the poet's discoveries. The two parts of *Poèmes et prose choisis* are connected by Char's faith and confidence in Poetry, the main theme of *La Parole en archipel*.

La Parole en archipel (1961) consists of six sections: 1) the second version of *Lettera amorosa*; 2) *La Paroi et la prairie*; 3) *Poèmes des deux années*; 4) *La Bibliothèque est en feu et autres poèmes*; 5) *Au-Dessus du vent*, and 6) *Quitter*. This work includes all of Char's major poetry published during his fifth stage of development. Through the arrangement of the six sections and the choice of title, Char shows why Poetry is a moral necessity for man and how Poetry replaces philosophy.

It is significant that the first part of *La Parole en archipel* is *Lettera amorosa*, Char's first work of synthesis of life and poetry, the major concern and accomplishment of his fifth stage of development. In a strict sense, the texts of *La Paroi et la prairie* belong to his fourth stage because they were composed between 1948 and 1951. However, this work was first published in 1952, at the beginning of his fifth period. By including it in *La Parole en archipel*, Char recalls *Les Matinaux* and his discovery of harmony between man and nature, a discovery essential to his revelation of

---

[35] The poems are selected from the following works: *Placard pour un chemin des écoliers* (1937), *Dehors la nuit est gouvernée* (1938), *Fureur et mystère* (1948), *Les Matinaux* (1950), *La Paroi et la prairie* (1952), *Poèmes des deux années* (1955), and *La Bibliothèque est en feu et autres poèmes* (1957).

[36] The aphorisms are chosen from the following groups: *Moulin premier* (1936), *Partage formel* (*Seuls demeurent*, 1945), *Rougeur des Matinaux* (*Les Matinaux*, 1950), *A une sérénité crispée* (1951), *Le Rempart de brindilles* (1953), *La Bibliothèque est en feu* (1956), *Les Compagnons dans le jardin* (1957), and *Sur une nuit sans ornement* (*La Bibliothèque est en feu et autres poèmes*, 1957).

the fusion attained in *Lettera amorosa*. *Poème des deux années* also joins previous works to *Lettera amorosa* and initiates the expansion of that work to include the community of men at large. By placing *Poèmes des deux années* after *La Paroi et la prairie*, Char insures the continuity and unity of his poetic proof of totality. *La Bibliothèque est en feu et autres poèmes* is based on the experiences of sexual and fraternal love, of fusion of man and the universe; this work concentrates on the poet's duty to guide man to live creatively. The first four sections of *La Parole en archipel* prepare the presentation of the necessity of Poetry for a better present and future, which is expressed in the last two parts.

Au-Dessus du vent consists of 18 texts written between 1958 and 1960. The first three poems were originally written and published in 1958 in *Cinq poésies en hommage à Georges Braque*, and eight of the remaining 15 texts appeared as "minuscules." [37] The title of *Au-Dessus du vent* suggests that there is totality and immortality beyond destruction and fragmentation.

The poet in *Au-Dessus du vent* is no longer a participant in the struggle of everyday life, but an observer of man and the universe. He acts only to guide man, to reveal to man the possibility of experiencing totality. Moreover, the poet's communications are creative acts beyond death:

> Alors la mort, en dessous, n'aura capté que ton écho. La parole bouclée se confond toujours avec la vapeur exhalée par nos bouches. [38]

In other words, the role of the poet has replaced that of the philosopher. It is the poet who understands the truth which underlies all knowledge and being:

> La réalité sans l'énergie disloquante de la poésie, qu'est-ce? [39]

---

[37] *L'Issue* (1960), *Le Pas ouvert de René Crevel* (1956), *L'Escalier de Flore* (1958), *Traverse* (1958), *De 1943* (1961), *La Faux relevée* (1959), *Eros suspendu* (1960), and *La Montée de la nuit* (1961).
[38] "Le Pas ouvert de René Crevel," *Au-Dessus du vent* in *La Parole en archipel* (Paris, 1961).
[39] "Pour un Prométhée saxifrage."

The poet shows man how to confront contradiction and injustice: "Je cours le malheur des humains, le dépulpe de son loisir." [40] He shows man the value of revolt against the forces of destruction and fragmentation: "Pleine sera la vigne/Où combat ton épaule." [41] Through the coincidence of an act of living and an act of poetry, that is by following the poet's method of creative activity, man is able to bring into being a better present and realize his possibilities of nobility:

> La méchanceté dort. Il est tel qu'il se rêvait. [42]

Because man's first experience of totality occurs in union with woman, the important role of woman is reemphasized in *Au-Dessus du vent*. Woman projects man into the future, assures him of his continuity of being:

> Eve solaire, possible de chair et de poussière, je ne crois pas au dévoilement des astres, mais au tien seul. [43]

The future of man seems to receive more attention in *Au-Dessus du vent* than in any other group of Char's texts. However, this does not mean that either man's present or past is neglected in favor of his future. On the contrary, the present is the predominant tense; the present remains as man's only time in which to act and as the poet's major concern in his role as man's moral guide. Even the past is treated respectfully, perhaps more respectfully in this section than in Char's previous works. In *Au-Dessus du vent*, Char maintains his earlier denial of History, but he never rejects man's heritage, expressed in *Les Matinaux* (1950) and *La Paroi et la prairie* (1952). It is the knowledge of universal experience based on union in the past which strengthens man and makes him able to confront the present:

> Je te vis, la première et la seule, divine femelle dans les sphères bouleversées. [44]

---

[40] "L'Oiseau spirituel."
[41] "L'Issue."
[42] "Traverse."
[43] "L'Avenir non prédit."
[44] "Eros suspendu."

Char rejects historical determinism, but not man's historical existence. In "Déclarer son nom," he acknowledges that each man's childhood and youth influence his maturity, his present:

> J'avais dix ans. La Sorgue m'enchâssait... Mais quelle roue dans le coeur d'enfant aux aguets tournait plus fort, tournait plus vite que celle du moulin dans son incendie blanc?

Man has only the present in which to live and act, in which to become; he is "entre le vieil absent et le nouveau venu." [45] The exact character of this future is unknown, "l'avenir non prédit," but it does exist:

> Noble semence, guerre et faveur de mon prochain, devant la sourde aurore je te garde avec mon guignon, attendant ce jour prévu de haute pluie, de limon vert, qui viendra pour les brûlants, et pour les obstinés. [46]

Confidence in Poetry to help man makes the future possible, even accessible.

The optimism of *Au-Dessus du vent* is expressed not only through emphasis on the continuity of man (his past, present, and future), but also through a reaffirmation of the immortality attainable through creative activity:

> Quand le bouvier des morts frappera du bâton,
> Dédiez à l'été ma couleur dispersée.
> Avec mes poings trop bleus étonnez un enfant.
> Disposez sur ses joues ma lampe et mes épis. [47]

It is significant to note the importance that Char places on the need to expose youth to the poet's enlightened discovery of totality, "lampe," and its communication in his poems, "épis." It is procreation through the creative activity of Poetry which affirms man's present and future. Poetic knowledge of unity and continuity is to be procreated from generation to generation:

---

[45] "La Faux relevée."
[46] "Pour un Prométhée saxifrage."
[47] "La Faux relevée."

La fleur que je réchauffe, je double ses pétales, j'assombris sa corolle. [48]

The establishment of a better world in which all men may act in the knowledge that the universe is "toute liée" [49] depends upon the poet's optimistic communication that creative activity is man's only means to become in the present and be projected into the future. The poet reveals the universal truth of existence: "Ces légers mots immortels jamais endeuillés." [50]

The optimism of *Au-Dessus du vent* is continued in *Quitter*, the last part of *La Parole en archipel*. This section of seven poems and one group of aphorisms ("Les Dentelles de Montmirail") affirms man through Poetry. In *Quitter*, Char fuses all elements and individuals into the a-spatial and a-temporal universe of Poetry. As the title of *Au-Dessus du vent* suggests totality beyond fragmentation, the title of *Quitter* is a call, almost a command, to man to participate in this unity through poetic activity and to abandon his feeling of alienation and vulnerability. *Quitter* contains Char's most positive and most explicit presentation of the role of Poetry as man's only justification for being, his only means for self-realization and self-affirmation.

According to Pierre Guerre,[51] *Quitter* was written between 1959 and 1960. However, these dates do not apply to the first text, "Nous avons," which was originally published in 1958. The remaining seven texts were most likely composed between 1959 and 1960 although only one is dated by Char ("Aux Riverains de la Sorgue," 1959) while "L'Eternité à Lourmarin" "could not have been written before January 1960 because it treats Camus's death.

Char is supremely confident in man and the realization of his possibilities through Poetry, but his optimism is tempered by an acute awareness of the baser side of human nature: "Nous restons gens d'inclémence." [52] As there have always been "époques de détresse," [53] there will always be struggle to confront not only the forces which daily threaten man's existence, but also man's inner

---

[48] "La Montée de la nuit."
[49] "Nous tombons."
[50] *Ibid.*
[51] Pierre Guerre, *René Char* (Paris, 1961), p. 157.
[52] "Contrevenir," *Quitter* in *La Parole en archipel* (Paris, 1961).
[53] "Les Dentelles de Montmirail."

weaknesses: "Comment rejeter dans les ténèbres notre coeur antérieur et son droit de retour?"[54] Char never prophesizes the creation of a paradise, for the risk of the struggle is essential to the attainment of human dignity: "Les pluies sauvages favorisent les passants profonds."[55] However, the baser side of man is opposed by "un mystère plus fort,"[56] man's historically stubborn refusal to succumb to suffering and disaster:

> Tyrannies sans delta, que midi jamais n'illumine, pour vous nous sommes le jour vieilli; mais vous ignorez que nous sommes aussi l'oeil vorace, bien que voilé, de l'origine.[57]

Man's "fureur et mystère" have enabled him to survive.

Poetry can help man go beyond mere survival through the development of the possibilities of man's "mystère" and lead him to the experience of fulfillment. In Poetry, all contradictions and fragmentation cease:

> Le temps de la famine et celui de la moisson, l'un sous l'autre ...ont effacé leur différence. Ils filent ensemble, ils bivaguent![58]

Man can participate in the totality offered by Poetry by performing an act of Poetry, the only act which fuses opposites into one entity:

> La poésie à la fois parole et provocation silencieuse, désespérée de notre être-exigeant pour la venue d'une réalité qui sera sans concurrente. Imputrescible celle-là. Impérissable, non; car elle court les dangers de tous. Mais la seule qui visiblement triomphe de la mort matérielle. Telle est la Beauté...[59]

Poetry conquers death, man's most unrelenting enemy: "Nous n'avons qu'une ressource avec la mort: faire de l'art avant elle."[60]

---

[54] "Nous avons."
[55] "Les Dentelles de Montmirail."
[56] "Nous avons."
[57] Ibid.
[58] "L'Allégresse."
[59] "Dans la marche."
[60] "Les Dentelles de Montmirail."

"Faire," in its infinitive form, is the main verb in *Quitter*. "Faire" is a verb of action, of doing, not of being, and it is frequently used in a creative context. Its usage in the infinitive form is important; it implies an injunction or command to someone to do something now, immediately. In addition, the infinitive has not only the force of an imperative, but it also excludes fixed time divisions. The infinitive represents the all-inclusive present which dominates Char's poetry. "Faire" is synonymous with to act. In order to become, man must "faire de l'art," [61] "faire un poème," [62] act poetically.

In "Nous avons," Char explains how to use Poetry effectively, how to act creatively:

> Faire un poème, c'est prendre possession d'un au-delà nuptial qui se trouve bien dans cette vie, très-rattaché à elle, et cependant à proximité des urnes de la mort.

Man must neither reject nor attempt to transcend this world: rather, he must participate in the concrete world of everyday existence, "cette vie." He has only to act creatively, "faire un poème," in order to realize himself and his ideals.

Furthermore, man's action must be creative fraternally in order to be just:

> Il faut s'établir à l'extérieur de soi ...si nous voulons que quelque chose hors du commun se produise... [63]

Man's failure not to go beyond mere survival in the past was caused by his lack of responsible creative activity. The poet is not only responsible for guiding the community of men, but each member of that community is also responsible to it.

Fraternal love, expressed by the predominant usage of "nous" throughout *Quitter*, is inseparable from the authentic act of Poetry, which leads to the establishment of a better present and future:

> La quête d'un frère signifie presque toujours la recherche d'un être, notre égal, à qui nous désirons offrir des trans-

---

[61] "Les Dentelles de Montmirail."
[62] "Nous avons."
[63] *Ibid.*

cendences dont nous finissons à peine de dégauchir les signes. [64]

Fraternal love and fraternal creative action are necessary to end human injustice and alleviate much human suffering.

In *Quitter*, it is significant to note that Char mentions neither sexual love nor union with woman. Moreover, the poet's constant companion, "tu," does not appear at all. *Quitter* is the only group of texts in which Char omits all references to woman and to "tu." While woman plays an essential role in Char's poetics, she is only the first means for the attainment of his ultimate vision: communication of the fusion of life and Poetry. Fraternal love is more important than sexual love. The absence of "tu" emphasizes the change in the poet's role from participant to that of witness and guide which emerges throughout *La Parole en archipel*, specifically in *Au-Dessus du vent*.

The omission of "tu" and the role of woman in *Quitter* reveals the architectural character of Char's poetics of fusion. It begins with the role of union with woman and its value to individual man in *Lettera amorosa*. This role is expanded to its fraternal possibilities in the next four sections until the end in *Quitter* where the role of fraternal love emerges as the actual goal of Char's emphasis on union and exchange.

Through fraternal creative activity, "le Chant reprendrait." [65] Because man has the possibility to "faire un poème," he has the possibility of living in happiness. The celestial becomes terrestrial, the ideal is concrete, and the future belongs to the present: "nous sommes irrésistiblement jetés en avant." [66] The impossible becomes possible through "Poésie, unique montée des hommes." [67]

La Parole en archipel represents Char's successful fusion of life and Poetry on individual and fraternal levels. The archipelago of the title refers to the discontinuity and flux which characterize man's world. But, beneath the fragmented surface lies a solid mass, a unified structure. "La Parole" communicates this hidden continuity, unity, and totality of being. It appears "en archipel" because

---

[64] "Les Dentelles de Montmirail."
[65] "Nous avons."
[66] "Dans la marche."
[67] "Nous avons."

it mirrors reality. Each poem, "parole," acts upon the fragments in order to reveal that each fragment is a part of the total structure, the archipelago or principal sea [68] of the universe. The poem is an active agent of discovery and communication. The poet, and therefore man, must do, "faire." Man must reject (*Quitter*) notions of isolation and fragmentation and ascend (*Au-Dessus du vent*) to the totality to which he belongs. He is not alone; his union with woman (*Lettera amorosa*) makes possible fraternal exchange (*Les Compagnons dans le jardin*) and participation in the oneness of the cosmos. The poet's duty is to reveal this oneness and rouse man to respond to it (*La Bibliothèque est en feu*). He must present to man the moral necessity of Poetry, for only Poetry justifies man's existence in the present, leads him to the experience of cosmic harmony and unity, and guarantees his future. This is the theme of *La Parole en archipel* and, indeed, of all of Char's poetry.

---

[68] Georges Blin, "L'Instant multiple dans la poésie de René Char," *L'Arc* (été 1963), p. 20.

CHAPTER VI

CONCLUSION: 1962-1966: A POETICS OF RENEWAL

René Char's poetics and poetry form an integral whole which reflects the development of his discovery of the cosmic totality which characterizes all existence. His work from *Les Cloches sur le coeur* to *La Parole en archipel* elucidates this fusion of opposites through the examination of man, nature, and the role of the poet. In his examination of each subject, Char finds that Poetry contains the solution, that is, Poetry overcomes contradiction and fragmentation. Poetry is the common fact of truth and being; it is the principle of unity, the "commune présence" in which each element and each individual participate.

Char's sixth stage of development dates from 1962 to 1966 and includes only three works: *Commune présence* (1964), *L'Age cassant* (1966), and *Retour amont* (1966). In these three volumes, Char undertakes a profound investigation of his poetics and poetry from 1923 to 1966. His painstaking and rigorous review of his aesthetic journey through life leads him to a renewal of confidence in his discovery that Poetry is the macrocosm of all existence. Char finds that his efforts to reveal this singular truth are attained in his own creative acts. His vision of the fusion of life and poetry is represented by his own being.[1] In the study and evolution of René Char, the man and poet, René Char concludes that his course

---

[1] Further evidence that this sixth period is one of review and self-examination is found in Char's decision to reassess, revise where necessary, and republish his previous major collections: *Fureur et mystère* (1962), *Le Marteau sans maître* suivi de *Moulin premier* (1964), *Les Matinaux* (1964), and *Recherche de la base et du sommet* (1965).

justifies his own existence and that this course is the only one by which each individual may assert his dignity of being.

Commune présence

Commune présence (1964) is the most comprehensive presentation of Char's poetics and poetry. This work consists of texts selected from all his collective editions, from *Le Marteau sans maître* (1934)[2] to *La Parole en archipel* (1961), and it includes 12 texts[3] from *Retour amont*.[4] The significance of *Commune présence* lies in the organization of the texts into eight sections.

Before *Commune présence*, Char's collective editions were organized according to a pragmatic method which is a common practice among poets. As soon as several small volumes of texts were published, he placed them in a larger and more accessible edition in the order of their publication although the order of the texts within any group was not strictly chronological. The title of each small volume became the section title for each group within the larger edition. This method of organization characterizes *Le Marteau sans maître* (1934), *Fureur et mystère* (1948), and *La Parole en archipel* (1961). *Poèmes et prose choisis* (1957), Char's major anthology prior to *Commune présence*, represents the first change in this organizational pattern because the poems are separated from the aphorisms. However, this departure from Char's usual method is not radical, for the texts are still arranged in order of publication. In *Commune présence*, Char disregards this organizational approach.

Each section of *Commune présence* is composed of texts selected from previous collective editions, rather than from small volumes,[5] and each text is placed according to the relation of its theme to the section title. All indications of the date of com-

---

[2] *Commune présence* contains texts from *Le Marteau sans maître*, a work not included in any of Char's anthologies, particularly *Poèmes et prose choisis* (1957), before 1964.

[3] A thirteenth poem, "Effacement du peuplier," was published in *L'Arc* (été 1963), p. 48.

[4] *Commune présence* also contains one text, "Avec Braque, peut-être, on s'était dit...," which was not previously published; this text is included, however, in the section on Georges Braque in *Alliés substantiels* in *Recherche de la base et du sommet*, 1965.

[5] The exception is *Retour amont*.

CONCLUSION: 1962-1966: A POETICS OF RENEWAL 197

position and that of publication are obscured. *Commune présence* is not a collective work in the usual sense; it does not merely assemble a number of small volumes. *Commune présence* is a mosaic composition of diverse pieces which are combined for the formation of an integrated whole. Earlier collective works are disarranged; texts are displaced from their established position and rearranged in a new pattern. Char "pulverises" his original structures and forges a new order with the fragments. The configuration of *Commune présence* parallels Char's theory of constructive destruction. He risks the unity of his work in order to give concrete evidence of the unity of Poetry: "Essaime ta poussière / Nul ne décèlera votre union." [6]

Although the organizational structure of *Commune présence* is strictly non chronological, the arrangement of the eight sections follows an architectural order which seems chronological. These sections reflect and summarize the evolution of Char's poetry: 1) *Cette fumée qui nous portait*, 2) *Battre tout bas*, 3) *Haine du peu d'amour*, 4) *Lettera amorosa* (definitive text), 5) *L'Amitié se succède*, 6) *Les Frères de mémoire*, 7) *L'Ecarlate*, and 8) *Vallée close*.

Cette fumée qui nous portait begins with an evocation of Char's childhood and adolescence in Isle-sur-Sorgue and describes the poet's personal experiences of communion with nature. His early awareness of the possibility of reconciling man with his world leads him to the singular discovery that the human and the elemental participate in a "commune présence" of existence. His desire to communicate this vision of a harmonious universe appears early in his life. The event of war [7] precipitates him into participation with men of varying individual traits, yet men who are willing to risk their individuality in the struggle against an immediate danger. In the revolt of fraternal action, the poet discovers that each man has a mystery of being, "une fumée," which enables him to survive despite the constant threat of destruction. This inexplicable "fumée" causes man to act, and it justifies his existence. He becomes "l'homme debout."

---

[6] "Commune présence," *Cette fumée qui nous portait* in *Commune présence* (Paris, 1964).

[7] In *Cette fumée qui nous portait*, 15 of the 24 texts refer to World War II.

In *Battre tout bas*, the poet examines "l'homme debout" and finds that when man fails to risk his being he ceases to communicate with others; he returns to his illusion of isolation and estrangement. The poet must dispel this illusion, "battre tout bas," and show man the totality offered by poetic truth. The individual has an immediate means with which to end his isolation; through a sexual union with woman, he obtains the strength necessary to act, to accept the risk of exposure which characterizes "l'homme debout." Moreover, man's union with woman prepares him for an exchange of self-knowledge with others.

The theme of love is continued in *Haine du peu d'amour*. The cause of man's alienation from the world lies in his past failure to act creatively. The act of love is the human expression of the poetic act. The celebration of exchange in the present, the only time which exists for action, guarantees human continuity because the desire to reexperience the totality of union projects man into the future. The fusion of man and woman is no different from that of poet and the written word; the act of living is synthesized with the act of poetry in *Lettera amorosa*.

L'Amitié se succède brings together the first four sections by expanding the role of exchange. Union with woman leads to fraternal communion; it also enables man to understand the external world, nature. When man acts constructively toward nature, he finds that the role of exchange and its ensuing vision of totality are equally attainable in the world. Man and nature are mutually dependent for a meaningful existence; man needs nature in which to be threatened to act, and nature needs man to enrich its possibilities. Only creative activity can reconcile the individual with his world.

Creative activity is no longer restricted to the poet; it includes all men who fuse an act of living and an act of poetry. The poetization of man enables each individual to become one of *Les Frères de mémoire* and participate in artistic immortality. Any expression of art is an expression of Poetry:

> L'Art est une route qui finit en sentier, en tremplin, mais dans un champ à nous.[8]

---

[8] "Avec Braque, peut-être, on s'était dit...," *Les Frères de mémoire*.

In *Les Frères de mémoire*, Char pays hommage to those artists who have accepted the risk of creativity in order to guide man to an understanding of himself and an acceptance of his world. The efforts of these artists endure beyond death. In this section, Char includes not only well known figures (Corot, Courbet, Mozart, Giacometti, and Braque) but also the unknown caveman whose sketches on the walls of the Lascoux grotto defy time. Art, not history, expresses man's heritage of survival; the individual who acts creatively overcomes death, "se réfléchissant ...dans le miroir de notre regard, provisoire receveur universel pour les yeux futurs." [9]

Because Poetry, that is all forms of artistic expression and representation, offers a guide for man's conduct, the poet's method serves man. *L'Ecarlate* is a concise summary of the poet's role and responsibility. Although he is aware of the baser side of man, he also knows that man's inner resistance can be channeled into a constructive revolt against his condition. The poet's "épidémie de feu" [10] combines apparent contradictions within man and his world into one harmonious reality in which each individual has unlimited possibilities to act, to become, to live creatively, poetically. Poetry gives man self-confidence in his present and hope in his potential:

> Porteront rameaux ceux dont l'endurance sait user la nuit noueuse qui précède et suit l'éclair. Leur parole reçoit existence du fruit intermittant qui la propage en se délacérant. [11]

Poetry not only unifies the cosmos, but also constricts and humanizes it in order that each member of the human community may understand his part in the *Vallée close*, the oneness of all existence. Poetry demands the risk of activity; man and poet alike must maintain a constant state of response in order to assault the destructive forces and construct a better present:

> ...à la poursuite de la vie qui ne peut être encore imaginée, il y a des volontés qui frémissent, des murmures qui

---

[9] "Célébrer Giacometti."
[10] "La Récolte injuriée," *L'Ecarlate*.
[11] "Les Parages d'Alsace."

vont s'affronter et des enfants sains et saufs qui *découvrent.*[12]

There can be no respite from the risk of confrontation: "la poésie vit d'insomnie perpétuelle."[13] Man's essential dignity lies in his creative acts of living, which permit him to discover his integral place in the "vallée," the world. Furthermore, this "vallée" is "close" because "le poète est *combinable*";[14] he fuses absence and presence, the concrete and the abstract, the past and the future, that which is solid and that which is becoming, object and emotion, being and destruction. Without Poetry, man is isolated, and his existence is fragmented. Through Poetry, his dignity and justification for being are made manifest to him. Because he can fuse an act of living and an act of poetry, he realizes his own possibilities and participation in the unity of the cosmos. Man's reality and cosmic totality form one order of existence; "la poésie, c'est le monde à sa meilleure place."[15]

Commune présence demonstrates the unity and continuity of Poetry, the theme of the whole body of Char's work. Each text reveals one aspect of the oneness of Char's poetic universe. However, it is significant that Char's deliberate disregard for chronological organization in *Commune présence* results in a succinct presentation of the evolution of his poetics and poetry. Each of the eight sections of *Commune présence* evokes a given stage of thematic concern which characterizes Char's quest for the discovery and communication of poetic truth. Each section contains at least one text or phrase which refers to Char's historical existence.[16] Char's poetic evolution is one of resolution, which follows a deliberative course of development. One problem is overcome before another is undertaken, and each problem raised is one that has its foundation in Char's personal experience. The non-chronological structure of *Commune présence* is paradoxically chronological. Char has constructed an orderly and well-integrated

---

[12] "Jacquemard et Julia," *Vallée close.*
[13] "Les Dentelles de Montmirail."
[14] Pierre Berger, "Conversation avec René Char," *La Gazette des lettres* (11 juin 1952), p. 13.
[15] *Ibid.*, p. 9.
[16] The most frequent references are: Névons, Sorgue, Moulin du Calavon, Thor, Vosges, Alsace, and "partisan."

work in which dates of composition and publication are obscured only to affirm the successive stages of his own poetic development.

Char's Present Position

Char's subtle confirmation of the stages of development of his poetics and poetry in *Commune présence* provides the main theme of *L'Age cassant* (1966) and *Retour amont* (1966). These two volumes summarize Char's present position. He reviews in detail his aesthetic evolution, previously presented as a successive but integrally unified whole in *Commune présence*. In this self-examination, Char finds that he has reached a time of poetic maturity, "âge cassant." The very arrival at this positive time of life imposes upon him the personal demand and the artistic summons that he reaffirm the value of the poet's risk to discover and reveal the fusion of life and poetry. *L'Age cassant* contains Char's frank admission that a reassessment of his poetry justifies his right to continue his task. *Retour amont* presents his serious reflections on his own past efforts. This reexamination leads him to a renewal of confidence in his chosen vocation and its possibilities for all men and the immediate future.

A second major characteristic which shows the interrelationship between *L'Age cassant* and *Retour amont* and further identifies them with *Commune présence* is the use of "je." It becomes increasingly more difficult to distinguish between the "je" of Char the poet and the "je" of Char the man. In *L'Age cassant* and *Retour amont*, there seem to be examples which refer to incidents and impressions of a personal or historical nature and others of a more general aspect. Prior to 1962, that is prior to the first publication of texts from *Retour amont*, Char's use of "je" had evolved to the point where it included every man involved in creative activity. In *L'Age cassant* and *Retour amont*, Char goes beyond this fusion of man and poet; indeed, no fusion is necessary. Poet and man were never opposite elements or contradictory forces to be fused into a single entity. On the contrary, Char's retrospective self-study shows that the poet and the man are one and the same. Each experience and insight known by the man are essential to the poet, and each artistic effort and discovery is significant in the growth of the man and his response to his world:

"...j'entrai dans l'âge cassant." [17] It is Char who has attained this point in space and time; it is neither Char the man nor Char the poet; it is the harmony of these elements and experiences, personal and aesthetic, which identify René Char. Life and poetry are inseparable; if life determines poetry, Poetry determines life; it is this latter vision which Char emphasizes in these two volumes. If each man will look back upon his past, "retour amont," he will discover that the same "commune présence," the same harmony of life and poetry, reside within him. By describing the evolution of his "je," Char reveals the poet and the role of poetry in each individual.

A third significant trait which links *Commune présence* to *L'Age cassant* and *Retour amont* is found in the dates of composition and arrangement. Although *Commune présence* is an anthology which covers Char's creative development from 1934 to 1962, it also contains 12 of the 30 texts of *Retour amont*. This indicates that much of the composition of *Retour amont* coincided with the preparation of *Commune présence*. More importantly, it shows that Char had conceived of the need for such a retrospective and cogitative work before 1962, when two texts were published separately with the reference *Retour amont* inédit. It is probable that as soon as *La Parole en archipel* (specifically *Quitter* and *Au-Dessus du vent*) was completed Char began *Retour amont* as a concrete demonstration of his poetics of the totality of life. *L'Age cassant*, although most likely undertaken after the completion of *Commune présence*, was composed concurrently with *Retour amont*. In fact, *L'Age cassant* is the companion work to *Retour amont* and places the inner experience and reflections of *Retour amont* in their proper perspective.

L'Age cassant consists of 43 aphorisms which summarize Char's present aesthetic position. In this volume, he affirms the value of his poetry and his poetic direction. The tone of the work is one of authority and decisiveness; it is the voice of one who has made no concessions in his search to justify life and who has succeeded. The quest has been difficult, at times turbulent and seemingly without direction, but the end result is worthwhile.

In *L'Age cassant*, Char reiterates and reemphasizes previous themes. He warns against complacency: "Confort est crime"

---

[17] *L'Age cassant*, I (Paris, 1966).

(XIV). He praises the threat of destruction, the lack of security, and the necessity of crispation: "...nous apprenons à n'être jamais consolés" (V). The poet, that is the one who has accepted the writing of poetry as a means to guide man, must make man see that he must not be patronized: "L'histoire des hommes est la longue succession des synonymes d'un même vocable. Y contredire est un devoir" (XXII). Life must be continually assaulted and confronted:

> "Je me révolte, donc je me ramifie." Ainsi devraient parler les hommes au bûcher qui élève leur rébellion (XXXIV).

Man must be in a constant state of action: "Nul homme, à moins d'être un mort-vivant, ne peut se sentir à l'ancre en cette vie" (XXI); there is no excuse for inactivity. Moreover, man must not look to the future; he must concentrate on the present:

> Ce qui fut n'est plus. Ce qui n'est pas doit devenir. Du labyrinthe aux deux entrées jaillissent deux mains pleines d'ardeur. A défaut d'un esprit, qu'est-ce qui inspire la livide, l'atroce, ou la rougissante dispensatrice? (XXIII).

Acceptance of the risk of being in the knowledge of human fragility and mortality is essential in the construction of a better present.

In addition to a review of the main themes of his poetry, Char reviews his own course of development. He justifies his efforts to liberate poetry and man:

> Qui oserait dire que ce que nous avons détruit valait cent fois mieux que ce que nous avions rêvé et transfiguré sans relâche en murmurant aux ruines? (XX).

He evokes his childhood in Isle-sur-Sorgue: "L'aubépine en fleurs fut mon premier alphabet" (XIII). Nature and the important lessons she contains are stressed in several aphorisms, notably "Venasque."

L'Age cassant is Char's poetics of life. In his reaffirmation of the major tenets of the whole body of his work, he demonstrates the compatibility of his life and poetry. He has attained his "âge cassant" historically and aesthetically through a constant assault on life: "J'ai de naissance la respiration agressive" (VII). Others can attain this point of maturity and self-justification by accepting his lead:

> Se mettre en chemin sur ses deux pieds, et, jusqu'au soir, le presser, le reconnaître, le bien traiter ce chemin qui, en dépit de ses relais haineux, nous montre les fétus souhaits exaucés et la terre croisée des oiseaux (XLIII).

In *L'Age cassant*, Char presents a positive and forceful resumé of his poetics. The reason for his absolute confidence in his work is found in *Retour amont*. The title of this volume reflects the more important aspects of its 30 texts. In the first place, *Retour amont* means literally the action of returning upstream, that is of movement in the direction of the source. In the second place, it refers to an inner voyage of self-examination.

Char is going back to the original source of poetry, his own formation. He is strongly influenced by his native region of Provence and the specific references to this area are numerous: Luberon, Vaudois, Mérindol, Vaucluse, Thouzon. It was here that he first felt within him the stirrings of poetry and here that he first became aware of the vital lesson of homogeneity that nature holds: "Notre figure terrestre n'est que le second tiers d'une poursuite continue, un point, amont."[18]

The term "amont" is taken from the world of nature, a significant factor in all of Char's work. It is from nature that he has learned the constructive role of destruction. When the river Thouzon overflows, it damages the surrounding area; but, when its waters recede, the result is enrichment: "Dans le creux de la ville immergée, la corne de la lune mêlait le dernier sang et le premier limon."[19] From the fig tree described in "Devancier" comes the knowledge of nature's cyclical process: being-nothingness-being. Char poses the rhetorical question: "La terre est quelque chose ou quelqu'un?"[20] It is; it exists and daily surrounds man. It is composed of menacing elements and peaceful, beneficent ones; each serves the other. "Retour" means repetition and reciprocity; it refers directly to the process of recurrence in nature.

---

[18] "Lenteur de l'avenir," *Retour amont* (Paris, 1966).
[19] "Chérir Thouzon."
[20] "Pause au château cloaque."

Man is a part of this homogeneous framework and he must participate fully in this world: "Dans le ciel des hommes, le pain des étoiles me sembla ténébreux et durci, mais dans leurs mains étroites je lus la joute des étoiles; j'en recueillis la sueur dorée, et par moi la terre cessa de mourir."[21] This demand for struggle and action is also inherent in the title, for it is considered more difficult to go upstream than downstream, that is to go in the opposite direction, to contradict the usual course of movement. It is a risk to act in an opposing fashion, but the risk must be accepted as necessary for a meaningful existence: "Qui a creusé le puits et hisse l'eau gisante/Risque son coeur dans l'écart de ses mains."[22] This risk of action must occur in the present: "Lâcher un passé négligeable."[23] The present is man's only time of being for acting:

> Le passé retarderait l'éclosion du présent si nos souvenirs érodés n'y sommeillaient sans cesse. Nous nous retournons sur l'un tandis que l'autre marque un élan avant de se jeter sur nous.[24]

The use of the verb "retourner" indicates that the past has a contributive role. Study of past activity explains certain problems of the present; one of these problems is liberty. Char recalls his participation in "la drôle de guerre" in "Les Parages d'Alsace" and in the maquis in World War II in "Faction du muet." While there is no immediate and easily identifiable outside threat of destruction, man's tendency towards complacency can undo in the present the successful risks and acts of the past: "...le loriot.../Au lieu de faim, périt d'amour."[25] This symbol of peace and liberty must be vigilantly and actively maintained: "Le vin de la liberté aigrit s'il n'est, à demi bu, rejeté au cep."[26] Man's inactivity can return him to adversity. Moreover, the reason that the present is better than the past is found in the courageous acts of the past. If this present is to be better, man must act now: "Revers des

---

[21] "Lutteurs."
[22] "La Soif hospitalière."
[23] "Traversée."
[24] "Pause au château cloaque."
[25] "Lied du figuier."
[26] "Pause au château cloaque."

sources: pays d'amont, pays sans biens, hôte pelé, je roule ma chance vers vous." [27]

Char's going back in space and time in *Retour amont* is an additional example of his negation of temporality and spatiality. In his travel backwards, he is actually going forward; it is this very return to an examination of the past that renews his confidence in himself and in his work to challenge the future: "J'ai renversé le dernier mur..." [28] In his inner journey he finds that he carries within him the past, that he belongs to the present, but that he is also future; he is a "convergence des multiples" as is his poetry: "Des années de gisant s'éclairèrent soudain sous ce fanal vivant et altéré de nous." [29] In "Célébrer Giacometti," Char emphasizes the survival of man's creative acts. His poems have hopefully helped man to understand his essential dignity of being: "Tu es une fois encore la bougie où sombrent les ténèbres autour d'un nouvel insurgé." [30]

Char's search for the discovery and possession of the knowledge of being unfolds in *Retour amont*. This serious and careful self-investigation confirms his belief in the whole body of his poetry. Scrutiny of his own formation and the course of his subsequent development justifies his work and his life. *Retour amont* offers demonstrable proof that his risk and all risk is worthwhile, that man's possibilities of fulfillment lie in his own creative acts, and, most importantly, that life and poetry spring from the same source. From this vantage point, Char acknowledges the truth of his discovery of unity:

> Le point fond. Les sources versent. Amont éclate. Et en bas le delta verdit. Le chant des frontières s'étend jusqu'au belvédère d'aval. [31]

This is the message of Char's poetics and poetry and the meaning of his life.

---

[27] "Aiguevive."
[28] "Lenteur de l'avenir."
[29] "Le Banc d'ocre."
[30] "Servante."
[31] "L'Ouest derrière soi perdu."

APPENDIX I

Poems: Known dates of composition

Les Cloches sur le coeur 1922-1926

  "Jouvence" 1923-1925

Le Marteau sans maître 1927-1933

  Arsenal 1927-1928
  Artine 1930
  L'Action de la justice est éteinte 1931
  Poèmes militants 1931-1933
    "La Luxure" 1932
  Abondance viendra 1932-1933
    "Devant soi" 1927-1934

Le Tombeau des secrets 1929-1930

Hommage à Paul Eluard (Summer) 1932

Moulin premier 1935-1936

  "Commune présence" 1935-1936

Placard pour un chemin des écoliers 1936-1937

  "Dédicace" (March) 1937
  "Compagnie de l'écolière" 1936-1937

Dehors la nuit est gouvernée 1937-1938

  "Dehors la nuit est gouvernée" 1937
  "Tous compagnons de lit" 1937
  "La Récolte injuriée" 1937-1938
  "Remise" 1937

Premières alluvions 1923-1929

    "Jouvence I" 1923-1925
    "Sur le volet d'une fenêtre" 1923-1925
    "Sur une table de mairie" 1939
    "Avertissement" 1946

Fureur et mystère

    Seuls demeurent 1938-1944

        L'Avant-monde 1938-1944
            "Argument" 1938
            "Envoûtement à la Renardière" (December) 1941
            "Le Loriot" (September 3) 1938
            "Le Bouge de l'historien" 1942

        Le Visage nuptial
            "Le Visage nuptial" 1938
            "Gravité" 1937-1938

        Partage formel
            "Partage formel" 1942
            "Mission et révocation" 1938-1944

    Feuillets d'Hypnos 1941-1944

    Le Soleil des eaux 1946

    Les Loyaux adversaires
        "Chaume des Vosges" 1939
        "Le Thor" (September 15) 1947

    Le Poème pulvérisé 1945-1947
        "Argument" 1946
        "Les Trois soeurs" 1946
        "Biens égaux" 1937
        "Hymne à voix basse" 1946
        "Le Muguet" 1946
        "Pulvérin" 1946
        "Le Requin et la mouette" 1946
        "Chanson du velours à côtes" (April) 1947

    La Fontaine narrative 1947
        "A une ferveur belliqueuse" 1943
        "Allégeance" (February) 1948

Les Matinaux

La Sieste blanche
  "Complainte du lézard amoureux" (April) 1947
  "Montagne déchirée" (August 29) 1949

Un Adieu, un salut
  "Antonin Artaud" 1948
  "Georges Braque intro muros" (June) 1947

Le Consentement tacite
  "Anoukis et plus tard Jeanne" (September 18) 1949
  "Le Masque funèbre" (June) 1948
  "Les Lichens" 1948

Joue et dors
  "Les Inventeurs" (September 30) 1949

Rougeur des Matinaux 1948

À une sérénité crispée

  "A ***" 1950

Lettera amorosa 1952 ("version originelle")

Art bref

Amis peintres
  "Jean Villeri I" 1939 (date of revision)
  "Jean Villeri II" 1948
  "Pierre Charbonnier" 1948
  "Balthus" 1946
  "Ciska Grillet" 1949
  "Georges Braque" 1947

Madeleine qui veillait (January 27) 1948

Huis de la mort salutaire 1948

Lettera amorosa: 2ème version 1953-1960

Recherche de la base et du sommet 1941-1948

  "Billets à F. C."
    "Premier billet" (December 18) 1941
    "Deuxième billet" (March 14) 1943
    "Troisième billet" (September 20) 1946
    "Quatrième billet" (April 12) 1948

"La Lune d'Hypnos" 1945
"La Liberté passe en trombe" (August) 1946
"Heureuse la magie" 1948

Pauvreté et privilège 1948-1954

La Corde sensible
"Héraclite d'Ephèse" 1948
"Sur René Crevel" (March 7) 1948
"A la mort d'Eluard" "(November 20) 1952

Y a-t-il des incompatibilités? 1950

La Lettre hors commerce (February 18) 1947

Une Communication
"Nous resterons attachés" 1954

Poèmes des deux années 1953-1954

Le Rempart de brindilles (January-March) 1953

L'Amie qui ne restait pas (September) 1953 - (January) 1954
"La Double tresse" 1939 and 1953

La Bibliothèque est en feu et autres poèmes

La Bibliothèque est en feu (July-August) 1955

Les Compagnons dans le jardin
"Les Compagnons dans le jardin" 1957

Autres poèmes
"Deuil des Névons" 1954
"L'Une et l'autre" (September 10) 1957
"Aiguillon" 1957

Sur une nuit sans ornement 1957

Cinq poésies en hommage à Georges Braque (Spring-Summer) 1958

La Parole en archipel 1952-1960

Au-Dessus du vent 1958-1960

Quitter 1959-1960
"Aux riverains de la Sorgue" 1959

RECHERCHE DE LA BASE ET DU SOMMET 1965

Pauvreté et privilège
"Dédicace" 1954
"Roger Bernard" 1944
"Le Mariage d'un esprit de vingt ans..." 1963
"Jeanne qu'on brûla verte" 1952

Alliés substantiels
"Braque, lorsqu'il peignait" 1963
"Octantaine de Braque" 1962
"Songer à ses dettes" 1963
"Avec Braque, peut-être, on s'était dit..." 1963
"Visage de semence" 1938
"Lelia Caetani" 1954
"Jean Hugo" 1957
"Dansez, montagnes" 1961
"Ban" 1963
"Francis Picabia" 1952
"Le Coup" 1961
"Nicolas de Stael" 1952
"Viera da Silva" 1960
"Jean Villeri III" 1958

La Conversation souveraine
"Hommage à Maurice Blanchard" 1960
"Je veux parler d'un ami" 1957
"Feuillet de garde" 1947
"L'Accueil à un livre..." 1953
"Jacques Dupin" 1950
"Jean Senac" 1954
"Présence chaleureuse de Franz Hellens" 1956
"Au revoir, Mademoiselle" 1955
"Violette blanche pour Jean-Paul Samson" 1964
"Impressions anciennes" 1950, 1952, 1964

APPENDIX II

Editions of Char's Poems (in alphabetical order)

A la santé du serpent

1946
1947: *Le Poème pulvérisé*
1948: *Fureur et mystère*
1953: *Arrière-histoire du Poème pulvérisé*
1954
1962: *Fureur et mystère*
1964: (*Vallée close*) *Commune présence*

A une sérénité crispée

1951: original edition
1957: *Poèmes et prose choisis*
1964: *Commune présence*
1965: *Recherche de la base et du sommet*

L'Action de la justice est éteinte

1931: original edition
1934: *Le Marteau sans maître*
1945: *Le Marteau sans maître* suivi de *Moulin premier*
1963: *Le Marteau sans maître* suivi de *Moulin premier*

L'Age cassant

1966: original edition

Anthologie

1960

Arrière-histoire du Poème pulvérisé

1953: original edition

Arsenal

    1929: original edition
    1930: revised edition
    1934: *Le Marteau sans maître*
    1945: *Le Marteau sans maître* suivi de *Moulin premier*
    1963: *Le Marteau sans maître* suivi de *Moulin premier*

Art bref

    1950: suivi de *Premières alluvions*

Artine

    1930: original edition
    1934: *Le Marteau sans maître*
    1945: *Le Marteau sans maître* suivi de *Moulin premier*
    1963: *Le Marteau sans maître* suivi de *Moulin premier*

La Bibliothèque est en feu

    1956: original edition
    1957: *La Bibliothèque est en feu et autres poèmes*
    1957: *Poèmes et prose choisis*
    1961: *La Parole en archipel*
    1964: (*Les Frères de mémoire*) *Commune présence*

Cinq poésies en hommage à Georges Braque

    1958: original edition

Claire

    1949: original edition

Les Cloches sur le coeur

    1928: original edition, largely destroyed

Commune présence

    1964: collective edition:
        Premières alluvions
        Le Marteau sans maître
        Placard pour un chemin des écoliers
        Dehors la nuit est gouvernée
        Fureur et mystère
        Les Matinaux
        A une sérénité crispée
        La Parole en archipel

Lettera amorosa
Retour amont

LES COMPAGNONS DANS LE JARDIN

    1957: original edition
    1957: *La Bibliothèque est en feu et autres poèmes*
    1957: *Poèmes et prose choisis*
    1961: *La Parole en archipel*

LA CONJURATION

    1947: original edition
    1948: *Fureur et mystère*

DEHORS LA NUIT EST GOUVERNÉE

    1938: original edition
    1949: preceded by *Placard pour un chemin des écoliers*
    1957: *Poèmes et prose choisis*
    1964: *Commune présence*

DE MOMENT EN MOMENT

    1957: original edition
    1957: *Poèmes et prose choisis*

LES DENTELLES DE MONTMIRAIL

    1960: original edition
    1961: *(Quitter)*, *La Parole en archipel*
    1964: *(Vallée close) Commune présence*

DÉPENDANCE DE L'ADIEU

    1936: original edition
    1949: *Dehors la nuit est gouvernée* précédé par *Placard pour un chemin des écoliers*

LE DEUIL DES NÉVONS

    1954: original edition
    1957: *La Bibliothèque est en feu et autres poèmes*
    1957: *Poèmes et prose choisis*
    1961: *La Parole en archipel*
    1964: *(L'Amitié se succède) Commune présence*

EN TRENTE-TROIS MORCEAUX

    1956: collective edition

L'Escalier de Flore

    1958: original edition
    1961: (*Au-Dessus du vent*) *La Parole en archipel*
    1964: (*L'Ecarlate*) *Commune présence*

La Fauvette des roseaux

    1955: original edition
    1957: *La Bibliothèque est en feu et autres poèmes*
    1962: *La Parole en archipel*

Fête des arbres et du chasseur

    1948: original edition
    1950: *Les Matinaux*
    1957: *Poèmes et prose choisis*
    1964: (*L'Amitie se succède*) *Commune présence*
    1964: new edition of *Les Matinaux*

Feuillets d'Hypnos

    1946: original edition
    1948: *Fureur et mystère*
    1957: extracts in *Poèmes et prose choisis*
    1962: new edition of *Fureur et mystère*

Fureur et mystère

    1948: collective edition, in part original
        Seuls demeurent
        Feuillets d'Hypnos
        La Conjuration
        Le Poème pulvérisé
        La Fontaine narrative
    1957: *Poèmes et prose choisis*
    1962: new edition
    1964: *Commune présence*

L'Inclémence lointaine

    1961: original edition

Lettera amorosa

    1953: original edition
    1957: *Poèmes et prose choisis*
    1961: revised version in *La Parole en archipel*
    1964: definitive version in *Commune présence*

LE MARTEAU SANS MAÎTRE

> 1934: collective edition, in part original
> *Arsenal*
> *Artine*
> *L'Action de la justice est éteinte*
> *Poèmes militants*
> *Abondance viendra*
> 1945: definitive edition, followed by *Moulin premier*
> 1963
> 1964: *Commune présence*

LES MATINAUX

> 1950: collective edition, in part original
> *Fête des arbres et du chasseur*
> *La Sieste blanche*
> *Un Adieu, un salut*
> *Le Consentement tacite*
> *Joue et dors*
> *Rougeur des matinaux*
> *L'Homme qui marchait dans un rayon de soleil*
> *Ils sont privilégiés...*
> *Pourquoi se rendre?*
> *Toute vie...*
> 1957: *Poèmes et prose choisis*
> 1964: *Commune présence*
> 1964: new edition

LA MONTÉE DE LA NUIT

> 1961: original edition
> 1961: (*Au-Dessus du vent*) *La Parole en archipel*

MOULIN PREMIER

> 1936: original edition
> 1945: appended to *Le Marteau sans maître*
> 1957: *Poèmes et prose choisis*
> 1963: appended to *Le Marteau sans maître*

NOUS AVONS

> 1958: original edition
> 1959
> 1961: (*Quitter*) in *La Parole en archipel*
> 1964: (*L'Ecarlate*) *Commune présence*

La Paroi et la prairie

    1952: collective edition, in part original
        Lascaux
        Transir
        Quatre fascinants
        La Minutieuse
    1957: *Poèmes et prose choisis*
    1961: *La Parole en archipel*

La Parole en archipel

    1957: *Poèmes et prose choisis*
    1961: collective edition, in part original
        Lettera amorosa, second version
        La Paroi et la prairie
        Poèmes des deux années 1953-1954
        La Bibliothèque est en feu et autres poèmes
        Au-Dessus du vent
        Quitter
    1964: *Commune présence*

Paul Eluard (Hommage à)

    1933: original edition

Placard pour un chemin des écoliers

    1937: original edition
    1949: precedes *Dehors la nuit est gouvernée*
    1957: *Poèmes et prose choisis*
    1964: *Commune présence*

Le Poème pulvérisé

    1947: original edition
    1948: *Fureur et mystère*
    1953: *Arrière-histoire du Poème pulvérisé*
    1962: *Fureur et mystère*

Poèmes

    1951: anthology

Poèmes des deux annés 1953-1954

    1955: collective edition, in part original
        Le Rempart de brindilles
        L'Amie qui ne restait pas
        Pourquoi la journée vole
    1961: *La Parole en archipel*

Poèmes et prose choisis

    1957: collective anthology
        Moulin premier
        Placard pour un chemin des écoliers
        Dehors la nuit est gouvernée
        Fureur et mystère
        Les Matinaux
        A une sérénité crispée
        La Paroi et la prairie
        Lettera amorosa
        Recherche de la base et du sommet suivi de *Pauvreté et privilège*

Premières alluvions

    1946: collective edition, in part original
        Les Cloches sur le coeur
    1950: preceded by *Art bref*
    1964: *Commune présence*

Quatre fascinants. La Minutieuse

    1951: original edition
    1952: *La Paroi et la prairie*
    1957: *Poèmes et prose choisis*
    1961: *La Parole en archipel*
    1964: *Commune présence*

Recherche de la base et du sommet suivi de Pauvreté et privilège

    1955: original edition
    1957: *Poèmes et prose choisis*
    1965: new edition

Le Rempart de brindilles

    1953: original edition
    1955: *Poèmes des deux années 1953-1954*
    1961: *La Parole en archipel*

Retour amont

    1966: original edition

Seuls demeurent

    1945: collective edition, in large part original
        L'Avant-monde

    Le Visage nuptial
    Partage formel
    1948: *Fureur et mystère*
    1957: *Poèmes et prose choisis*
    1962: *Fureur et mystère*, new edition
    1964: *Commune présence*

Le Soleil des eaux

    1949: original edition
    1951

Le Tombeau des secrets

    1930: original edition

Le Visage nuptial

    1938: original edition
    1945: *Seuls demeurent*
    1948: *Fureur et mystère*
    1957: *Poèmes et prose choisis*
    1962: *Fureur et mystère*, new edition
    1964: (*Haine du peu d'amour*) *Commune présence*

APPENDIX III

VARIANTS

Char's poetic variants may be divided into nine categories: line and phrase deletions, line and phrase additions, line and phrase changes, word changes, title changes, consolidation of two or more lines, form changes, order of appearance, and punctuation changes. Appendix III contains all of these variants, except those of punctuation; the punctuation changes, including spelling differences (as they may be typographical errors, rather than actual revisions) are omitted from this Appendix due to the difficulty of a meaningful presentation of such changes.

Appendix III is arranged by order of publication date. Under each volume of poems, there are listed the omissions of entire poems, the additions of entire poems, the inclusion of poems previously published, and the variants of each poem. In order to facilitate the location of the variants, Roman numerals have been assigned to each aphorism which is unnumbered by Char and the page numbers have been listed for those variants included in the two anthologies, *Poèmes et prose choisis* and *Commune présence*, which are not arranged according to a specific volume of poems. In addition, I have established the following key: the stanza number is represented by a Roman numeral, P signifies paragraph, and an Arabic number refers to either a line of verse or a prose sentence. Wherever possible, the actual revision has been included in parentheses; where stanzas or paragraphs were greatly reworked, the variants have been noted only.

LES CLOCHES SUR LE COEUR 1928

    previously published
        Témoignages de grandeur 1927

ARSENAL 1929

    from *Les Cloches sur le coeur* 1928

Flexibilité de l'oubli
    V, VI, VIII, IX deleted
    III, 1 and 3-5 deleted
    X, 4-5 deleted
    XI, 2, 4-8 deleted
    III, 1 plural changed to singular (*Pèlerins* to *Pèlerin*)
    V, 4-5 added (*Se lancent leurs linges fumants/Étoile rose et rose blanche*)
    V, 1 word change (*Les grands prêtres* to *Les putains*)

ARSENAL 1930

  omissions
    La Délivrance naturelle
    Récit funèbre prend forme de poème

  additions
    Le Sujet
    Bonne aventure
        phrase in last line (*gagner le soleil*) from last line of *La Délivrance naturelle* (*Arsenal*, 1929)
    L'
    Masque de fer
        phrase (*viande secrète*) from line 10 of *La Délivrance naturelle* (*loc. cit.*)
    L'Amour
    L'Egalité

  variants
    La Tête sous l'oreiller
        II deleted and form changed
        I, 1 phrase deleted (*se complait aux lanternes*)
        III, 1 phrase deleted (*qui s'était assoupi*)
    Flexibilité de l'oubli
        VI, 1 and 6 positions reversed
        VII, 3-4 deleted (*Clown musical/Aux braises des sunlights*)
    Le Grand travail
        II, 1-2 revised (*On voit la tête/calculer* to *Tête à tête/N'est pas calculer*)
    L'Exhibitionniste
        not listed in table of contents

LE TOMBEAU DES SECRETS 1930

  previously published
    Bel édifice ou les pressentiments 1930
    L'Amour (1929)

L'Action de la justice est éteinte 1931

  previously published
    L'Esprit poétique (1931)

Le Marteau sans maître 1934

  Arsenal

  omissions
      Le Sujet
      Bonne aventure
      Probable
      La Tête sous l'oreiller
      L'Amour
      Puissance négative
      Flexibilité de l'oubli
      L'Embaumé
      Le Grand travail
      L'

  additions
      Détachement
      from Le Tombeau des secrets (1930)
          Bel édifice ou les pressentiments
              title changed to Bel édifice et les pressentiments
              II added
              last line, phrase added (en pleurant)
          L'Ambition
              rewritten
              2 retained (Comme je m'approche je m'éloigne)
          L'Amour
          Sosie
              IV, 2 phrase deleted (qui est)
          La Respiration
              title changed to Les Poumons
              form changed from two stanzas to one stanza

  variants
      L'Emploi
          I, 1 word change (trottoir to enclos)
      La Vérité continue
          original title: La Vérité
          I, 1 changed (L'oiseau maquis de paradis to Le novateur de la lézarde)
      Possible
          form of Stanza III expanded from 2 to 5 lines
          11 word change (oiseau to aigle)
          form of last stanza changed

Transfuges: original title: *La Guerre sous roche*
Masque de fer
   1 word change (*viande* to *rage*)
   2 added (*Sans diplomatie*)
L'Egalité
   2 changed (*Sous les verrous* to *Dans un carcan*)
A l'horizon remarquable
   original title: *La plus heureuse*
Singulier: II added
Leçon sévère
   completely rewritten
   last line retained (*D'un sang jamais entendu*)
Popularité
   reworks *Flexibilité de l'oubli*

ARTINE

   P 10, footnote deleted (*Jésus-Christ*)

L'ACTION DE LA JUSTICE EST ÉTEINTE

Sommeil fatal
   II, 3 word change (*prédiction* to *prédilection*)
Voyager sans tunnel
   II, 3 added (*Mobiles du grand oranger*)
Le Retour de Lola Abat
   original title: *Le Fantôme de Lola Abat*
   II, 1 word change (*coin* to *angle*)
Poètes
   epitaph added (*Le cercle est la figure conformée par une ligne circulaire. Raymond Lulle*)
   order change to precede *L'Artisanat*
L'Artisanat
   order change to follow *Poètes*
L'Esprit poétique
   dedication omitted
   letter to Artine (*Chère Artine*)
      II word change (*taille de guêpe* to *taille d'amanite*)
      final phrase added (*Ambassade déportée*)
Les Soleils chanteurs
   13 word change (*fleur* to *mauve*)
   15 added (*Ceux qui canalisent l'écume du monde souterrain*)
   19 added (*Les magiciens à l'épi*)
   22 added (*Le blasphème exterminateur*)
L'Amour
   last line added (*Moelle de la digitale*)

POÈMES MILITANTS: added

Abondance viendra: added

Le Marteau sans maître suivi de Moulin premier 1945

Arsenal

addition
- *Robustes météores*
  - 12 II from *La Délivrance naturelle* 9-12 (*Arsenal*, 1929)

variants
- *La Torche du prodigue*
  - original title: *L'Emploi*
- *La Vérité continue*
  - form changed to 2 stanzas (1-2/3-7)
- *Possible*
  - III condensed to 3 lines
  - 8 separated as stanza V
- *Tréma de l'émondeur*
  - original title: *L'Exhibitionniste*
- *Transfuges*
  - II, last line from *Bonne aventure* (1930)
  - I, 1 added (*Sang enfin libérable*)
  - I, 3 new (*Respire comme une plante*)
- *Un Levain barbare*
  - original title: *L'Egalité*
  - last line deleted (*La première tête qui tombe*)
- *Leçon sévère*
  - form change to 3 stanzas (6/2/5)
  - I, 4 deleted (*Faute d'hérédité*)
- *La Rose violente*
  - original title: *L'Ambition*
- *Voici*
  - original title: *Popularité*
- *Sosie*
  - VI, 2 deleted (*L'homme*)
  - VI, last line reworked (*Je ne suis pas au bout de tes misères* to *Je ne vais pas au bout de ta pauvreté*)
- *Dentelée*
  - original title: *Détachement*
  - 1 deleted (*La fleur du pissenlit a perdu son identité*)
  - 2 & 3 reworked

L'Action de la justice est éteinte

omission
- *L'Esprit poétique*

APPENDIX III - VARIANTS

addition
> *Le Climat de la chasse ou l'accomplissement de la poésie*
> I, Cf. *La Mère du vinaigre* (Poèmes militants, 1934) II
> VII, 3-4 *Le Cheval de corrida* (Poèmes militants, 1934)
> II, Cf. II, 1-3 *La Mère du vinaigre* (*loc. cit.*) II, 4-6 *Le Cheval de corrida* (*loc. cit.*)
> III Cf. *L'Esprit poétique* XII
> IV Cf. V, 4-7 *Drames* (Poèmes militants, 1934)
> V Cf. III, 4-6 *L'Accomplissement de la poésie* (Poèmes militants, 1934)
> VI Cf. Vi, 1 & VII, 6-7 *Drames* (*loc. cit.*)
> VII Cf. *L'Esprit poétique*, final P of letter to Artine
> VIII Cf. IV *La Mère du vinaigre* (*loc. cit.*)

variants
> *Sommeil fatal*
> I, 1 reworked, in part from 3 *Les Liaisons sentimentales de l'image* (Poèmes militants, 1934) (*chemin des sources ancien chemin des sables*)
> I, 3 reworked
> II, 3 word change (*prédilection* to *prédiction*)
> *L'Oracle du grand oranger*
> original title: *Voyageur sans tunnel*
> I, II deleted
> *La Manne de Lola Abba*
> former title: *Le Retour de Lola Abat*
> introduction in italics added
> I, II deleted
> V, 1 deleted
> *La Main de Lacenaire*
> footnote deleted (**Je lisais l'Album d'un pessimiste quand cette phrase est venue s'interposer entre le text de Rabbe et moi avec l'énergie du désespoir.*)
> *Poètes*
> epigraph deleted
> *L'Artisanat furieux*
> original title: *L'Artisanat*
> *Les Messagers de la poésie frénétique*
> original title: *Les Messagers délirants de la poésie frénétique*
> 4 word change (*papier* to *copeaux*)
> *Les Soleils chanteurs*
> 20-22 deleted (*Les artisans incendiaires*
>   *La traite des vampires*
>   *Le blasphème exterminateur*)
> 13 added (*Ceux qui hivernent à l'hôpital et que leur linge éclaté enivre encore*)

15-17 added (*L'ortie des prisons*
Le pariétaire des prisons
Le figuier allaiteur de ruines)
last 2 lines consolidated
L'Instituteur révoqué
dedication deleted (*à Paul Eluard*)
L'Amour
1-2 deleted (*Les mains neutres des squelettes stoïciens pour caresser tes cheveux/Réglisse noire les mois de disette*)
3 word change (*fermes* to *ouvres*)
last line reworked

POÈMES MILITANTS

omissions
Le Cheval de corrida
II, 4-6; VII, 3-4 to *Le Climat de la chasse* (*L'Action de la justice est éteinte*, 1945)
Drames
IV, 4-6; V, 1; VI, 6-7 to *Le Climat de la chasse* (*loc. cit.*)
L'Accomplissement de la poésie
III, 4-6 to *Le Climat de la chasse* (*loc. cit.*)
La Mère du vinaigre
II, 2-3, 5; IV, 1-3 to *Le Climat de la chasse* (*loc. cit.*)
Les Liaisons sentimentales de l'image
3 to *Sommeil fatal* (*loc. cit.*)

variants
La Luxure
III, 6 definite article deleted (*les*)
Métaux refroidis
III, 12 added (*Cette tête ne vaut pas*)
Chaîne
7-8 consolidated into one line
Les Asciens
original title: *Minerai*
nine lines deleted: 3-5, 12, 24-28
18-19 consolidated into line 18
change in order: 13 originally preceded 8
Vivante demain
I, II deleted
III becomes I, 1-2 and II, 1-2
I, 2 word change (*toute chaude* to *votive*)
Les Observateurs et les rêveurs
dedication added (*à Maurice Blanchard*)
II, 4-6 deleted
III, 4 phrase deleted (*la croisse brûlante des angles*)

APPENDIX III - VARIANTS

La Plaine
   original title: *L'Accident dans la plaine*
   7 deleted (*Au suc gastrique de la bêtise infaillible*)
   11 deleted (*Et le roulement de la tôle qui voile la vue des monuments*)

Confronts
   original title: *A la faveur de la peau*
   dedication added (*à Maurice Fourrier*)
   III, 3-4 line order reversed
   IV, part of 8, deleted
   IV, 8 phrase changed (*à la sortie* to *après la chimie*)
   IV, 9 deleted
   IV, 7-9 consolidated
   IV, 10 changed from plural to singular (*plante souple*)
   V, 1 form changed to separate stanza V
   V, 2-13 form VI

L'Historienne
   II, 3-6 definite articles changed to possessive adjectives
   III, 4 deleted (*Happé comme l'aimant happe l'épingle*)
   III, 7-8 consolidated
   IV, 4-5 consolidated

Sade, l'amour enfin sauvé de la boue du ciel, cet héritage suffira aux hommes contre la famine
   original title: *La Puma de D. A. F. Sade*

Le Supplice improvisé
   12-13 deleted (*Je suis passé/Sans lyrisme*)
   14 word changes
      word deleted (*Du*)
      word change (*au* to *ô*)
   8-9 consolidated
   17 deleted (*L'absence se rapièce comme un sac*)

Cruauté
   original title: *Fanatisme*
   dedication omitted (*à Tristan Tzara*)

Sommaire
   I, 3 word change (*roue vitrée* to *solstice*)
   I, 3 phrase change *saute au* to *sur le*
   I, 4 reworked and added to 3
   form divided into 2 stanzas (1-7/8-9)

Pour Mamouque
   original title: *Trianon*
   dedication deleted (*Pour Mamouque*)
   I, 2; II, 1-2 added
   I, 1 was original poem

Crésus
   dedication added (*à Georges Mounin*)
   II, 3 deleted (*Longs amants moulés dans les draps*)

II, 11 deleted (*Passagers du Rêve, asymétrique*)
V, 1-2 deleted (*Une conjonction d'astres impurs Trombes clémentes aux communes*)
Bourreaux de solitude
　form changed to two stanzas (1/2-3)
Versant
　5 phrase deleted (*Fractures symphoniques*)

Abondance viendra

L'Eclaircie
　P 2, 1 phrase deleted (*à ses auditeurs inintéressés*)
Eaux-mères
　P 2, 5 phrase change (*qui est à la forge* to *une forge*)
　P 2, 35 phrase added (*des bourgs?*)
　P 2, 36 phrase deleted (*A l'aide d'un gant de boxe*)
　P 2, 58 phrase added (*A Paris*)
　P 2, 83 word change (*dégoûtantes* to *odieuses*)
Les Rapports entre parasites
　II last line deleted (*Pour être logique avec la nature il sème des peignes et récolte des cheveux.*)
Migration
　dedication added (*à Yvonne Zervos*)
Domaine
　form changed from a block form to a paragraph form
　V deleted
Intégration
　dedication added (*à Christian Zervos*)
Devant soi
　II, III consolidated into II
　II, 2 deleted (*Le grisou, entre autres inspirations sublimées cessait d'être l'auxiliaire occulte, fascinant des érections irrépressibles*)
　II divided

Moulin premier

*** form changed to 2 stanzas (1-12/13-18)
I word change (*battre* to *démanteler*)
IV form changed from 3 to 2 paragraphs (1/2-3)
XIV addition from *L'Esprit poétique* (*L'Action de la justice est éteinte*, 1934) (*Les statuts de l'érotisme*)
XV addition from *L'Esprit poétique* III (*loc. cit.*)
　(*Je ne plaisante pas avec les porcs.*)
XVII word change (*oiseau tuteur* to *oiseau-missel*)
XVIII reworked: footnote deleted and incorporated into text
XXIII P1 & 2 consolidated into P1
XXV form consolidated to 1 P

APPENDIX III - VARIANTS   229

XXVI reworked and expanded
XXVII P2, next-to-last line direct object deleted (*le*)
XXXII 2-3 consolidated into P2
XXXIV 2 phrase changed (*rigoureux, offensant, en 'maconnerie'* to *offensant, tige de maçonnerie*)
   3 word deleted (*permanent*)
XXXVII 3 word change (*évanouissement* to *anéantissement*)
XLI addition from *L'Esprit poétique* P 10 (*loc. cit.*)
   (*Je commence à croire que la nuit m'attend toujours*)
   word deleted (*Je*)
   word change (*m'* to *t'*)
XLII addition (*La bêtise aime gouverner. Lui arracher ses chances. Nous débuterons en ouvrant le feu sur ces villages du bon sens.*)
XLIV 1 phrase addition (*suave sécheresse*)
XLV 4 added (*Contemporain d'une Saint-Barthélemy des lucides*)
XLVI P 1 reworked into 2 P
XLVII P 1 reworked
XLVIII addition from *L'Esprit poétique* P 14 (*loc. cit.*)
   (*Les longues promenades silencieuses, à deux, la nuit, à travers la campagne déserte, en compagnie de la panthère somnambule, terreur des maçons.*)
L consolidated to 1 P
LIII consolidated to 1 P
LIV P2 added (*O monnaie d'hélium au visage lauré!*)
   P1, 2 change from singular to plural (*vaines*)
LIX addition from *L'Esprit poétique* P 4 (*loc. cit.*) (*Le chien errant n'atteint pas forcément la forêt.*)
LX addition from *L'Esprit poétique* (*loc. cit.*) P 7. (*Au bout du bras du fleuve il y a la main de sable qui écrit tout ce qui passe par le fleuve.*)
LXII 2 added (*Toujours plus larges fiançailles des regards*)
LVIII-LXIV changed in order of appearance
LXV footnote deleted and incorporated into text (*Aime, riveraine*)
Commune présence
   I, 4-5 consolidated into 4
   II, 3-5 consolidated into 3

SEULS DEMEURENT 1945

   previously published
      Le Visage nuptial 1938

         variants
            IV, 6 word change (*lynchés* to *lapidés*)

    additions
        Conduite
        Gravité
            from *Dehors la nuit est gouvernée* 1938
        Evadné
        Post-scriptum

PREMIÈRES ALLUVIONS 1946

    from *Les Cloches sur le coeur* 1928
        Prêt au dépouillement
        14 Juin 1924
            original title: *Harmonium*
            1, 4, 9-14 deleted
            reworked
        Poème pour la voir
            original title: *Profession de foi*
            II, 2-4 deleted
            III deleted
            new last stanza
            rewoked
        Sillage noir
            original title: *Sillage*
            II added from *La Tête sous l'oreiller* (*Arsenal*, 1930)
        Morte saison
            3-5, 7-9, 13 deleted
            II, 3 word and tense change (*avait faim* to *eût soin*)
        Le Veilleur naïf
            original title: *Intérieur*
            13 and 19 deleted
            13 word change (*mâchoirs raides* to *mâchoires*)
            14 reworked
            15 word change (*se bloquait* to *cédait*)
            17 word change (*armoire à glaces* to *glâce*)
            22 phrase change (*envahit son champs visuel* to *lui prit la main*)
        Fanemousse
            original title: *Pour une vierge*
            I, II, III, deleted
            II from *Présage* I
        Témoignage de la grandeur
            parts II and III deleted
            part I reworked
        Le Sol de la nuit
            original title: *Parallèle du coeur*
            I, II, III deleted
            VI, 2 rewritten

Le Poème pulvérisé 1947
   from *Dehors la nuit est gouvernée* 1938
      Biens égaux
         I, II consolidated and reworked considerably

Fureur et mystère
   FEUILLETS D'HYPNOS (1946)
      dedication added (*à Albert Camus*)
      230 added (*Toute la vertu du ciel d'Août, de notre angoisse confidente, dans la voix d'or du météore.*)
      231 added (*Peu de jours avant son supplice, Roger Chaudon me disait: "Sur cette terre, on est un peu dessus, beaucoup dessous. L'ordre des époques ne peut être inverse. C'est, au fond, ce qui me tranquillise, malgré la joie de vivre qui me secoue comme un tonnerre..."*)
   LES LOYAUX ADVERSAIRES
      from *Premières alluvions* (1946)
         Sur le volet d'une fenêtre
         Chaume des Vosges
            original title: *Sur une table de mairie*
   LE POÈME PULVÉRISÉ
      Seuil
         last line divided into 2 lines
      Jacquemard et Julia
         II, last line, word change (*allégi* to *allégé*)
      Météore du 13 août
         introduction in italics added

Dehors la nuit est gouvernée précédé par Placard pour un chemin des écoliers 1949

Introduction added

   PLACARD POUR UN CHEMIN DES ÉCOLIERS
      Dédicace
         II, 10 word deleted (*automne*)
      Allée du confident
         V, VI redivided
      Exploit du cylindre à vapeur
         V divided (1-7/8-20)
      Les Vivres du retour
         I last line deleted (*Embellir ton haleine malmenée par la rixe*)

   Dehors la nuit est gouvernée
      omissions
         Gravité to *Le Visage nuptial* (*Seuls demeurent*, 1945)

Biens égaux to *Le Poème pulvérisé* 1947
addition previously published
Dépendance de l'adieu 1936

variants
Tous compagnons de lit
IV, 1 word changed (*de légumes* to *de l'amertume*)
Passerelle
II, last line deleted (*Par la morne amnistie clairsemée*)
Confins
III, 5 deleted (*Les filles nous oublient, les mères nous regardent*)
L'Essentiel intelligible
form change from blocks to individual stanzas
IV, 1 deleted (*Cris guérisseurs en collier de persiennes*)
VII, 1 deleted (*Mes ordonnances, vos oreilles se sont secouées du pastel*)
Une Italienne de Corot
IV, last line deleted (*Du vice à soûler une cave*)
Dire aux miens
original title: *Sulfater*
A un fantôme de la réflexion surpris chez les pleutres de la providence
I, 8 deleted (*Le verbe et le désir interprètent l'espace*)
Le Temps du store
IV, 3-4 deleted (*Dussé-je tourner morphine en m'imposer tumeur à l'os / C'est postiche d'admettre que des mains se dévouent*)
Versions
X, 4 changed (*Tué de faim des colons* to *Elargi l'orage de front*)
La Récolte injuriée
I, II consolidated into I
Postface
original title: *Validité*

ART BREF suivi de PREMIÈRES ALLUVIONS 1950

ART BREF

from *Premières alluvions* (1946)
Jean Villeri I
original title: *L'Ami peintre*
reorganized
II last sentence added

PREMIÈRES ALLUVIONS

from *Les Cloches sur le coeur* (1928)

Sans pardon
   I 4-6, II, III, IV deleted
   reworked
omissions:
   L'Ami peintre to *Art bref* (1950)
   Sur le volet d'une fenêtre to *Les Loyaux adversaires* (*Fureur et mystère*, 1948)
   Sur une table de mairie to *Les Loyaux adversaires* (*loc. cit.*)
additions
   Avant de...
   Moi qui...
variants
   Avertissement
      II, 1 phrase added (*de provende*)
   Jouvence
      II added from *A l'horizon* (*Le Tombeau des secrets*, 1930)
   Pour qu'une forêt...
      original title: *Ecrit avec du sang de cochon*
      subtitles deleted (*Plus tard, Guerre*)

LES MATINAUX 1950

previously published
   Fête des arbres et du chasseur 1948

LE SOLEIL DES EAUX 1951

documents added
Pourquoi du Soleil des eaux added

LA PAROI ET LA PRAIRIE 1952

previously published
   Quatre fascinants 1951
   La Minutieuse 1951
   from *Amitié cachetée* 1951
      Transir: reworked

ARRIÈRE-HISTOIRE DU POÈME PULVÉRISÉ 1953

Argument
   1 not set off from rest of poem
Seuil: last 2 lines fused
Jacquemard et Julia
   P2, last line, word change (*allégé* to *allégi*)

omission
> *Le Météore du 13 août*

A LA SANTÉ DU SERPENT 1954
> previously published as part of *Le Poème pulvérisé* 1947, 1948

POÈMES DES DEUX ANNÉES *1953-1954* 1955
> *La Double tresse*
> > I *Chaume des Vosges* from *Les Loyaux adversaires* (*Fureur et mystère*, 1948)
> > II *Sur la paume de Dabo* added
>
> previously published
> > *Le Rempart de brindilles* 1953

RECHERCHE DE LA BASE ET DU SOMMET suivi de PAUVRETÉ ET PRIVILÈGE 1955

> RECHERCHE DE LA BASE ET DU SOMMET
> > from *Cinq parmi d'autres* 1947
> > > *Dominique Corticchiato*
> >
> > from *Art bref* 1950
> > > *Huis de la mort salutaire*
>
> PAUVRETÉ ET PRIVILÈGE
> > from *Art bref* 1950
> > > *Madeleine qui veillait*
> >
> > from the avant-propos to the translation of Héraclite d'Ephèse (1948)
> > > *Héraclite d'Ephèse*
> >
> > previously published separately
> > > *Bandeau de Fureur et mystère* 1948
> > > *Bandeau de Claire* 1949
> > > > reworked
> > >
> > > *Bandeau des Matinaux* 1950
> > > *Louis Fernandez* 1950
> > > *Bois de Stael* 1951
> > > *Victor Brauner peintre* 1952
> > > *Entre la prairie et le laurier* 1954
> > > *Y a-t-il des incompatibilités?* 1950

LA BIBLIOTHÈQUE EST EN FEU ET AUTRES POÈMES 1957
> addition
> > *Sur une nuit sans ornement*
>
> previously published
> > *Les Compagnons dans le jardin* 1957
> > > *A un enfant* 1956

APPENDIX III – VARIANTS

    La Passante des Sceaux
        from *Bonne grâce d'un temps d'avril* 1955
    Epitaphe 1957
    Berceuse pour chaque jour... 1956
    La fauvette des roseaux 1955
  Le Deuil des Névons 1954
  L'Une et l'autre 1957
  Aiguillon 1957

variants
    La Bibliothèque est en feu
        P 9 added (*L'éclair me dure*)
        P 10 next-to-last line, final phrase deleted (*ne le peuvent*)
        P 13 added (*La poésie me volera ma mort*)
        P 17 added (*On naît avec les hommes, on meurt inconsolé parmi les dieux*)

POÈMES ET PROSE CHOISIS 1957

  p. 195
    Commune présence (*Moulin premier*, 1945)
      I deleted
      title appears as *Tu es pressé d'écrire*
(*Fureur et mystère*)
  (*Seuls demeurent*)
    (*L'Avant-monde*)
      pp. 18-26
        order change in grouping under *Neuf poèmes pour vaincre*
  (*Le Visage nuptial*)
      pp. 27-28
        order change: *Gravité* precedes *Conduite*
(*Les Loyaux adversaires*)
    p. 101
      Dis...
        original title: *Loyal avec la vie*
    p. 179
      Chaume des Vosges reworked
(*Le Poème pulvérisé*)
    p. 64
      Donnerbach mühle: P 1 consolidated
    p. 69
      Seuil: last line divided into 2 lines
    p. 83
      A la santé du serpent
        XXV last line divided into 2 lines
(*La Fontaine narrative*)
    p. 89

> *A une ferveur belliqueuse*
>> I last line reworked (*un peu de charité* to *un regard d'ici-bas*)
>> III, 1 phrase changed (*d'être épuisés* to *l'épuisement*)
>> III, 2 phrase changed (*qui vous fut témoigné* to *dont vous fûtes couverte*)
>> IV, 3 changed (*J'ai le coeur assez fort, folle, pour vous gifler...* to *J'ai la tête assez chaude pour vous mettre en débris...*)
>> IV, 4 changed (*A vous de vous défendre* to *Vous êtes sans défense*)
>> V, 3 phrase changed (*obéir à leur voix* to *bâtir pour eux*)
>> VI, last line changed (*et femme devenez, mais femme qui se plie* to *coeur enfant devenez sous le nuage noir*)
>> VII last line changed (*campagnarde effrontée, les lumières sont froides où les hommes sont nés* to *servante de hasard, les lumières se rendent où l'affamé les voit*)

(*Les Matinaux*)
> p. 132
>> *Hermétiques ouvriers*
>>> original title: *Doléances du feutre*

(*A une sérénité crispée*)
> pp. 231-244
>> abridged
>> omissions: 4-6, 8-13, 15, 19, 22, 24-25, 29-30, 34, 36-37, 41, 46-48, 50-51, 53, 55-61, 63, 65, 68, 70-71, 77, 79, 84-86, 88, 90, 92, 94, 97

>> variants
>>> 28 word deleted (*grand*)
>>> 35 word added (*allègre*)
>>> 45 added (*Le poète au sortir des demeures: les toiliers de l'espace lui offrent un orchestre.*)
>>> 54 last lines deleted (*Exemple d'image jactée qui ne me satisfait pas. Je la rapporte pour m'alerter. Profit du phare.*)
>>> 66 last phrase deleted (*nous convertissons*)
>>> 67 last line deleted (*Pour notre dommage, car il ne sera plus désormais fraternel par le fond.*) order changed to 70
>>> 73 last line added
>>> 74 word changed (*le poète* to *je*)
>>> 78 sentence 2 deleted

APPENDIX III - VARIANTS 237

  82 last phrase deleted (*du bonheur soustrait aux regards et à sa propre nature*)
  89 indefinite article changed (*des faits* to *les faits*)
  Post-merci title omitted
   no longer appears as a separate section
   omissions: 2, 4, 5, 9, 10
   7 deletion of P 2
   introduction paragraphs appear as 2 aphorisms

(*Poèmes des deux années 1953-1954*)
 (*Le Rempart de brindilles*)
  pp. 245-249
   P 14 line 1 word change (*nous* to *lui*)
    line 2 added (*L'énigme a fini de rougir*)
   P 16 reworked
  p. 117
   Le Mortel partenaire
    dedication added (*à Maurice Blanchot*)
  p. 178
   Front de la rose
    P 1, line 6 verb changed (*vit* to *resurgit*)
    P 2, line 3 word deleted (*aussitôt*)
 (*L'Amie qui ne restait pas*)
  p. 182
   Vermillon
    epigraph added (*Réponse à un peintre*)
  p. 187
   Le Risque et le pendule
    dedication added (*à René Ménard*)

(*La Bibliothèque est en feu et autres poèmes*)
 p. 256
  La Bibliothèque est en feu
   XXIX P 1, line 1 abridged (*n'est rien moins que prévenu, qu'insaisissable* to *est peu saisissable*)
 p. 262
  Les Compagnons dans le jardin
   P 4, line 1 phrase abridged (*Au XX siècle* to *XXe siècle*)
   P 7, line 2 phrase changed (*notre accomplissement* to *nous accomplir*)
 p. 166
  Epitaphe
   1 change from plural to singular (*à l'éparse douleur*)
 p. 167
  L'Arbre frappé added to *Bonne grâce d'un temps d'avril*

pp. 168-170
Neuf merci pour Veira da Silva grouping

CINQ POÉSIES EN HOMMAGE À GEORGES BRAQUE 1958

Le Hasard chante
last 2 lines from *Prompte* 1960

LA PAROLE EN ARCHIPEL 1961

LA PAROI ET LA PRAIRIE
Transir appears as part of *Lascaux*
Quatre fascinants
  Le Serpent: 1-3 reworked
  La Minutieuse
    reworked
    included as part of *Quatre fascinants*

LETTERA AMOROSA (*Deuxième version*)

introduction changed from French to Italian
Dédicace
  title omitted
  P 4 deleted
I P1, line 3 phrase deleted (*très fort*)
  P 1, 4-6 deleted
V phrase changed (*ironise la rampe* to *raille l'alto*)
VI omitted
VIII 1-2 deleted
  4 last phrase deleted (*les uns les autres*)
  5-7 consolidated and reworked
  10 reworked
IX 1 deleted
  2 word changed (*quelquefois* to *parfois*)
X 2 word deleted (*pareillement*)
XI phrase changed (*te ralliant* to *s'il te traverse*)
XIII omitted
XVI omitted
XVII omitted
XVIII 1 word deleted (*arbitrairement*)
  1 final phrase deleted
  2 deleted
XIX P1, line 1 word deleted (*réciproquement*)
  phrase deleted (*dans cet ajustement*)
  2 word deleted (*Pourtant*)
  4-6 deleted
XX omitted
XXI 2 word changed (*beaucoup* to *longtemps*)
XXII 3 deleted

XXIII omitted
XXIV last line deleted
   order changed to follow XXVII
XXV 1 last phrase deleted
  2 phrase deleted (*Il est*)
XXVIII omitted
XXX omitted
XXXIII P2 word changed (*cauchemar* to *mauvais songe*)
XXXVII omitted
XXXIX word changed (*à nouveau* to *encore*)

Poèmes des deux années 1953-1954
  Le Rempart de brindilles
    Le Mortel partenaire
      dedication deleted (*à Maurice Blanchot*)
  L'Amie qui ne restait pas
    Le Risque et le pendule
      dedication deleted (*à René Ménard*)
  Pourquoi la journée vole
    P 1 deleted
    P 2, line 2 rewritten
        3 word changed (*étreinte* to *saisir*)
         verb changed (*n'ont-ils pas* to *ont*)
        4 verb changed (*il doit répondre* to *il répond*)
    P 3, line 1 phrase changed (*Très vieux* to *Au soir*)

La Bibliothèque est en feu et autres poèmes

La Bibliothèque est en feu
  X divided into 2 paragraphs
A deux enfants
  I added (*A Elisabeth*) — published 1958 as *Elisabeth petite fille*
  A une enfant becomes II: (*A Hélène*)
Neuf merci
  previously grouped as *Neuf merci pour Veira da Silva*
Débris mortels et Mozart
  order changed from last position in *Les Compagnons dans le jardin* to first position in *Autres poèmes*

Au-Dessus du vent

from *Cinq poésies en hommage à Georges Braque* 1958
  Attenants
  Captifs
  L'Oiseau spirituel
previously published
  L'Issue 1961
  L'Escalier de Flore 1958

>
> reworked
>
> *Déclarer son nom* 1959
> *Traverse* 1959
> *Eros suspendu* 1960
> *Si...* 1959
> *De 1943* 1961
> > original title: *Non résurrection* 1951
>
> *La Faux relevée* 1959
> *L'Avenir non prédit* 1960
> *La Montée de la nuit* 1961
> *Le Pas ouvert de René Crevel*
> > original title: *Le Pas de René Crevel* 1956

Quitter
> previously published
> > *Nous avons* 1958, 1959
> > *Dans la marche* 1959
> > *Contrevenir* 1959
> > *Les Dentelles de Montmirail* 1961
> > *Fontis* 1961

Fureur et mystère 1962

omission
LA CONJURATION

Seuls demeurent
> *L'Avant-monde*
> > order returned to that of 1948
>
> ## LE VISAGE NUPTIAL
> > *Conduite* precedes *Gravité*

Feuillets d'hypnos
> 65 name changed (*Marcel Grillet* to *André Grillet*)
> 87 name changed and footnote added (*Léon Saingermain* to *León Zyngermain *alias Saingermain*)

Les loyaux adversaires
> *La Patience*
> > III, 3 phrase changed (*fait pleurer* to *met en pleurs*)
> > III, 5 phrase changed (*on a perdu la clé* to *la clé fut perdue*)
> > IV, 6 phrase changed (*va les chasser* to *soudain les chasse*)

Le poème pulvérisé
> *Donnerbach mühle*: P 1 divided
> *Le Météore du 13 août*
> > introduction in italics deleted
> > P 9, first line word changed (*Aime* to *Ame*)

APPENDIX III - VARIANTS   241

Le Marteau sans maître suivi de Moulin premier 1963
   Arsenal
      Vérité continue
         form restored to 3 stanzas (1-2/3-4/5-7)
      Un Levain barbare
         last line of 1930 and 1934 texts restored (*La première tête qui tombe*)
      Sosie
         VI, last line word change (*ta pauvreté* to *ton dénuement*)
   L'Action de la justice est éteinte
      Sommeil fatal
         I, 1 restored to 1931, 1934 text (*Les animaux à tête de navire cernent le visage de la femme que j'aime.*)
         II omitted (*L'homme se refuse à ne pas croire à la sincérité des lettres qu'une inconnue lui écrivait lorsqu'il était enfant. Celle-ci lui dévoilait le côté prophétique de son écriture. La couleur précisément noire de l'avenir l'autorisait à formuler une prédiction: il embrasserait une carrière qui est la perdition des bolides, ces virtuoses de passage oubliant volontiers leur tête comestible sur la planche d'un garde-manger, au petit jour.*)
      Tu ouvres les yeux...
         original title: *L'Amour*
   Poèmes militants
      La Luxure
         III, 6 definite article restored (*les*)
      Confronts
         I, 3 phrase change to return to 1934 text (*sur le* to *saute au*)
         III, 3-4 reversed to 1934 order
      Bourreaux de solitude
         form restored to one stanza
   Abondance viendra
      Les Rapports entre parasites
         last paragraph divided into 2 P after fifth sentence
   Moulin premier
      X word change (*où* to *que*)
      XI line deleted (*Tels, ces canaris, comme conçus dans l'urine des concierges, dont la cage est une seconde loge qui avance sur la rue pour indisposer le promeneur.*)
      XX phrase deleted (*Toute cette confiserie*)
      XXIV phrase deleted (*têteur de chatte*)
      XXVI form changed to 2 stanzas (1-2/3-4)

Les Matinaux 1964

omissions
Un Adieu, un salut
Antonin Artaud
Georges Braque intro muros
L'Homme qui marchait dans un rayon de soleil

Commune présence 1964

Lettera amorosa (version définitive)
Dédicace: title restored
I P2, line 6 phrase deleted (*en vérité*)
XII added (*Absent partout où l'on fête un absent.*)
XVII added (*Après le vent c'était toujours plus beau, bien que la douleur de la nature continuât.*)
XXIII added (*La terre veule, les nuits de pariade. Un complot de branches mortes n'y pourrait tenir.*)
XXVI order changed from XXVIII in 1953
   1 adjective deleted (*opaque*)
   2 deleted (*Je les distingue, les détruis.*)
   4 deleted (*Anéantis par mon irruption luxurieuse.*)
   last line added (*Blasons, durcis, ce matin, comme du miel de cerisier.*)
XXIX added (*Pourquoi le champ de la blessure est-il de tous le plus prospère? Les hommes aux vieux regards, qui ont eu un ordre du ciel transpercé, en reçoivent sans s'étonner la nouvelle.*)
XXX added (*Affileur de mon mal je souffre d'entendre les fontaines de ta route se partager la pomme des orages.*)
XXXIV added (*Je ne confonds pas la solitude avec la lyre du désert. Le nuage cette nuit qui cerne ton oreille n'est pas de neige endormante, mais d'embruns enlevés au printemps.*)
(*Arsenal, Le Marteau sans maître*)
  p. 111
    Sade
      former title: Sade, *l'amour enfin sauvé de la boue du ciel, cet héritage suffira aux hommes contre la famine*
(*Le Visage nuptial — Seuls demeurent, Fureur et mystère*) no longer appears as a group.
(*Moulin premier*)
  p. 6
    Commune présence
      II formerly entitled *Tu es pressé d'écrire*

previously published
  Aux portes d'Aérea

APPENDIX III - VARIANTS

    original title: *Apparition* 1962
Chérir Thouzon 1962
    original title: *Thouzon*
additions from RETOUR AMONT
    Devancier
    Sept parcelles de Lubéron I, II
    La Soif hospitalière
    Tracé sur le gouffre
    Le Gaucher
    Le Nu perdu
    Mirage des aiguilles
    Les Parages d'Alsace
    Célébrer Giacometti
    Lied du figuier
addition from *Recherche de la base et du sommet*
    Avec Braque, peut-être, on s'était dit...

RETOUR AMONT 1966

    previously published
        Passe au château cloaque
            P 8 from *Nous ne jalousons pas les dieux...* (1962)
    published in *Commune presence* (1964)
        Sept parcelles de Lubéron
            I
                form change: asterisks between stanzas 4 and 5, 5 and 6 omitted
        Tracé sur le gouffre
        Chérir Thouzon
            form changed to 1 P
        Mirage des aiguilles
        Aux portes d'Aérea
            P 3 and P 4 fused
        Devancier
            dedication omitted (*à Yves de Bayser*)
        Les Parages d'Alsace
        La Soif hospitalière
        Le Nu perdu
            form changed from 2 P to 1 P
        Célébrer Giacometti
            sentence 2 word deleted (*sa sombre alvéole* to *son alvéole*)
        Lied du figuier
        Le Gaucher

RECHERCHE DE LA BASE ET DU SOMMET 1965

    PAUVRETÉ ET PRIVILÈGE

        additions
            Dédicace
            Le Mariage d'un esprit de vingt ans...
        from *Recherche de la base et du sommet* 1955
            Huis de la mort solitaire
            Dominique Corticchiato
        previously published
            Jeanne qu'on brûla verte 1956
            Après in *Le Dernier couac* 1958

        variants
            Trois respirations
                original title: *Il existe un printemps*

    ALLIÉS SUBSTANTIELS

        additions
            Braque, lorsqu'il peignait
            Octantaine de Braque
            Songer à ses dettes
            Avec Braque, peut-être, on s'était dit
            Visage de semence
            Lelia Caetani
            N. Ghika
            Dansez, montagnes
            Ban
            Francis Picabia
            Le Coup

        from *Art bref* 1950
            Georges Braque
            Le Dard dans la fleur
                original title: *Balthus*
            Pierre Charbonnier I
            Ciska Grillet
            Jean Villeri I
            Jean Villeri II

        from *Les Matinaux* 1950
            Georges Braque intro muros
        previously published
            Secrets d'hirondelles 1946
            Nouvelles-Hebrides, Nouvelle-Guinée 1962
            Pierre Charbonnier II 1958
            Jean Hugo 1957

Jean Villeri III 1958
Roger Bernard 1945

LA CONVERSATION SOUVERAINE

additions
    Page d'ascendants pour l'an 1964
    Hommage à Maurice Blanchard
    Je veux parler d'un ami
    Feuillet de garde
    L'Accueil à un livre...
    Présence chaleureuse de Franz Hellens
    Au revoir, Mademoiselle
    Violette blanche pour Jean-Paul Samson
    La Poésie indispensable
    Impressions anciennes

from *Les Matinaux* 1950
    Antonin Artaud

previously published
    Paul Eluard 1933
        original title: *Hommage à Paul Eluard*
    Arthur Rimbaud 1957
        original title: *Introduction aux oeuvres d'Arthur Rimbaud*
    Hommage à D.-A.-F. de Sade 1933
    A Saint Jean Perse
    Jacques Dupin 1950
    Jean Senac 1954

A UNE SÉRÉNITÉ CRISPÉE
addition
    Préliminaire
omissions: 1, 25, 29, 34, 37, 41, 46, 50, 53, 60, 61, 63, 66, 68, 71, 73, 78, 85, 86, 90

variants
    2 phrase deleted (*L'appétit de quelques esprits a complètement décraqué l'estomac des hommes.*)
    6 word change (*mes* to *les*)
    11 word change (*en* to *dans*)
    15 word change (*volume* to *souffle*)
    19 last sentence deleted (*Nous ne goûtons guère, d'être au même moment l'élu régnant de l'une et le guillotiné de l'autre.*)
    33 last line from deleted 34 (*L'ennemi le plus sournois est l'actualité.*)

35 last line added (*Certains survivent, promus à la parole, glaciers.*)
51 last line deleted (*N'étant l'obligé d'aucun, tu seras clément pour tous!*)
54 last three sentences deleted (*Example d'image jactée qui ne me satisfait pas. Je la rapporte pour m'alerter. Profit du phare!*)
55 only first line retained
56 P1 deleted (*L'idéal, disait ce prestidigitateur, serait d'édifier une ville sans plis.*)
   P2 last phrase deleted (*à la statue déféquée...*)
58 phrase deleted (*Honteux résultat!*)
82 final phrase deleted (*du bonheur soustrait aux regards et à sa propre nature.*)
 4 first line deleted (*Les faibles, parce qu'ils se débattent, réconfortent souvent les forts.*)

BIBLIOGRAPHY

A. WORKS BY RENÉ CHAR (IN ORDER OF PUBLICATION)

Major Editions

1928 *Les Cloches sur le coeur.* Paris: Le Rouge et le noir.
1929 *Arsenal.* Nîmes: Meridiens.
1930 *Arsenal.* Nîmes: De la main à la main.
1930 *Le Tombeau des secrets.* Nîmes: Imprimerie Larguier.
1930 *Artine.* Paris: Editions surréalistes.
1931 *L'Action de la justice est éteinte.* Paris: Editions surréalistes.
1933 *Hommage à Paul Eluard.* Paris.
1933 *Hommage à D.-A.-F. de Sade.* Paris.
1934 *Le Marteau sans maître.* Paris: Editions surréalistes.
1936 *Dépendence de l'adieu.* Paris: G.L.M.
1936 *Moulin premier.* Paris: G.L.M.
1937 *Placard pour un chemin des écoliers.* Paris: G.L.M.
1938 *Dehors la nuit est gouvernée.* Paris: G.L.M.
1938 *Le Visage nuptial.* Paris.
1945 *Seuls demeurent.* Paris: Gallimard.
1945 *Le Marteau sans maître suivi de Moulin premier.* Paris: Librairie José Corti.
1946 *Premières alluvions.* Paris: Editions de la revue Fontaine.
1947 *La Conjuration.* Paris.
1947 *Le Poème pulvérisé.* Paris: Editions de la revue Fontaine.
1948 *Fureur et mystère.* Paris: Gallimard.
1948 *Fête des arbres et du chasseur.* Paris: G.L.M.
1949 *Dehors la nuit est gouvernée précédé par Placard pour un chemin des écoliers.* Paris: G.L.M.
1949 *Claire.* Paris: Gallimard.
1949 *Le Soleil des eaux.* Paris: Librairie Henri Matarasso.
1950 *Les Matinaux.* Paris: Gallimard.
1950 *Art bref suivi de Premières alluvions.* Paris: G.L.M.
1951 *Quatre fascinants. La Minutieuse.* Paris: Imprimerie André Tournon.
1951 *Le Soleil des eaux.* Paris: Gallimard.
1951 *A une sérénité crispée.* Paris: Gallimard.
1951 *Poèmes.* Paris: Galerie Jacques Dubourg.
1952 *La Paroi et la prairie.* Paris: G.L.M.
1953 *Lettera amorosa.* Paris: N.R.F., collection "Espoir."
1953 *Arrière-histoire du Poème pulvérisé.* Paris: Jean Hugues.

1953 *Le Rempart de brindilles.* Paris: Louis Broder.
1954 *A la santé du serpent.* Paris: G.L.M.
1955 *Recherche de la base et du sommet suivi de Pauvreté et privilège.* Paris: N.R.F., collection "Espoir."
1955 *Poèmes des deux années 1953-1954.* Paris: G.L.M.
1956 *La Bibliothèque est en feu.* Paris: Louis Broder.
1956 *En trente-trois morceaux.* Paris: G.L.M.
1956 *L'Abominable homme des neiges.* Le Caire: Librairie L.D.F.
1956 *Pour nous, Rimbaud.* Paris: G.L.M.
1957 *Les Compagnons dans le jardin.* Paris: Louis Broder.
1957 *La Bibliothèque est en feu et autres poèmes.* Paris: G.L.M.
1957 *Poèmes et prose choisis.* Paris: Gallimard.
1958 *Sur la poésie.* Paris: G.L.M.
1958 *Le Dernier couac.* Paris: G.L.M.
1958 *Cinq poésies en hommage à Georges Braque.* Geneva: Edwin Engleberts.
1958 *L'Escalier de Flore.* Alès: P.A.B.
1959 *Nous avons.* Paris: Louis Broder.
1960 *Anthologie.* Paris: G.L.M.
1960 *Les Dentelles de Montmirail.* Alès: P.A.B.
1961 *L'Inclémence lointaine.* Paris: Pierre Bérès.
1961 *La Parole en archipel.* Paris: Gallimard.
1962 *Fureur et mystère.* Paris: Gallimard.
1963 *Lettera amorosa.* Geneva: Edwin Engleberts.
1963 *Le Marteau sans maître suivi de Moulin premier.* Paris: José Corti.
1964 *Commune présence.* Paris: Gallimard.
1964 *Les Matinaux.* Paris: Gallimard.
1965 *La Recherche de la base et du sommet.* Paris: Gallimard.
1966 *L'Age cassant.* Paris: José Corti.
1966 *Retour amont.* Paris: Gallimard.

"Minuscules"

1951 *Amitié cachetée.* Alès: P.A.B.
1951 *La Lettre 1 du dictionnaire.* Alès: P.A.B.
1952 *Pourquoi le ciel se voûte-t-il?* Alès: P.A.B.
1953 *Homo poeticus.* Alès: P.A.B.
1954 *Rengaine d'odin le roc.* Alès: P.A.B.
1954 *L'Alouette.* Paris: G.L.M.
1954 *Contre l'éphémère.* Alès: P.A.B.
1954 *Pour renouer.* Alès: P.A.B.
1954 *Epitaphe.* Alès: P.A.B.
1955 *La Fauvette des roseaux.* Alès: P.A.B.
1955 *Bonne grâce d'un temps d'avril.* Alès: P.A.B.
1955 *Chanson des étages.* Alès: P.A.B.
1955 *A une enfant.* Alès: P.A.B.
1956 *Jeanne qu'on brûla verte.* Alès: P.A.B.
1956 *Berceuse pour chaque jour jusqu'au dernier.* Alès: P.A.B.
1956 *Le Pas de René Crevel.* Alès: P.A.B.
1957 *De moment en moment.* Alès: P.A.B.
1957 *Le Poète au sortir des demeures.* Alès: P.A.B.
1957 *L'Une et l'autre.* Alès: P.A.B.

1957 *Aiguillon.* Alès: P.A.B.
1958 *Elisabeth petite fille.* Alès: P.A.B.
1958 *Nous avons.* Alès: P.A.B.
1958 *Traverse.* Alès: P.A.B.
1959 *La Faux relevée.* Alès: P.A.B.
1959 *Aux riverains de la Sorgue.* Alès: P.A.B.
1960 *Eros suspendu.* Alès: P.A.B.
1960 *Prompte.* Alès: P.A.B.
1960 *La Quête d'un frère.* Alès: P.A.B.
1960 *Pourquoi la journée vole.* Alès: P.A.B.
1960 *Le Rebanque.* Alès: P.A.B.
1960 *Page d'ascendants.* Alès: P.A.B.
1960 *L'Allégresse.* Alès: P.A.B.
1961 *La Montée de la nuit.* Alès: P.A.B.
1961 *Poésies.* Alès: P.A.B.
1961 *L'Arbre frappé.* Alès: P.A.B.
1961 *De 1943.* Alès: P.A.B.
1961 *L'Issue.* Alès: P.A.B.
1962 *Apparition d'Aérea.* Alès: P.A.B.
1962 *Thouzon.* Alès: P.A.B.
1962 *Buoux.* Alès: P.A.B.
1962 *Nous ne jalousons pas les dieux.* Alès: P.A.B.
1966 *Provence, point Oméga.*
1966 *Le Flux de l'aimant.* Paris: Gaston Puel.

Works in Collaboration

1930 *Ralentir travaux*, with André Breton and Paul Eluard. Paris: Editions surréalistes.
1945 *Rêves d'encre*, with José Corti, Paul Eluard, Julian Gracq, and Gaston Bachelard. Paris: Editions José Corti.
1947 *Cinq parmi d'autres*, with Edith Thomas, J. Lecompte-Boinet, Général de Larminat, Vercors. Paris: Editions de minuit.
1951 *Arthur Rimbaud boulevard d'enfer*, with Jacques Dupin. Paris.
1960 *Deux poèmes*, with Paul Eluard. Paris: Jean Hugues.

Prefaces

1939 Roux, Les Quatre frères. *Quand le soir menace.* Paris: G.L.M.
1945 BERNARD, ROGER. *Ma Faim noire déjà.* Paris: Cahiers d'art.
1947 BATTISTINI, YVES. *A la droite de l'oiseau.* Paris: Editions de la revue Fontaine, collection "L'Age d'or."
1948 *Héraclite d'Ephèse*, trans. Yves Battistini. Paris: Editions Cahiers d'art.
1950 DUPIN, JACQUES. *Cendrier du voyage.* Paris: G.L.M.
1950 ADAMOV, ARTHUR. *La Parodie. L'Invasion.* Paris: Charlot.
1952 *Poésie partagée.* Le Temps de la poésie. Paris: G.L.M.
1952 *Catalogue abrégé des éditions G.L.M.* Paris: G.L.M.
1953 GAZELLES, RENÉ. *De Terre et d'envolée.* Paris: G.L.M.
1954 L., M. et M. de B. *Petit dictionnaire de santé.* Paris: G.L.M.
1954 SENAC, JEAN. *Poèmes.* Paris: N.R.F., collection "Espoir."

1954 PILON, JEAN GUY. *Les Cloîtres de l'été.* Montreal: Editions de l'Hexagone.
1957 RIMBAUD, ARTHUR. *Oeuvres.* Paris: Club Français du livre.
1965 CAMUS, ALBERT. *La Postérité du soleil.* Geneva: Edwin Engleberts.

PREFACES TO ART EXHIBITION CATALOGUES

1938 *Dessins et gouaches de J. M. Prassinos.* Paris: Galerie Billiet.
1939 *Jean Villeri.* Paris: Galerie Henriette.
1947 *Georges Braque.* Paris: Galerie Maeght.
1948 *Pierre Charbonnier.* Paris: Galerie Claude.
1948 *Jean Villeri.* Paris: Galerie Maeght.
1949 *Ciska Grillet.* Paris: Galerie Claude.
1950 *Louis Fernandez.* Paris: Galerie Pierre.
1950 *Georges Braque.* Paris: Galerie Maeght.
1951 *Nicolas de Staël.* Paris: Galerie Jacques Dubourg.
1951 *Assortiment de dessins de Picabia.* Alès: P.A.B.
1952 *Victor Brauner.* Paris: Galerie de France.
1952 *Exposition de 66 minuscules de P.A.B.* Paris: Librairie Jean Loize.
1953 *Wilfredo Lam.* Paris: Galerie Maeght.
1957 *Jean Hugo.* Paris: Galerie des Cahiers d'art.
1958 *Jean Villeri.* Paris: Galerie Creuze.
1958 *Georges Braque. Oeuvre graphique.* Geneva: Cabinet des Estampes.
1958 *Pierre Charbonnier.* Paris: Galerie J.C. de Chaudun.
1961 *Joan Miró.* Paris: Galerie Maeght.
1963 *Victor Brauner.* Paris: Le Point Cardinal.

SURREALIST DOCUMENTS AND TEXTS SIGNED BY CHAR (1929-1934) [a]

1930 *Second Manifeste du Surréalisme.* (First appeared in *La Révolution surréaliste,* 15 décembre 1929).
1931 *(L'Age d'or) Aspect social. Questionnaire.* (In defense of the film *L'Age d'or* by Louis Buñuel and Salvador Dali.)
1931 *Ne Visitez pas l'Exposition coloniale.* (Against the policies of colonialism.)
1931 *Au Feu!* (Against the intolerances of the Spanish riots).
1931 *Premier Bilan de l'Exposition coloniale.*
1932 *L'Affaire Aragon.* (In defense of Aragon's poem "Front rouge.")
1932 *Paillasse!* (Condemnation of Aragon and his adherence to the Communist party.)
1933 *La Mobilisation contre la guerre n'est pas la paix.*
1934 *Appel à la lutte.* (Against the threat of Fascism.)
1934 *La Planète sans visa.* (Against the expulsion of Leon Trotsky from France and all French territory.)

---

[a] MAURICE NADEAU, *Histoire du surréalisme* (Paris, 1964).

B. CRITICAL WORKS

AMER, HENRI. "René Char: *La Parole en archipel*," *NNRF*, 113 (mai 1962), 907-909.

AUDEJEAN, CHRISTIAN. "René Char: *L'Age cassant* (José Corti), *Province, point Oméga* (chez l'auteur), *Le Flux de l'aimant* (Gaston Puel)," *Esprit* (mars 1966), 509-510.

BALAKIAN, ANNA. *Surrealism: The Road to the Absolute*. New York: The Noonday Press, 1959.

BATAILLE, GEORGES. "René Char et la force de la poésie," *Critique*, VIII (octobre 1951), 819-823.

BATTISTINI, YVES. "Les Couleurs dans l'oeuvre de René Char," *L'Arc*, 22 (été 1963), 50-57.

———. "Héraclite d'Ephèse," *Trois Contemporains*. Paris: Gallimard, 1955.

BAUDELAIRE, CHARLES. *Les Fleurs du mal*. Paris: Garnier Frères, 1959.

BEAUFRET, JEAN. "L'Entretien sous le marronier," *L'Arc*, 22 (été 1963), 1-7.

BENOÎT, P. A. *Bibliographie des oeuvres de René Char de 1928 à 1963*. Paris: Le Demi-jour, 1964.

BERGER, PIERRE. "Conversation avec René Char," *La Gazette des lettres*, VIII (15 juin 1952), 8-14.

———. "René Char," *Poètes d'aujourd'hui*. Paris: Editions Pierre Seghers, 1951.

BERNARD, SUZANNE. *Le Poème en prose de Baudelaire jusqu'à nos jours*. Paris: Librairie Nizet, 1959.

BLANCHOT, MAURICE. *La Part du feu*. Paris: Gallimard, 1949.

———. "René Char," *Critique* (octobre 1946), 387-399.

———. "René Char et la pensée neutre," *L'Arc*, 22 (été 1963), 9-14.

BLIN, GEORGES. "Avant-propos," *Georges Braque, René Char*, Catalogue pour l'exposition du livre *Lettera amorosa*. Paris: Bibliothèque littéraire Jacques Doucet, 1963.

———. "L'Instant multiple dans la poésie de René Char," *L'Arc*, 22 (été 1963), 15-24.

———. "Préface," *Commune présence*. Paris: Librairie Gallimard, 1964, vii-xxiv.

BOISDEFFRE, PIERRE DE. "Poésie vivante — René Char," *Les Nouvelles littéraires* (12 février 1959), 7.

BOSQUET, ALAIN. "René Char ou le verbe est une éthique," *La Revue de Paris*, 62 (septembre 1955), 117-126.

———. "René Char: *Recherche de la base et du sommet et Poèmes des deux années*," *La Table ronde*, 90 (juin 1955), 196-197.

BOUNOURE, GABRIEL. "Base et sommet de la poésie de Char," *NNRF*, 38 (février 1956), 300-307.

———. "Céreste et la Sorgue," *L'Arc*, 22 (été 1963), 25-32.

———. *Marelles sur le parvis*. Paris: Librairie Plon, 1958.

BRETON, ANDRÉ. *Entretiens*. Paris: Gallimard, 1952.

———. *Manifestes du surréalisme*. Paris: Gallimard, collection d'Idées, 1963.

BRODIN PIERRE. *Présences contemporaines*, I. Paris: Editions Debresse, 1956.

CASSOU, JEAN. *Georges Braque*. New York: Harry N. Abrams, Inc., 1964.

CIOCCHINI, HECTOR. "La Parole habitable," *L'Arc*, 22 (été 1963), 58-63.

CLANCIER, G.-E. "Une Salve d'avenir," *Mercure de France*, 1136 (avril 1958), 702-708.
DECAUNES, LUC. "René Char ou la poésie fortifiée," *Esprit*, 30 (décembre 1962), 1008-1017.
Dictionnaire biographique français contemporain. Paris: Agence Internationale de Documentation contemporaine "Pharos," 1954.
DU BOUCHET, ANDRÉ. "Fureur et mystère," *Les Temps modernes*, 42 (avril 1949), 745-748.
DUPIN, JACQUES. "Dehors la nuit est gouvernée," *L'Arc*, 22 (été 1963), 64-68.
FRONTÈS, STÉPHANE. "Char: l'arme nommé parole," *Carrefour* (23 mars 1955), 9.
Georges Braque, René Char. Bibliothèque littéraire Jacques Doucet. Catalogue avec avant-propos de Georges Blin et l'étude de François Chapon, pour l'exposition du livre *Lettera amorosa*. Paris: 1963.
GRENIER, JEAN. "L'Amour de la vie," *L'Arc*, 22 (été 1963), 69.
GROS, LEÓN-GABRIEL. "Cette Conquête en avant de nous...," *Cahiers du sud*, 345 (avril 1958), 287-293.
———. "René Char: De l'éclair à la rose," *Cahiers du sud*, 366 (juin 1962), 282-286.
GUERRE, PIERRE. "René Char," *Poètes d'aujourd'hui*. Paris: Pierre Seghers, 1961.
HACKETT, C. A. "An Introduction to the Poetry of René Char," *FMLS*, II (1966), 347-355.
———. "La Lumière dans l'oeuvre de René Char," *L'Arc*, 22 (été 1963), 70-75.
JUIN, HERBERT. "La Poésie et la fraternité," *Critique*, 96 (mai 1955), 409-414.
LANES, JERROLD B. "Lecture de *Partage formel*," *L'Arc*, 22 (été 1963), 76-81.
LAURENT, G-A. "*Seuls demeurent* par René Char," *Paru*, 10 (août-septembre 1945), 50-51.
MÉNARD, RENÉ. "Aura de *Lettera amorosa*," *Critique*, 77 (octobre 1953), 830-836.
———. *La Condition poétique: Cinq essais pour interpréter Char.* Paris: Gallimard, 1959.
———. "Le Coeur, la poésie, René Char...," *L'Arc*, 22 (été 1963), 82-86.
MIGUEL, ANDRÉ. "Poésie et vérité de René Char," *NNRF*, 63 (mars 1958), 518-521.
MILLS, RALPH J., JR. "Char and Michaux: Magicians of Insecurity," *Chicago Review*, 15 (Autumn 1961), 40-56.
MOUNIN, GEORGES. *Avez-vous lu Char?* Paris: Gallimard, 1946.
———. "Les Images de la vitre," *L'Arc*, 22 (été 1963), 87-90.
———. "Situation présente de René Char," *Les Temps modernes* 137-138 (juillet-août 1957), 272-288.
———. "Vers l'arbre-frère aux jours comptés," *Cahiers du sud*, 342 (septembre 1957), 306-309.
NADEAU, MAURICE. *Histoire du surréalisme.* Paris: Editions du Seuil, 1964.
Nomenclature des journaux et revues en langue française paraissant dans le monde entier. Paris: L'Argus de la Presse, 1930-1931.
OSTER, PIERRE. "René Char: *Poèmes des deux années: 1953-1954: Recherche de la base et du sommet suivi de Pauvreté et privilège*," *NNRF*, 29 (mai 1955), 903-904.
PATRI, AIMÉ. "*Fête des arbres et du chasseur* par René Char," *Paru*, 54 (octobre 1949), 39.
———. "*Fureur et mystère* par René Char," *Paru*, 49 (décembre 1948), 31.

Picon, Gaëtan. *Panorama de la nouvelle littérature française.* Paris: Librairie Gallimard, 1960.

———. "René Char et l'avenir de la poésie," *Fontaine*, 63 (novembre 1947), 826-834.

———. *L'Usage de la lecture.* Paris: Mercure de France, 1960.

Pilon, Jean-Guy. "La Condition poétique: II," *La Revue de l'Université Laval*, XIV (juin 1960), 899-903.

Poulet, Georges. "René Char: de la constriction à la dissémination," *L'Arc*, 22 (été 1963), 33-45.

Rau, Greta. *René Char ou la poésie accrue.* Paris: Librairie José Corti, 1957.

Raymond, Marcel. *De Baudelaire au surréalisme.* Paris: Librairie José Corti, 1963.

Richard, Jean-Pierre. "René Char ou la contradiction résolue," *Onze études sur la poésie moderne.* Paris: Editions du Seuil, 1964.

Rousseaux, André. "Valeur de René Char," *Littérature du vingtième siècle.* Paris: Editions Albin Michel, 1949.

Rousselot, Jean. *Panorama critique des nouveaux poètes français.* Paris: Pierre Seghers, Editeur, 1952.

Saillet, Maurice. "A une sérénité crispée," *Mercure de France*, 1059 (premier novembre 1951), 512-519.

Tilliette, Xavier. "Poètes français contemporain II: Surréalistes," *Etudes*, 266 (septembre, 1950), 241-245.

Thomas, Henri. *La Chasse aux trésors.* Paris: Gallimard, 1961.

Verboud, Jean-Jacques. "L'Age cassant par René Char," *Cahiers du sud* (1966), 330-331.

Verhesen, Fernand. "Avec René Char vers un ordre insurgé," *Le Journal des poètes*, 10 (décembre, 1953), 3.

———. *Voies et voix de la poésie française contemporaine.* Brussels: Editions des artistes, 1960.

Vigée, Claude. "Deux aspects de la sensibilité poétique française depuis la guerre (1944-1958)," *Révolte et louanges.* Paris: Librairie José Corti, 1962.

Who's Who in France 1955-1956. Paris: Editions Jacques Lafitte, 1955.

Wurm, Franz. "Poésie et traduction," *L'Arc*, 22 (été 1963), 91-98.

INDEX

"***," 68, 70-72
"A****," 137-139
"A deux enfants," 181
"A l'horizon," 45, 46
"A la santé du serpent," 103, 132, 173
"A un fantôme de la réflexion surpris chez les pleutres de la providence," 81-82
"A une ferveur belliqueuse," 104
A une sérénité crispée, 111, 112, 131-139, 148, 162
Abondance viendra, 42, 65-67, 68, 75
Absence-presence, dialectic of, 19, 25, 160, 173-174
"L'Accident dans la plaine," 63
Act versus activity, 34, 37-38, 40, 43-44, 56
L'Action de la justice est éteinte, 42, 57-61, 67, 68, 75
Un Adieu, un salut, 122-123
L'Age cassant, 195, 201-204
Alliés substantiels, 145
L'Amie qui ne restait pas, 167, 170-175
L'Amitié se succède, 197, 198
"Amour," 36, 44
"L'Amour," 44, 45, 58
"L'Amoureuse en secret," 123
"Antonin Artaud," 122
Aphorism, 36, 37, 59, 69, 91-92, 128, 147-148, 154n
Apollinaire, Guillaume, 22, 24, 26, 27, 28, 30, 35, 131, 143
"L'Arbre frappé," 181
"Argument," 89, 100
Arrière-histoire du Poème pulvérisé, 17, 100
Arsenal, 15, 16, 19, 27, 29-39, 42-48, 57, 60, 61, 67, 68, 75
Art, 142-151, 152-153, 199
Artaud, Antonin, 122, 143
Art bref, 112, 145-146, 148, 149, 173
Artine, 42, 48-57 59, 60, 61, 67n, 71, 75, 117, 141
"Les Asciens," 62-63, 64
Au-Dessus du vent, 186, 187-190, 193, 194, 202
Autres poèmes, 176, 182, 183-184
L'Avant-monde, 77, 87, 88, 89-90, 94, 95

Battre tout bas, 197, 198
Baudelaire, Charles, 22-23, 26-27, 28, 30, 143

"Bel édifice ou les pressentiments," 45, 47-48
La Bibliothèque est en feu, 176-179, 182, 194
La Bibliothèque est en feu et autres poèmes, 153, 176-184, 186, 187
"Biens égaux," 81, 100-102
Blake, William, 25
Bloodpoisoning, crisis, 78, 138
"Bonne aventure," 35-36, 37, 38
Bonne grâce d'un temps d'avril, 181, 182
"Le Bouge de l'historien," 89-90
Braque, Georges, 123, 146-148
Breton, André, 29, 38, 41, 46, 148-149

"Caesia," 26, 27
Capitaine Alexandre, 96
"Carte du 8 novembre," 89
"Centon," 125
"Ce Soir...," 18-19
Cette fumée qui nous portait, 197
"Chaîne," 63
Chance, 100-101
"Chant du refus," 89
"Chaume des Vosges," 98, 171-172
"Chère Artine," 59
"Le Cheval de corrida," 60, 61
Cinq poésies en hommage à Georges Braque, 146, 187
Claire, 112, 115-117, 118
"Le Climat de la chasse ou l'accomplissement de la poésie," 58, 60-62
Les Cloches sur le coeur, 15, 16, 18, 19-28, 30, 32, 34, 35, 36, 109, 122, 145, 157, 163, 195
"Commune présence," 68, 72-74
Commune présence, 154, 195, 196-201, 202
Les Compagnons dans le jardin, 176, 179-183, 194
"Conduite," 85, 86
"Confronts," 64
La Conjuration, 87-88, 117, 147
Le Consentement tacite, 123-125
Constriction for dissemination, 156, 157
La Conversation souveraine, 142, 143-144
La Corde sensible, 144-150
"Crésus," 64
Crispation, 137, 138, 144, 162
"Cruauté," 64

Death, 22-23, 74, 97, 120, 135, 183, 187
"Débris mortels et Mozart," 182-183
"Dédicace," 79, 80
Dehors la nuit est gouvernée, 77, 78-79, 81-84, 87, 88, 91, 98, 100, 106, 121, 159, 180, 184
"La Délivrance naturelle," 35-36, 37, 38
Dépendance de l'adieu, 81, 117
"Le Deuil des Névons," 183-184
"Devant soi," 66
"Domaine," 65

"Donnerbach Mühle," 102, 173
"La double tresse," 171-172
"Drames," 60, 61
Dream, 31, 35-36, 38, 42, 48-53, 56, 59, 63, 64

"L'Eclaircie," 67
L'Ecarlate, 197, 199
Education, 18, 19; Ecole communale, 18; Ecole de Commerce, 19; Lycée d'Avignon, 18; Université d'Aix, 19
"L'Egalité," 36
Eluard, Paul, 29-30, 33, 41, 75, 143
"L'Emploi," 35
"Entre la prairie et le laurier," 146
"En vue de Georges Braque," 147
"Epitaphe," 181
"L'Esprit poétique," 58, 59-61, 68
"Evadné," 85-86, 87
"L'Exhibitionniste," 43
Experience, 112-113

Fête des arbres et du chasseur, 112, 115, 117, 118-119, 121
Feuillets d'Hypnos, 65, 77, 83, 87, 94-98, 101, 106, 159
"Fièvre de la petite pierre d'Alsace," 173
"Flexibilité de l'oubli," 30-33, 35, 42, 44
La Fontaine narrative, 78, 104, 173
Les Frères de mémoire, 197, 198-199
Fureur et mystère, 81, 86, 87, 88-108, 109, 110, 112, 114-115, 121, 131, 138, 157, 163, 170, 179, 196

"Georges Braque intro muros," 123, 147
"Le Grand travail," 33, 35, 44
"Gravité," 81, 85, 86-87

Haine du peu d'amour, 197, 198
"Harmonium," 21
Heraclitus, 143, 145
History, denial of, 65, 134, 188-189
Hommage à Paul Eluard, 75
L'Homme qui marchait dans un rayon de soleil, 129-130
Humanization of the poet, 82-83, 91-92, 106-107

"L'Illusion imitée," 45, 47
"Ils sont privilégiés...," 130
"Intégration," 65
"Intérieur," 25, 26
"Introduction," 78-79
"Les Inventeurs," 126
"Invitation," 173-174
Isle-sur-Sorgue, 16, 17, 18, 30, 33, 119, 184, 197, 203

"Jacquemard et Julia," 17
Je, 82-83, 119, 121, 129, 136, 159, 160-161, 162, 201-202
Joue et dors, 125, 127
"Jouvence," 15, 20, 21, 45, 46
"Jouvence des Névons," 119, 183

"L'," 36, 44
Lascaux, 139, 140, 163
La Tour, Georges de, 104, 145
Lautréamont, 143
Lettera amorosa, 72, 82, 139, 153-165, 166, 167, 170, 171, 172, 173, 174, 176, 186-187, 193, 194, 197, 198
La Lettre hors commerce, 148-149
"Lèvres incorrigibles," 146
"Liberté," 90
"La Lisière du trouble," 173
"**Le Loriot**," 89
"Louis Curel de la Sorgue," 17-18, 89, 95
Les Loyaux adversaires, 77, 98, 99, 102, 106, 109, 171
"La Luxure," 63

"Madeleine qui veillait," 145n, 148-149
Mallarmé, Stéphane, 24, 26
Maquis, 96, 104, 205
"Marmonnement," 173-174
Le Marteau sans maître, 29n, 41-67, 68, 70, 71, 74-76, 77, 80, 82, 106, 109, 110, 112, 121, 138, 157, 179, 196
"Masque de fer," 36
Les Matinaux, 17, 79, 111, 112, 115, 117-131, 132, 133, 139, 142, 157, 173, 181, 186, 188
Méridiens, 19
"Minerai," 63
La Minutieuse, 139, 141
Monteverdi, Claudio, 154, 157
Moulin premier, 37, 41, 59, 60, 61, 67-76, 77, 80, 90, 91, 92, 93, 94, 106, 129, 148
Multiplication, 161-162, 164

Nadja, 148-149
Nature, 17, 26, 109-110, 111, 112-142, 152, 204
Neuf merçi, 182
"Neuf poèmes pour vaincre," 89-90
Nostalgia for harmony, 79, 98, 99, 102-103, 119
Nous, 82-83, 121, 129, 159, 168, 192
"Nous avons," 190, 192
"Les Observateurs et les rêveurs," 64
Organization of collective editions, 179-180, 182, 196-197, 200-201

La Paroi et la prairie, 17, 112, 117, 139-142, 175, 186, 188
La Parole en archipel, 71, 139, 153, 154, 186-194, 195, 196, 202
Partage formel, 77, 82, 88, 90-94, 101, 106, 111, 148, 157
Pauvreté et privilège, 22, 112, 142-151, 173
Placard pour un chemin des écoliers, 65, 77, 78-80, 106
Plastic arts, 145-148, 150, 179
"Poème," 58, 60
Le Poème pulvérisé, 70, 71, 77-78, 81, 99-104, 106, 109, 120, 129, 132, 161, 173
Poèmes des deux années, 153, 166-176, 186, 187
Poèmes et prose choisis, 86, 89n, 91, 153, 181, 186, 196
Poèmes militants, 42, 57, 61-65, 66-67, 68, 75
Poetization of man, 159, 167

"Possible," 43
Post-merci, 132
"Post-scriptum," 86
"Pour Mamouque," 63
Pourquoi la journée vole, 167, 175-176
Premières alluvions, 19-21, 46, 145, 171
"Présage," 27
"Prêt au dépouillement," 27
Prophecy, 46, 92
"Puissance négative," 44
Pulverization, 103, 136, 162, 197

Quatre fascinants, 139, 140
Quitter, 186, 190-193, 194, 202

Ralentir travaux, 41
"Ravages de la lune," 27
Recherche de la base et du sommet, 78, 104-106, 123n, 138, 142, 146, 186
"Récit funèbre prend forme de poème," 35-36, 37, 38
Le Rempart de brindilles, 167-169, 171, 172
Retour amont, 195, 196, 201, 202, 204-206
Reverdy, Pierre, 18, 31, 143
Rimbaud, Arthur, 22-23, 26, 28, 30, 104, 143-144
Rougeur des Matinaux, 127-129, 135, 148

"Sade," 63, 64
"Sans pardon," 26
Second Manifeste du surréalisme, 40
"Le Serpent," 140-141, 173
Seuls demeurent, 17, 81, 88-94, 106
La Sieste blanche, 27n, 119-122, 126
Le Soleil des eaux, 17, 18, 112, 113-115, 117, 118
"Sosie," 45, 46
Sous la verrière, 146
Spaciality, 82, 163, 164, 184-185, 206
Subconscious, 36, 50
Surrealism, 21, 29-30, 32, 35, 38-39, 40-76, 107, 110, 138; rejection of, 77, 89, 90-91, 111, 129, 149
Sur une nuit sans ornement, 176, 184-185
"Le Sujet," 36-37, 38

"Témoignage de grandeur," 15
Temporality, 163-164, 185, 206
"Le Temps du store," 81
"La Tête sous l'oreiller," 33, 44
Le Tombeau des secrets, 42-43, 44-48, 57
"Tous compagnons de lit," 83, 84, 180
"Toute poésie," 15-16, 18, 20, 21
Toute vie, 131
Transir, 139, 140
"Trianon," 63
Tu, 19, 28, 159, 160-161, 162, 164, 193

"Un Oiseau suffit à la vie," 27

"Validité," 81
Vallée close, 197, 199-200
"Variation en caractères," 27
Vaucluse, 16, 17, 19, 110, 204
"La Vérité," 43-44, 46
"La Vérité continue," 43
"Vermillon," 173
"Versant," 64-65
"Le Vipéreau," 173
"Le Visage nuptial," 84-85, 86
Le Visage nuptial, 77, 81, 82, 84, 85-87, 88, 92, 98, 106, 115, 153, 157, 170, 172
"Les Vivres du retour," 80

World War II, 17, 77, 80, 88-98, 99, 104-105, 133, 138, 197, 205

The Department of Romance Studies Digital Arts and Collaboration Lab at the University of North Carolina at Chapel Hill is proud to support the digitization of the North Carolina Studies in the Romance Languages and Literatures series.

www.ingramcontent.com/pod-product-compliance
Lightning Source LLC
Chambersburg PA
CBHW030618230426
43661CB00053B/2040